Security Awareness:
Applying Practical Security in Your World
Second Edition

Mark Ciampa

THOMSON

COURSE TECHNOLOGY

Australia • Canada • Mexico • Singapore • Spain • United Kingdom • United States

THOMSON
COURSE TECHNOLOGY

Security Awareness: Applying Practical Security in Your World, Second Edition
is published by Course Technology

Senior Editor
William Pitkin III

Product Manager
Amy M. Lyon

Developmental Editor
Lisa Ruffolo

Production Editor
Marissa Falco

Senior Manufacturing Coordinator
George Morrison

Product Marketing Manager
Dennis Williams

Technical Editor
Sydney Shewchuk

Quality Assurance Testing
Christian Kunciw

Associate Product Manager
Sarah Santoro

Editorial Assistant
Allison Murphy

Cover Design
Nancy Goulet

Text Design
GEX Publishing Services

Compositor
GEX Publishing Services

BRIEF

Contents

TABLE OF
Contents

Introduction

The single most important topic in the computer world today is *security*. It's easy to see why. There was a 142 percent increase in the number of computer attacks in the first six months of 2005 compared to the same period the previous year. During that same time in 2005, almost 11,000 new viruses and worms were released, which was an increase of 48 percent over the 7,300 released in the second half of 2004 (and an increase of 142 percent over the first half of 2004). Almost 150,000 computers *each day* are infected and turned into remote control "robots" that attack other computers—and the owners of these computers don't even know their computers are doing this. Everywhere you turn, you see evidence of new attacks and warnings to keep your computer secure.

Yet knowing how to make a computer and home or small office network secure and keep it safe still remains a mystery to many. What type of attacks will antivirus software prevent? How do I set up a firewall? How can I test my computer to be sure that attackers cannot reach it through the Internet? Do I really need antispyware software and where can I find it? When should I install Windows updates? For most people, knowing how to keep computers secure from attacks can seem like a daunting task.

This book provides you with the tools you need to make your computer and network secure. *Security Awareness: Applying Practical Security in Your World 2ed* presents a basic introduction to practical computer security for all users, from students to home users to business professionals. Security topics are introduced through a series of real-life user experiences, showing why computer security is necessary and providing the essential elements for making and keeping computers secure. Going beyond learning the concepts of computer security, you will gain practical skills on how to protect your computers and networks from increasingly sophisticated attacks.

Each chapter in the book contains hands-on projects that cover making computers secure. In addition, projects that show how to use and configure security hardware and software are also included. These projects are designed to make what you learn come alive through actually performing the tasks. Besides the hands-on projects, each chapter gives you experience through realistic security case projects that put you in the role of a security consultant who works in different scenarios to solve the problems of clients. Every chapter also includes review questions to reinforce your knowledge while helping you to apply practical security in your world.

Approach

The approach of *Security Awareness: Applying Practical Security in Your World 2ed* is hands-on and practical. You will learn all about the different attacks that a computer system faces today and how to make your computer secure. Because no previous in-depth knowledge of network, system hardware, or operating systems is required, you can begin immediately to learn the steps of keeping the attackers from infecting your computer.

Yet *Security Awareness* is much more than a step-by-step approach for practical security. Because all computer systems are as different as their users, you will also learn background material regarding computer security and the different types of attacks and defenses. This will help you be able to apply your practical security knowledge to computers that are different from yours and to new computers, networks, and software that continually being introduced. *Security Awareness: Applying Practical Security in Your World 2ed* helps you learn what security is and how to use it to protect your computer today as well as into the future.

With the growth of online delivery of computer courses, it is essential that a textbook be flexible enough to be used in either the classroom or as part of an online Web course. This book is intended to meet the needs of students in both a traditional classroom setting as well as in an online delivery of the course materials. Hands-on activities can be performed using either equipment installed on a college campus or using personal computer equipment at home. Almost all hands-on activities cover software that is included as part of the Windows operating system or is a free download from the Internet. This allows students to perform activities in either a classroom computer lab with other classmates or alone in a home or apartment in an online course.

A special classroom computer lab is not necessary in order to perform the hands-on activities in *Security Awareness: Applying Practical Security in Your World 2ed*. A standard computer lab with basic equipment can be easily used to learn about applying practical security.

Intended Audience

This book is intended to meet the needs of students and professionals who want to be able to protect their computers and networks from attacks. A basic working knowledge of computers is all that is required to use this book. The book's pedagogical features are designed to provide a truly interactive learning experience to help prepare you for the challenges of securing networking and computers. In addition to the information presented in the text, each chapter includes Hands-On Projects that guide you through implementing practical hardware, software, and network security step by step. Each chapter also contains a running case study that places you in the role of problem solver, requiring you to apply concepts presented in the chapter to achieve a successful solution.

Chapter Descriptions

The chapters in this book discuss the following topics:

Chapter 1, "Introduction to Security," explains what security is and why it is important and reveals who the attackers are and how they attack, in addition to outlining the basic defenses necessary for safeguarding a computer system.

Chapter 2, "Desktop Security," tells how to make a desktop or laptop computer secure by protecting the equipment and the data stored on it, as well as how to recover from an attack.

Chapter 3, "Internet Security," explains how attacks through the Internet can occur and what steps can be taken to reduce the risk of Internet attacks and e-mail vulnerabilities.

Chapter 4, "Personal Security," explains how attacks can steal personal information through spyware and what can be done to prevent attacks on your privacy.

Chapter 5, "Network Security," describes the different types of network security attacks and tells how to set up wired and wireless network security.

Chapter 6, "Enterprise Security," describes how an organization can implement a secure environment through security policies and plans, training, as well as a discussion on ethics.

Features

To aid you in fully understanding computer and network security, this book includes many features designed to enhance your learning experience.

- **Chapter Objectives.** Each chapter begins with a detailed list of the concepts to be mastered within that chapter. This list provides you with both a quick reference to the chapter's contents and a useful study aid.

- **Illustrations and Tables.** Numerous illustrations of security concepts and technologies help you visualize theories and concepts. In addition, the many tables provide details and comparisons of practical and theoretical information.

- **Hands-On Projects.** Although it is critical to understand the importance of security, nothing can substitute for real-world experience. To this end, each chapter provides several Hands-On Projects aimed at providing you with practical security experience. These projects use the Windows operating systems as well as software downloaded from the Internet.

- **Chapter Summaries.** Each chapter's text is followed by a summary of the concepts introduced in that chapter. These summaries provide a helpful way to review the ideas covered in each chapter.

- **Review Questions.** The end-of-chapter assessment begins with a set of review questions that reinforce the ideas introduced in each chapter. These questions help you evaluate and apply the material you have learned.

- **Case Projects.** Located at the end of each chapter are several Case Projects. In these extensive exercises, you implement the skills and knowledge gained in the chapter through real design and implementation scenarios.

Text and Graphic Conventions

Wherever appropriate, additional information and exercises have been added to this book to help you better understand the topic at hand. Icons throughout the text alert you to additional materials. The icons used in this textbook are described below.

NOTE

The Note icon draws your attention to additional helpful material related to the subject being described.

HANDS-ON PROJECTS

Each hands-on activity in this book is preceded by the Hands-On icon and a description of the exercise that follows.

CASE PROJECTS

Case Project icons mark scenario-based assignments. In these extensive case examples, you are asked to implement independently what you have learned.

BLOCK ATTACKS

The Castle icon identifies computer and network defenses that are designed to block attacks by creating a strong security perimeter much like a castle wall or moat.

UPDATE DEFENSES

The Flaming Arrow icon points out defenses that must be continually updated in order to remain effective.

The Bucket icon illustrates action to be taken to prepare for reacting quickly to attacks.

The Horse icon shows those swift and strong proactive steps to be taken to thwart attackers.

INSTRUCTOR'S MATERIALS

The following additional materials are available when this book is used in a classroom setting. All the supplements available with this book are provided to instructors on a single CD-ROM. You can also retrieve these supplemental materials from the Course Technology Web site, *www.course.com*, by going to the page for this book, under "Download Instructor Files & Teaching Tools."

Electronic Instructor's Manual. The Instructor's Manual that accompanies this book includes the following items: additional instructional material to assist in class preparation, including suggestions for lecture topics; recommended lab activities; and tips on setting up a lab for Hands-On Projects; and solutions to all end-of-chapter materials.

ExamView Test Bank. This cutting-edge Windows-based testing software helps instructors design and administer tests and pretests. In addition to generating tests that can be printed and administered, this full-featured program has an online testing component that allows students to take tests at the computer and have their exams automatically graded.

PowerPoint presentations. This book comes with a set of Microsoft PowerPoint slides for each chapter. These slides are meant to be used as a teaching aid for classroom presentations, to be made available to students on the network for chapter review, or to be printed for classroom distribution. Instructors are also at liberty to add their own slides for other topics introduced.

Figure files. All the figures in the book are reproduced on the Instructor's Resources CD. Similar to the PowerPoint presentations, they are included as a teaching aid for classroom presentation, to make available to students for review, or to be printed for classroom distribution.

LAB REQUIREMENTS

To the Student

This book helps you understand computer security. Every chapter is designed to present you with easy-to-understand information about security to help you plan and implement it in different settings. Each chapter of the book ends with review questions, hands-on projects, and cases that are written to be as realistic as the work you may be performing on the job. Your instructor can provide you with answers to the review questions and additional information about the hands-on projects.

Internet assignments. Some projects require Internet access for information searches. These projects will help train you in using this valuable resource for keeping abreast with the latest security issues.

Security assignments. To complete the projects in the book, you will need access to a computer. These projects will give you real hands-on experience in installing security software, configuring security settings, and implementing secure practices. A computer using the Windows XP operating system with a connection to the Internet will be used to learn hands-on security. A Linksys wireless local area network will also be used.

System requirements. The recommended software and hardware configurations are as follows:

Desktop Computer

- Windows XP operating system with Service Pack 2
- Microsoft Internet Explorer 6.0+ browser installed
- Minimum Pentium 1 GHz MHz processor
- Minimum 128 MB of RAM
- VGA monitor
- Mouse or pointing device
- Wireless NIC adapter or USB external wireless adapter
- Hard disk drive
- One high density 3.5-inch floppy disk drive

Access Point

- Linksys WRT54G access point

ACKNOWLEDGMENTS

Once again the Course Technology team that produced this book was excellent. Senior Editor Will Pitkin again showed his exceptional insight by directing the focus of the book to meet the needs of its audience. Product Manager Amy Lyon was, as always, wonderful in keeping this project on track and always being so supportive. Amy is a true delight to work with! Developmental Editor Lisa Ruffolo was excellent at managing countless details, making suggestions, providing input, and helping make each chapter complete. Production Editor Marissa Falco was great in finding my mistakes and making excellent suggestions. The Editorial Team would like to thank the Technical Editor, Sydney Shewchuk, and the Quality Assurance testers who carefully reviewed the book: Christian Kunciw, Danielle Shaw, Peter Stefanis, and Jeff Schwartz. In addition, we would like to thank our team of peer reviewers who evaluated each chapter and provided very helpful suggestions and contributions:

Mike O'Dowd	Colorado Technical University
Nina Milbauer	Madison Area Technical College
Mark Weiser	Oklahoma State University

The entire Course Technology staff was always helpful and worked very hard to create this finished product. I'm honored to be part of such an outstanding group professionals, and to these people and everyone on the team I extend my sincere thanks.

Also, I want to thank my sons Greg and Brian and daughter-in-law Amanda. Their interest in yet another of my projects meant much to me. Finally, I want to thank my wonderful wife Susan. Her continual love, support, and encouragement helped see me through another book. I could not have written the first word without her.

DEDICATION

To my wife Susan.

PHOTO CREDITS

Figure 2-9: Courtesy of Microsoft Corporation

Figure 2-15: Courtesy of Simple Tech Inc.

CHAPTER ONE

INTRODUCTION TO SECURITY

After completing this chapter you should be able to do the following:

➤ List the challenges of defending against attacks

➤ Explain why information security is important

➤ Describe the different types of attackers

➤ List the general principles for defending against attacks

ON THE JOB

Susan stopped by the electronics store in the mall to exchange the package of DVD-Rs she received for her birthday with rewritable DVD-RWs. Susan was surprised to see a long line of customers at the service desk with their personal computers. As she waited in line, Susan saw a report on one of the televisions in the store that the "W32-FireStorm" worm had been released through the Internet over the weekend. Susan remembers from talking with her brother that a worm is a "malicious" program that travels through the Internet and can infest computers and damage them, but she's not sure how. Perhaps these customer's computers had been attacked by the worm and needed to be repaired by a technician, Susan thought.

At the desk an elderly gentleman was telling the service technician that his brand new computer had been "hit" by the W32-FireStorm worm and he was demanding another computer. The technician asked the gentleman why he thought it was infected by the worm. "Well, I heard that everybody that was connected to the Internet on Saturday was infected, and that's the day I read my grandson's e-mail," the man said.

Behind Susan two women struck up a conversation about their experiences. "That worm infected my computer and now my screen won't turn on!" one woman complained. "Well, guess what he did to me?" said the other woman, "It made the color on my printer fade."

Two young men in line next to Susan were also talking about what happened. "Someone told me that anti-virus software cannot stop a worm but only a firewall can. What's a firewall?" The other man replied, "You don't need a firewall if you download the patches from Microsoft's Web site."

Susan was puzzled. She thought to herself, "I didn't know a worm could do all these things." But she wasn't completely sure that these problems were all caused by the worm. After all, the color on her printer started to fade last month because it ran out of ink. And she was connected the Internet on Saturday but nothing seemed wrong with her computer. Susan began to wonder if her computer had been infected. She left the store after exchanging her DVDs to hurry back to her apartment.

We are living in a world that is much different from that of only a few years ago. Just as national security has become an issue of primary importance to our country, so too has the security of our personal computers become important. We rely on our computers for everyday tasks more than ever before: they are essential tools for learning at school, working on the job, and managing the home. As the importance of computers in our lives continues to increase, so too do the number of malicious attacks upon these computers. For example, there was a 142 percent increase in the number of attacks in the first six months of 2005 compared to the same period the previous year.

All computer users today have heard about attacks that can threaten their computers. A host of new words have been introduced into our daily vocabulary about these threats and their prevention: worms, anti-virus software, firewalls, and patches, to name a few. Yet most people remain unsure about *how* to make their computers more secure. Ask yourself this question: if you knew that a particularly nasty Internet worm was to be released within the next hour, what would you do to prevent your computer from being infected? Install a firewall or use antivirus software? Download a patch? Unplug your Internet connection? Or just wait until your computer is infected and then take it to the electronics store to be repaired?

It is vital for today's computer users to be knowledgeable about security and what steps should be taken to defend against attacks. Applying practical security in your world has never been more important than it is today.

In this chapter we will introduce computer security. We'll begin by explaining the types of computer attacks that occur today and the challenges of keeping computers safe. Next, we will discuss what information security is and why it is important, and we will examine who is responsible for these attacks. Finally, we will look at the general principles for defending against attacks.

CHALLENGES OF SECURING INFORMATION

Several difficulties are involved in keeping computers and the information on them secure. These challenges can be illustrated by the sheer number of attacks as well as different types of attacks that occur. The volume and diversity of these attacks make it particularly hard to mount a defense against attackers.

Today's Security Attacks

The number and types of security attacks that occur today are frightening. Consider the following statistics:

- In the last six months of 2004, organizations faced an average of 13.6 attacks per day versus 10.6 the previous six months. During the same time, 7,360 new Windows viruses and worms appeared, up 64 percent from the previous period.

- During the second quarter of 2005, 422 Internet security vulnerabilities were discovered, an increase of 11 percent from the first quarter. The latest trend in new vulnerabilities was in music-downloading programs such as Apple iTunes.

- During the first six months of 2005, over 46.5 million Americans had their privacy breached through lost computer files or computer attackers. The lost data includes credit card numbers, Social Security numbers, addresses, and phone numbers.

- The Federal Information Security Management Act (FISMA) requires that the computer security for 24 government agencies be rated annually. The overall score for these agencies in 2004 was a D+. Table 1-1 illustrates some of the scores from 2003 and 2004.

Table 1-1   Federal computer security report card

Government Agency	2003 Grade	2004 Grade
Agency for International Development	C-	A+
Department of Transportation	D+	A-
Department of Justice	F	B-
National Science Foundation	A-	C+
Department of Commerce	C-	F
Department of Veterans Affairs	C	F
Department of Agriculture	F	F
Department of Health and Human Services	F	F
Department of Energy	F	F
Housing and Urban Development	F	F
Department of Homeland Security	F	F

- The Department of Defense records over 60,000 attempted intrusions annually against their unclassified networks, which is over 160 attempts per day.

- Companies worldwide will spend almost $13 billion on computer security in 2005.

- The total dollar and amount of damage caused by attackers in 2004 was over $17.5 billion, a 30 percent increase over 2003.

- The Federal Bureau of Investigation (FBI) in 2005 will spend only $150 million of its $5 billion budget on combating computer crime.

- In January of 2004, a new computer virus called MyDoom attacked the Web site of a computer software company. This program infected millions of other computers around the world and created a secret "back door" on each one. Eight days later, the attacker used that back door to download personal data from the computer owners and caused almost $5 billion in damage, the second most expensive software attack ever.

- A group known as ShadowCrew acquired credit card numbers and other valuable information through a variety of clever tricks, including sending millions of e-mail messages that appeared to be from legitimate companies such as Yahoo! Inc. and Juno Online Services, but turned out to be fakes designed to steal passwords and credit card numbers. This group also excelled at breaking into databases to steal personal account data, and even broke into the networks of 12 companies that were not aware their systems had been breached. Every Sunday night from 10 PM to 2 AM hundreds of attackers would then meet online, buying and selling credit card information, sometimes even as "package deals." A member of ShadowCrew sold 115,695 stolen credit card numbers in one trade. Besides stealing credit card numbers, the group made more than $4.3 million in fraudulent credit card purchases over a two-year period.

- The number of Internet fraud complaints rose from 6,087 in 2000 to 48,252 in 2002 and 207,449 in 2004.

- The Computer Security Institute (CSI) reported security losses for 2004 by category. Table 1-2 illustrates some of those losses.

Table 1-2   Selected 2004 computer losses

Category	Losses
Sabotage	$871,100
System penetration	$901,500
Web site defacing	$958,100
Unauthorized access	$4,278,205
Financial fraud	$7,760,500
Theft of proprietary information	$11,460,000
Virus attacks	$55,053,900

- In a five-month period in 2005, 25 of the 60 largest personal information breaches were at colleges and universities. These breaches resulted in students' personal information (such as name, Social Security number, grades, and other information) being available to unauthorized users. Table 1-3 lists some of those breaches.

Table 1-3   Selected college and university information breaches in 2005

Date Breach Made Public	School Name	Type of Breach	Number of Names Exposed
March 1	University of California, Berkeley	Stolen laptop	98,400
March 11	Boston College	Outside attack	120,000
March 22	California State University, Chino	Outside attack	59,900
April 11	Tufts University	Outside attack	106,000
April 29	Oklahoma State University	Stolen laptop	37,000
May 19	Valdosta State University	Outside attack	40,000
June 18	University of Hawaii	Dishonest insider	150,000
June 25	University of Connecticut	Outside attack	72,000
July 7	University of Southern California	Programming error	320,000

- An attacker defaced the President of Argentina's Web site, inserting insults into his published speeches.
- A Brazilian Web site that pretended to sell Visa cards online loaded a program on the computer of anyone who visited that Web site. This program secretly recorded the keystrokes of individuals when they accessed predetermined sites such as banks and financial institutions, and then sent that information to the attackers.

It is clear that despite the growing concern regarding computer security the number of attacks continues to skyrocket. Some security experts estimate that four out of every five computers are victims of malicious attacks. And perhaps most troubling of all, there appears to be no end in sight.

SECURITY IN YOUR WORLD

"Why all the fuss?" asked Rhonda, Susan's roommate, as Susan sat down at her computer. Susan repeated the conversations she overhead in the electronics store and said that she was now worried the Internet worm had attacked her computer, too. "So what if it did? What's the worst thing that can happen?" Rhonda asked. Susan said that she had heard stories of worms stealing or even erasing data from a computer. "Can't you just put it all back?" Rhonda asked. Susan replied, "Rhonda, this is the only place I have this stuff. If it's erased then it's all gone. And besides, remember when my computer broke last year and I couldn't use it for a whole week? I was completely lost!" Susan started to feverishly click her desktop and look over her screen. After several minutes Rhonda said, "Hey Susan, how do you know if you find the worm?" Susan suddenly stopped and stared at Rhonda. "I don't know."

Difficulties in Defending Against Attackers

The challenge of keeping computers secure has never been greater. A number of trends illustrate why security is becoming increasingly difficult. One is the speed of attacks that occur today. With modern tools at their disposal, attackers can quickly scan systems to find weaknesses and then launch attacks with unprecedented speed. For example, the Slammer worm infected 75,000 computers in the *first 11 minutes* after it was released in 2003, and the number of infections *doubled* every 8.5 seconds. At its peak, Slammer was scanning *55 million computers per second* looking for another computer to infect. Later that same year, the Blaster worm infected 138,000 computers in the *first four hours* and ended up infecting over 1.4 million computers. Many attack tools can now initiate new attacks without any human initiative, thus increasing the speed at which systems are attacked.

A second problem in defending against attackers is a greater sophistication of attacks. Security attacks are becoming more complex, making it more difficult to detect and defend against. Attackers now use common Internet tools, such as e-mail and Hypertext Transfer Protocol (HTTP), to send data or commands to attack computers, making it tricky to distinguish an attack from legitimate traffic. Other attack tools vary their behavior so the same attack appears different each time, complicating detection.

Thirdly, because attackers now detect weaknesses faster, they can quickly attempt to exploit these vulnerabilities. The number of newly discovered system vulnerabilities doubles annually, making it more difficult for software developers to keep pace by updating their products. In 2004, the time between the disclosure of a vulnerability and the release of an attack that took advantage of it was only 5.8 days.

One of the looming fears is the increasing number of zero day attacks. While most attacks take advantage of vulnerabilities that someone has already uncovered, a **zero day attack** occurs when an attacker discovers and exploits a previously unknown flaw. Providing "zero days" of warning, a zero day attack can be especially crippling to networks and computers because the attack runs rampant while precious time is spent trying to identify the vulnerability.

NOTE

By mid-2005, the average "window of exposure," or the time between when a zero day attack occurred and when a software "fix" was made available, was 56.07 hours, according to Blackspider Technologies.

A fourth difficulty in computer defense is that instead of attacks coming from only one source, they can be distributed attacks. Attackers can now use thousands of computers in an attack against a single computer or network. This "many against one" approach makes it impossible to stop an attack just by identifying and blocking the source.

The final difficulty in defending against attacks is one that many security experts believe may be the most difficult of all: user confusion. Increasingly users are called upon to make difficult security decisions regarding their computer systems, sometimes with little or no information to direct them to the most secure decision. For example, when using the Windows XP Service Pack 2 (Win XP SP2) operating system, users doing a variety of computer tasks are asked security questions such as:

- Is it okay to open this port?
- Is it safe to quarantine this attachment?
- Do you want to permit your bank to install this add-in?

With little or no direction, users might answer Yes to these questions without understanding the implications. What is a "port"? Will opening the port allow unauthorized users in? Will the port forever remain open? How can the port be closed? What happens if it is?

The problem of user confusion can be clearly seen in the delay in applying software patches. A **patch** is software used to repair security flaws or other problems in an existing software program or operating system, and is one of the primary defenses against attacks. However, managing patches and knowing which ones to install can be difficult. Many attacks have been successful due to users not applying patches that had been released long before the attack occurred. Table 1-4 shows the interval between the release of a patch to address a security weakness and an attack exploiting that particular weakness.

Table 1-4   Delay between patches and attacks

Attack Name	Impact of Attack	Date Patch First Issued	Date Attack Began	Days Between Patch and Attack
Bugbear	Over 2 million computers infected	5/16/01	9/30/02	502
Yaha	E-mail DDoS worm that unleashed 7,000 attacks per day	5/16/01	6/22/02	402
Frethem	12 variants in first 12 months of activity	5/16/01	06/01/02	381
ELKern	Found in over 40 countries	5/16/01	4/17/02	336
Klez	Infected 7.2% of computers worldwide	5/16/01	4/17/02	336
Nimda	Spread worldwide in 30 minutes	10/17/00	9/18/01	336
Badtrans	Almost half a million infections reported	5/16/01	11/24/01	192
SQL Slammer	Infections doubled every 8.5 seconds	7/24/02	1/25/03	185
Code Red	Infections doubled every 37 minutes	6/18/01	7/19/01	31
Blaster	Over 1.4 million computers infected	7/16/03	8/11/03	26
Zotob.d	Infected CNN, the Associated Press, the New York Times	8/7/05	8/16/05	9

User confusion regarding security is often considered to be one of the primary reasons that computers continue to be infected at such a high pace today. Although many technology tools can be used to defend against attackers, tools that are not properly implemented—or are altogether ignored—are of little value. Many security experts agree that solving the user confusion problem will go a long way towards winning the war against attackers.

WHAT IS INFORMATION SECURITY?

Before it is possible to adequately defend against attacks, it is important to know and understand what information security is. This section defines information security and examines the terminology commonly used to describe it. In addition, it explores why information security is so critically important today.

Defining Information Security

In a general sense, security can be considered as a state of freedom from a danger or risk. For example, a nation experiences security when its military has the strength to protect its citizens from a hostile outside force. This state or condition of freedom exists because protective measures are established and maintained. However, the presence of an army does not guarantee that a nation will never be attacked. Attacks from powerful outside forces may come at any time. The goal of national security is to be able to defend against these inevitable attacks so that the nation itself will not collapse.

The term **information security** describes the tasks of guarding information that is in a digital format. This digital information is typically manipulated by a microprocessor (like on a personal computer), stored on a magnetic or optical storage device (like a hard drive or a DVD), and is transmitted over a network (such as a local area network or the Internet). You can understand information security by examining its three goals and how it is accomplished.

First, information security ensures that protective measures are properly implemented. Just as with national security, information security cannot completely prevent attacks or guarantee that a system is totally secure. Rather, information security creates a defense that attempts to ward off attacks and prevents the collapse of the system when an attack occurs. Thus, information security is *protection*.

Second, information security is intended to protect information that has a high value to people and organizations; that value comes from the characteristics of the information. Three of the characteristics of information that must be protected by information security are:

1. *Confidentiality*—Confidentiality ensures that only authorized parties can view the information.

2. *Integrity*—Integrity ensures that the information is correct and no unauthorized person or malicious software has altered that data.

3. *Availability*—Although a secure computer must restrict access attempts by unauthorized users, it must still make the data immediately available to authorized users.

Information security attempts to safeguard these three characteristics of information (sometimes known as CIA). Thus, information security *protects the confidentiality, integrity, and availability of information.*

Information security, however, involves more than protecting the information itself. The third goal of information security is displayed in Figure 1-1. The center of the diagram shows what needs to be protected, which is the information. Because this information is stored on computer hardware, manipulated by software, and transmitted by communications, each of these areas must also be protected. Thus information security protects the integrity, confidentiality, and availability of information *on the devices that store, manipulate, and transmit the information.*

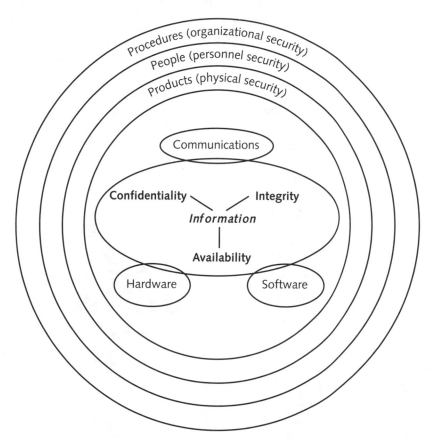

Figure 1-1   Information security components

Finally, information security is achieved through a combination of three entities. As shown in Figure 1-1, information, hardware, software, and communications are protected in three successive layers. The innermost layer consists of the products that provide the necessary security. These products may be as basic as door locks or as complicated as intrusion-detection systems and firewalls. They form the physical security around the data. The next layer is people. Without people implementing and properly using the security products, the data can never be protected. The final layer consists of procedures, which include the plans and policies established by an organization to ensure that people correctly use the products.

These three layers interact with each other. The procedures tell the people how to use the products in order to protect the information. Thus, information security protects the integrity, confidentiality, and availability of information on the devices that store, manipulate, and transmit the information *through the proper use of products, people, and procedures.*

Information Security Terminology

As with many advanced subjects, information security has specific terminology. The following scenario helps to illustrate information security terms and how they are used.

Suppose that Amanda wants to purchase a new stereo for her car. However, because several cars have been broken into near her apartment, she is concerned about someone stealing the stereo. Although she locks her car whenever she parks it, a hole in the fence surrounding her apartment complex makes it possible for someone to access the parking lot without restriction. Amanda's car and the threats to a car stereo are illustrated in Figure 1-2.

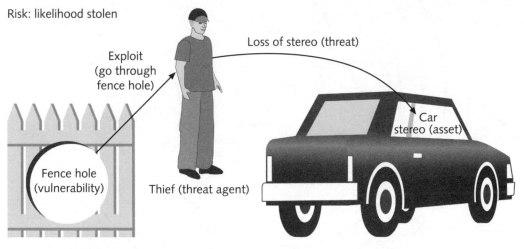

Figure 1-2   Amanda's car

Amanda's new car stereo is an **asset**, which is defined as something that has a value. Amanda is trying to protect her new car stereo from a **threat**, which is an event or object that may defeat the security measures in place and result in a loss. Information security threats are likewise events or actions that represent a danger to information. A threat by itself does not mean that security has been compromised; rather, it simply means that the potential for creating a loss is real. Although for Amanda the loss would be the theft of her stereo, in information security a loss can be the theft of information or a delay in information being transmitted, which can both result in a financial penalty or the loss of good will or a reputation.

A **threat agent** is a person or thing that has the power to carry out a threat. For Amanda the threat agent is a thief. In information security a threat agent could be a person attempting to break into a secure computer network. It could also be a force of nature such as a tornado or flood that could destroy computer equipment and thus destroy information, or it could be a virus that attacks a computer network.

Amanda wants to protect her new car stereo and is concerned about a hole in the fencing in her apartment's parking lot. The hole in the fencing is a **vulnerability** or weakness that allows a threat agent to bypass security. An example of a vulnerability that information security must deal with is a software defect in an operating system that allows an unauthorized user to gain access to a computer without a password.

If a thief can get to Amanda's car because of the hole in the fence, then that thief is taking advantage of the vulnerability. This is known as **exploiting** the security weakness. A hacker who knows an e-mail system does not scan attachments for viruses and thus sends infected e-mail messages to users is exploiting the vulnerability.

Amanda must decide if the risk of theft is high enough to keep her from purchasing the new stereo. A **risk** is the likelihood that the stereo will be stolen. In information security, a risk is the likelihood that a threat agent will exploit a vulnerability. Realistically, risk cannot ever be entirely eliminated; it would cost too much and take too long. Rather, some degree of risk must always be assumed. An organization should ask, "How much risk can we tolerate?" There are three options when dealing with risks: accept the risk, diminish the risk, or transfer the risk. In Amanda's case, she could accept the risk and buy the new stereo, knowing that the chances of it being stolen are high. Or she could diminish the risk by parking the car in a locked garage when possible and not letting anyone borrow her car keys. A third option is for Amanda to transfer the risk to someone else by purchasing additional car insurance. The insurance company then absorbs the loss and pays her if the stereo is stolen. In information security most risks should be diminished if possible. Table 1-5 summarizes information security terms.

Table 1-5 Security information terminology

Term	Example in Amanda's Scenario	Example in Information Security
Asset	Car stereo	Employee database
Threat	Steal stereo from car	Steal data
Threat agent	Thief	Attacker, virus, flood
Vulnerability	Hole in fence	Software defect
Exploit	Climb through hole in fence	Send virus to unprotected e-mail server
Diminish risk	Transfer to insurance company	Educate users

Understanding the Importance of Information Security

Information security is important to businesses and individuals to prevent data theft, thwart identify theft, avoid the legal consequences of not securing information, maintain productivity, and foil cyberterrorism. The following sections discuss these reasons in more detail.

Preventing Data Theft

Security is often associated with theft prevention. Drivers install security systems on their cars in order to prevent them from being stolen. The same is true with information security: preventing data from being stolen is often cited by businesses as the primary goal of information security. Business data theft involves stealing proprietary business information, such as research for a new drug or a list of customers that competitors are eager to acquire.

The theft of data is the single largest cause of financial loss due to a security breach. According to the 2005 FBI's annual Computer Crime and Security Survey, more than 600 U.S. businesses lost over $31 million as a result of data theft. The actual figure of estimated loss could be much higher, considering that some businesses might have been reluctant to report losses because of the bad publicity it could generate.

Data theft is not limited to businesses. Individuals can likewise be victims. The number of reported incidents of credit card numbers stolen from Internet computers continues to soar, with one bank reporting losses from the fraudulent use of online credit card information approaching $5 billion annually.

Thwarting Identity Theft

Identity theft involves using someone's personal information, such as a Social Security number, to establish bank or credit card accounts that are then left unpaid, leaving the victim with the debts and a damaged credit rating. In some instances, thieves have even bought cars and houses by taking out loans in someone else's name. According to the Federal Trade Commission (FTC), the number of identity theft victims increased 152 percent from 2002-2004, and the cost of identity theft for 2004 exceeded $52 billion. The age group that suffered the most identity theft was adults 18-29 years of age.

The four states in which identity theft occurs most frequently are (in order) Arizona, Nevada, California, and Texas.

NOTE

At the national, state, and local level, legislation that deals with this growing problem continues to be enacted. For example, the Fair and Accurate Credit Transactions Act of 2003 is a federal law that establishes a national system of fraud detection and alerts, and requires credit agencies to identify patterns common to identity theft to prevent its occurrence. Consumers can also receive free copies of their credit reports each year to help them recognize potential identify thefts more quickly. However, industry experts agree that the best defense against identity theft is to prevent private data from being stolen. Information security attempts to thwart identity theft by making it more difficult for thieves to break into computers and networks that contain personal information.

Identity theft is covered in detail in Chapter 4.

NOTE

Avoiding Legal Consequences

In recent years a number of federal and state laws have been enacted to protect the privacy of electronic data. Businesses that fail to protect data may face serious penalties. Some of these laws include the following:

- *The Health Insurance Portability and Accountability Act of 1996 (HIPAA)*—Under the **Health Insurance Portability and Accountability Act (HIPAA)**, healthcare enterprises must guard protected health information and implement policies and procedures to safeguard it, whether it be in paper or electronic format. HIPAA has two parts. Title I protects health insurance coverage for workers and their families. Title II deals with administrative simplification and puts a government agency in charge of national standards for electronic health care transactions and national identifiers for healthcare providers and employers. Those who wrongfully disclose individually identifiable health information with the intent to sell it can be fined up to $250,000 and spend 10 years in prison.

- *The Sarbanes-Oxley Act of 2002 (Sarbox)*—As a reaction to a rash of corporate fraud, the **Sarbanes–Oxley Act (Sarbox)** is an attempt to fight corporate corruption. Sarbox covers the corporate officers, auditors, and attorneys of publicly traded companies. Stringent reporting requirements and internal controls on electronic financial reporting systems are required. Corporate officers who willfully and knowingly certify a false financial report can be fined up to $5 million and serve 20 years in prison.

- *The Gramm-Leach-Bliley Act (GLBA)*—Like HIPAA, the **Gramm–Leach–Bliley Act (GLBA)**, passed in 1999, protects private data. GLBA requires banks and financial institutions to alert customers of their policies and practices in disclosing customer information. All electronic and paper formats containing personally identifiable financial information must be protected. The penalty for noncompliance for a class of individuals can be as high as $500,000.

- *USA Patriot Act of 2001*—Passed shortly after the terrorist attacks on September 11, 2001, the **USA Patriot Act** is designed to broaden the surveillance of law enforcement agencies so they can detect and suppress terrorism. Businesses, organizations, and colleges must provide information, including records and documents, to law enforcement agencies under the authority of a valid court order, subpoena, or other authorized agency. These records include borrowed print material from a college library, Internet site access, and e-mail and telephone communications. The Act also authorizes law enforcement to install electronic monitoring devices to assess computer and telephone usage. There are a variety of penalties for violating this Act.

- *The California Database Security Breach Act of 2003*—The **California Database Security Breach Act** is a state law that covers any state agency, person, or company that does business in California. It requires businesses to inform California residents within 48 hours if a breach of personal information has or is believed to have occurred. It defines personal information as a name with a Social Security number, driver's license number, state ID card, account number, credit card number, or debit card number, along with any required security access codes.

- *Children's Online Privacy Protection Act of 1998 (COPPA)*—In November 1998, the U.S. Congress passed the **Children's Online Privacy Protection Act (COPPA)** and directed the FTC to establish rules for its implementation. COPPA requires operators of online services or Web sites designed for children under the age of 13 to obtain parental consent prior to the collection, use, disclosure, or display of a child's personal information. The same requirements apply to general audience sites and services when the operator actually knows that it is collecting, using, or disclosing a child's personal information. COPPA also prohibits sites from limiting children's participation in an activity when the children (or their parents) choose not to disclose more personal information than is reasonably necessary to participate.

The penalties for violating these laws can be severe. Businesses and individuals must make every effort to keep electronic data secure from hostile outside forces in order to ensure compliance with these laws and avoid serious legal consequences.

Maintaining Productivity

Activities related to cleaning up after an attack divert resources, such as time and money, away from normal activities. When computers and networks don't function properly as a result of an attack, employees cannot be productive and complete important tasks. According to the ComputerVirus Prevalence Survey, the average cost for an organization to recover from an attack increased to more than $100,000 in 2004 in lost man-hours and related costs. Some businesses reported an average of more than 3,000 man-hours lost. Results from the latest Computer Crime and Security Survey indicate that virus attacks alone cost more than $42 million. These costs associated with "business continuity" can be significant. Table 1-6 provides an estimate of lost salary and productivity during a virus attack and cleanup.

Table 1-6 Cost of attacks

Number Total Employees	Average Hourly Salary	Number of Employees to Combat Attack	Hours Required to Stop Attack and Clean Up	Total Lost Salaries	Total Lost Hours of Productivity
100	$25	1	48	$4,066	81
250	$25	3	72	$17,050	300
500	$30	5	80	$28,333	483
1000	$30	10	96	$220,000	1,293

NOTE

The most expensive malicious attack on record, the 2000 Love Bug, cost an estimated $8.7 billion.

Spam, or unsolicited e-mail messages, was originally considered to be a nuisance rather than a security breach. However, because many computer attacks can be launched through e-mail messages, most network professionals now regard spam as a security risk. Although steps can be taken to restrict spam from entering a user's e-mail account, many unsolicited messages still slip through. According to the research group Postini, almost 230 million spam messages are sent each day, which is 67 percent of the total amount of e-mail transmitted. Almost 10 out of every 14 e-mails are spam. It is estimated that U.S. businesses forfeit $9 billion each year in lost productivity as employees spend time trying to restrict spam and deleting it from their e-mail accounts.

NOTE A major Internet service provider (ISP) set up filters to prevent unwanted "spam" e-mail from infecting users' inboxes. However, officials in one county in Florida found that the filtering had blocked e-mails sent to warn residents of hurricanes.

Foiling Cyberterrorism

An area of growing concern among many defense experts is surprise attacks by terrorist groups using computer technology and the Internet. These attacks could cripple a nation's electronic and commercial infrastructure. Such an attack is known as **cyberterrorism**. Utility companies, telecommunications, and financial services are considered prime targets of cyberterrorists because the terrorists can significantly disrupt business and personal activities by destroying a few targets. For example, disabling an electrical power plant could cripple businesses, homes, transportation services, and communications over a wide area.

NOTE In August 2003 a malicious program launched through the Internet disabled portions of the monitoring system at an Ohio nuclear power plant.

One of the challenges in combating cyberterrorism is that many prime targets are not owned and managed by the federal government. For example, almost 85 percent of the nation's most critical computer networks and infrastructures are owned and managed by private companies. Because these networks are not centrally controlled by the government, it is difficult to coordinate and maintain security.

Information security is the key to ensuring that the nation's ability to withstand an attack and respond appropriately is not compromised. Many industry experts believe that security to protect against cyberterrorism is vital in the nation's war against terrorism.

SECURITY IN YOUR WORLD

Susan set her drink on the table to listen to her friends as they ate lunch in the cafeteria. The W32-FireStorm worm had also attacked the school's computers and forced the school to disconnect from the Internet until the damage could be repaired and new security software could be installed. Susan's economics class was cancelled because they could not use the computers in the lab.

"Teenagers," said Frieda, one of Susan's friends. "They're the ones who write these kinds of sick programs. They've got too much free time on their hands and all they do is play games and write worms. They ought to be locked up for it!"

"I don't know," said Paula. "My younger brother's really smart about computers but I don't think he could do that. I wonder if the companies that sell security write the worms so people will have to buy their stuff."

Just then Professor Pitkin walked by their table. "Who do you think writes these worms?" Susan asked him. He smiled and said, "Teachers. They do it to cancel classes."

WHO ARE THE ATTACKERS?

The types of people behind computer attacks can be divided into several categories. These include hackers, crackers, script kiddies, employees, spies, and cyberterrorists.

Hackers

Although the term **hacker** is commonly used, computer experts and others debate its definition. Some people use "hacker" in a generic sense to identify anyone who illegally breaks into or attempts to break into a computer system. Used in this way, "hacker" is synonymous with "attacker." Others use the term "hacker" more narrowly to mean a person who uses his or her advanced computer skills to attack computers only to expose security flaws. Although breaking into another person's computer system is illegal, some hackers believe it is ethically acceptable as long as they do not commit theft, vandalism, or breach any confidentiality. These hackers (sometimes called "white hats") claim that their motive is to improve security by seeking out security holes so that they can be fixed.

However, security vulnerabilities can be exposed in ways other than attacking another computer without the owner's consent; most security professionals would not refer to themselves as hackers. Therefore, the general use of the term hacker to refer to someone who attacks computers is usually the more widely accepted usage of this word.

1

Crackers

A **cracker** sometimes refers to a person who violates system security with malicious intent. Like hackers, crackers have advanced knowledge of computers and networks and have the skills to exploit vulnerabilities in them. Unlike ethical hackers who claim to be only searching for security weaknesses, crackers (sometimes called "black hats") destroy data, deny legitimate users of service, or otherwise cause serious problems on computers and networks. Crackers can be identified by their malicious actions: they intend to do harm to any computer they can break into.

 NOTE The term cracker was coined around 1985 by some hackers who wanted to distance themselves from those who attack computer systems with malicious intent.

Script Kiddies

Much like crackers, **script kiddies** want to break into computers to create damage. However, whereas crackers have an advanced knowledge of computers and networks, script kiddies are unskilled users. Script kiddies do their work by downloading automated hacking software (scripts) from Web sites and then using it to break into computers.

While script kiddies lack the technical skills of crackers, they are sometimes considered more dangerous. Script kiddies tend to be computer users who have almost unlimited amounts of leisure time that they can use to attack systems. Their success in using automated software scripts tends to fuel their desire to break into more computers and cause even more harm. Because script kiddies do not understand the technology behind what they are doing, they often indiscriminately target a wide range of computers, causing problems for a large audience.

Spies

A computer **spy** is a person who has been hired to break into a computer and steal information. Spies do not randomly search for unsecured computers to attack as script kiddies, crackers, and hackers do. Rather, spies are hired to attack a specific computer that contains sensitive information. Their goal is to break into that computer and take the information without drawing any attention to their actions. Spies, like hackers, possess excellent computer skills.

Thieves

Unlike a spy who targets a specific source, thieves search for any unprotected computer and attempt to steal credit card numbers, banking passwords, or similar information. From July through December of 2004, 54 percent of the top 50 malicious Internet programs were designed to steal such confidential financial information. This is up from 44 percent from the previous six months. According to some security experts, these new Internet thieves make up the fastest growing segment of Internet attacks. Often the thieves are linked to organized crime syndicates operating from overseas.

Employees

One of the largest information security threats to a business comes from an unlikely source: its employees. Why would employees break into their company's computer? Sometimes an employee might want to show the company a weakness in their security. On other occasions, employees who have some reason to be disgruntled may be intent on retaliating against the company. Some employees may be motivated by money. For example, a competitor might approach an employee and offer money in exchange for stealing information. In some instances, employees have even been blackmailed into stealing from their employers.

Cyberterrorists

Many security experts fear that terrorists will turn their attacks to the network and computer infrastructure to cause panic among citizens and wreak havoc with vital information systems. Known as **cyberterrorists**, such people may attack because of their ideology—for the sake of their principles or beliefs. A report distributed by the Institute for Security Technology Studies at Dartmouth College lists three goals of a cyberattack: to deface electronic information (such as Web sites) to spread misinformation and propaganda; to deny service to legitimate computer users; and to commit unauthorized intrusions into systems and networks that result in outages of critical infrastructure and corruption of vital data.

NOTE

A White House cybersecurity adviser has urged greater attention to potential security breaches online. He cautioned, "As long as we have vulnerabilities in cyberspace, and as long as America has enemies, we are at the risk of the two coming together to severely damage our great country."

Cyberterrorists are sometimes considered the attackers that should be feared the most, for it is almost impossible to predict when or where an attack may occur. Unlike hackers or crackers who continuously probe systems or create attacks, cyberterrorists can lie dormant for several years and then suddenly strike a network in a new way. Their targets may include a small group of computers or networks that can affect the largest number of users, such as the computers that control the electrical power grid of a state or region. An isolated attack could cause a power blackout that would affect tens of millions of people.

Defending Against Attacks

Protecting computers against a wide range of attacks calls for a wide range of defense mechanisms. Although multiple defenses may be necessary to withstand attacks, these defenses should be based on five fundamental security principles: layering, limiting, diversity, obscurity, and simplicity. This section examines each of these principles, which provide a foundation for building a secure system.

Layering

The Hope diamond is a massive (45 carat) stone that by some estimates is worth one-quarter of a billion dollars. How are precious stones like the Hope diamond protected from theft? They are not openly displayed in public with a single security guard standing at the door. Instead, these stones are enclosed in protective cases that are bullet-proof, smash-proof, and resistant to almost any outside force. The cases are located in special rooms with massive walls and sensors that can detect slight movements or vibrations. The doors to the rooms are monitored around the clock by remote security cameras, and the video image from each camera is recorded on tape. The rooms are in buildings surrounded by fences and roaming security guards. In short, precious stones are protected by *layers* of security. If one layer is penetrated—such as the thief getting into the building—several more layers must still be breached, and each layer is often more difficult to breach than the previous. A layered approach has the advantage of creating a barrier of multiple defenses that can be coordinated to thwart a variety of attacks.

NOTE   The Hope diamond has not always had multiple layers of security. In 1958, this priceless diamond was placed in a plain brown paper wrapper and sent by registered first-class U.S. mail to the Smithsonian Institution! The envelope in which it was sent is on display at the Smithsonian along with the diamond itself.

Information security likewise must be created in layers. If there is only one defense mechanism, an attacker may be able to circumvent it. Instead, a security system must have layers, making it unlikely that an attacker has the tools and skills to break through *all* the layers of defenses. A layered approach can also be useful in resisting a variety of attacks. Layered security provides the most comprehensive protection.

Limiting

Consider again the issue of protecting a precious diamond. Although a diamond may be on display for the general public to view, permitting anyone to touch the stone increases the chances that it will be stolen. Only approved personnel should be authorized to handle the diamond. Limiting who can access the diamond reduces the threat against it.

The same is true with information security. Limiting access to information reduces the threat against it. Only those who must use data should have access to it. In addition, the amount of access granted to someone should be limited to what that person needs to know.

For example, access to the human resource database for an organization should be limited to approved employees, such as department managers and vice presidents. An entry-level computer technician might back up the database everyday, but he should not be able to view the data, such as employee salaries, because he has no job-related need to do so.

 What level of access should users have? The best answer is the *least amount necessary* to do their jobs, and no more.

NOTE

Some ways to limit access are technology based (such as assigning file permissions so that a user can only read but not modify a file), while others are procedural (prohibiting an employee from removing a sensitive document from the premises). The key is that access must be restricted to the bare minimum.

Diversity

Diversity is closely related to layering. Just as you should protect data with layers of security, so too must the layers be different (diverse) so that if attackers penetrate one layer, they cannot use the same techniques to break through the other layers. A jewel thief, for instance, might be able to foil the security camera by dressing in black clothes, but should not be able to use the same steps to trick the motion detection system.

Using diverse layers of defense means that breaching one security layer does not compromise the whole system. Diversity may be achieved in several ways. For example, some organizations use multiple security products provided by different vendors. An attacker who can circumvent a Brand A device would have more difficulty trying to break through a Brand B device because they are different.

Obscurity

Suppose a thief who wants to steal a precious diamond plans to do so during a shift change of the security guards. When the thief observes the guards, however, he finds that the guards do not change shifts at the same time each night. On Monday they rotate shifts at 7:15 PM, while on Tuesday they rotate at 6:50 PM, and the following Monday they rotate at 6:25 PM. The thief cannot find out the times of these changes because they are kept secret. Because the shift changes are confusing and not well known, an attack becomes more difficult. This technique is sometimes called "security by obscurity." Obscuring what goes on inside a system or organization and avoiding clear patterns of behavior make attacks from the outside much more difficult.

An example of obscurity would be to not reveal the type of computer, operating system, software, and network connection a computer uses. An attacker who knows that information can more easily determine the weaknesses of the system to attack it. If this information is hidden, then it takes much more effort to acquire the information and, in many instances, an attacker will then move on to another computer in which the information is easily available. Obscuring information can be an important way to protect information.

Simplicity

Because attacks can come from a variety of sources and in many forms, information security is by its very nature complex. The more complex something becomes, the more difficult it is to understand. A security guard who does not understand how motion detectors interact with infrared trip lights may not know what to do when one system alarm shows an intruder but the other does not. In addition, complex systems allow many opportunities for something to go wrong. In short, complex systems can be a thief's ally.

The same is true with information security. Complex security systems can be hard to understand, troubleshoot, and feel secure about. As much as possible, a secure system should be simple for those on the inside to understand and use. Complex security schemes are often compromised to make them easier for trusted users to work with—but this can also make it easier for the attackers. In short, creating a system that is simple from the inside but complex on the outside can be difficult, but it reaps a major benefit.

BUILDING A COMPREHENSIVE SECURITY STRATEGY

Defending against attacks through the fundamental security principles of layering, limiting, diversity, obscurity, and simplicity helps provide a theoretical model for building a secure system. Yet how are these principles put into practice? That is, what does a practical, comprehensive security strategy look like? There are four key elements to creating a practical security strategy. These elements are not new; rather, their origins can be traced back 1,000 years ago to the days of castles in medieval Europe. Understanding these key elements as they were used in castles during the Middle Ages helps to see how they can be applied when developing practical security strategies today.

Block Attacks

BLOCK ATTACKS

The word *castle* comes from a Latin word meaning *fortress,* and most castles served in this capacity. One of a castle's primary functions was to protect the king's family and citizens of the countryside in the event of an attack from a hostile enemy. A castle was designed to block enemy attacks in two distinct ways. First, a castle was surrounded by a deep moat that was filled with water, which prevented the enemy from getting close to the castle. In addition, many castles had a high protective stone wall between the moat and the outer walls of the castle. The purpose of the moat and protective wall was to create a *security perimeter* around the castle itself: any attacker would have to breach the strong perimeter first.

NOTE

The moat and the high stone wall are examples of using layers as well as diversity.

Effective information security today follows this same model of blocking attacks by having a strong security perimeter. Usually this security perimeter is part of the computer network to which a personal computer is attached. If attacks are blocked by the network security perimeter, then the attacker cannot reach the personal computers on which data is stored. Security devices can be added to a computer network that continually analyzes traffic coming into the network from the outside (such as e-mail or Web pages) and block unauthorized or malicious traffic.

In addition to perimeter security, most castles provided *local security*. Consider an arrow shot by an attacker that travels over the moat and outer wall. Those inside the castle defending it would be vulnerable to arrow attacks despite the strong security perimeter. One solution is to provide each defender with a shield that deflects the arrows.

This same is true for information security. As important as a strong network security perimeter is to blocking attacks, some will invariably slip through the defense. It is vital to also have local security on all of the personal computers as well to defend against any attack that breaches the perimeter.

NOTE

The latest technique in local security is for the network to automatically check the security settings of each personal computer. Those computers that lack the proper local security hardware or software to defend against attacks are immediately disconnected from the network until their configurations have been corrected.

Update Defenses

UPDATE DEFENSES

Imagine a castle in which each of the defenders has a personal leather shield to protect against arrows shot over the wall. The defenders may feel that they have adequate protection against the attacker's arrows. Yet what if a new attack involved arrows with their tips on fire? If the defenders had never seen flaming arrows before, they would not know how to prevent their leather shields from catching on fire when struck with a flaming arrow. This "new technology" of flaming arrows could prove to be disastrous if the defenders had no means to change their type of shields.

Today's information security attackers are as equally inventive as attackers were over 1,000 years ago. New types of attacks appear almost daily. Users protecting information today must be resourceful in continually updating defenses. This involves updating defensive hardware and software as well as applying operating system patches on a regular basis.

1

Minimize Losses

As a flaming arrow comes sailing over the wall of the castle, it may strike a bale of hay and set it ablaze. If the defenders were not prepared with a bucket of water to douse the flames, the entire contents of the castle could burn. Being prepared to minimize losses is essential in defending a castle.

Likewise, today's attacks might slip through security perimeters and local defenses. Action must be taken in advance to minimize losses. This may involve keeping backup copies of important data in a safe place such as CD-ROMs or other backup devices. For an organization, minimizing losses might mean having an entire business recovery solution policy that details what to do in the event of a successful attack.

Send Secure Information

A castle that is under siege for an extended period might require outside help from an ally. But how can these friendly distant forces receive the cry for help? In some instances, the castle sends a messenger on horseback to break through the enemy lines to reach the supporters. In order to accomplish this task, the messenger takes the swiftest horse and wears layers of protective body armor.

A parallel can be drawn to today's world of information security. As users send e-mail and other information over the Internet, the information must be protected and kept secure. This may involve "scrambling" the data so that unauthorized eyes cannot read it without knowing the correct code to unscramble it. In other instances, it may require establishing a secure electronic link between the sender and receiver that would prevent an attacker from reaching the information. Information security is more than being on the defensive; it often involves taking proactive steps to thwart attackers.

CHAPTER SUMMARY

- ❑ Several difficulties are involved in keeping computers and the information on them secure. These can be clearly seen by the number of attacks as well as different types of attacks that occur. The volume and diversity of these attacks make it particularly hard to mount a defense against them.

- ❑ A number of trends illustrate why information security is becoming more difficult. One is the speed of attacks. With modern tools at their disposal, attackers can quickly scan systems to find weaknesses and then launch attacks with unprecedented speed. Another problem in defending against attackers is the increased sophistication of attacks. Security attacks are becoming more difficult to detect and defend against. Conversely, because attackers can detect computer weaknesses faster, they can also more quickly attempt to exploit vulnerabilities. Instead of an attack coming from one source, attacks today can be distributed by using thousands of computers to access or harm a single computer or network. Finally, user confusion is often considered one of the primary reasons that the rate of computer infections continues at such a high pace today. Although a variety of technology tools can be used to defend against attackers, security tools that are not properly implemented are of little value.

❑ Information security protects the integrity, confidentiality, and availability of information on the devices that store, manipulate, and transmit the information through products, people, and procedures.

❑ Information security has its own set of terminology. A threat is an event or an action that can defeat security measures and result in a loss. A threat agent is a person or thing that has the power to carry out a threat. A vulnerability is a weakness that allows a threat agent to bypass security. Taking advantage of a vulnerability is called an exploit. A risk is the likelihood that a threat agent will exploit a vulnerability.

❑ Preventing the theft of information is accepted as the single most important reason for protecting data. Other reasons include avoiding legal consequences, maintaining productivity, foiling cyberterrorism, and thwarting identity theft.

❑ A hacker possesses advanced computer skills far beyond the average user. Hackers use these skills to attempt to access computer resources by circumventing any protective measures that are in place. Some hackers commit their acts to seek out and report security flaws; others may attack out of boredom or curiosity. A cracker violates system security with a malicious intent. Crackers use their advanced computer knowledge and skills to destroy data, deny legitimate users of service, or otherwise cause serious problems on computers and networks. Script kiddies download automated hacking software from Web sites and then use it to break into computers. A computer spy is someone hired to break into a computer and steal information for financial gain. Employees attack systems out of egotism, vengeance, or financial gain. Cyberterrorists have an ideological motivation for attacking computers and networks.

❑ The basic principles for creating a secure environment are layering, limiting, diversity, obscurity, and simplicity. Layering involves creating a barrier of many defenses that eliminates a single point of failure. Limiting means restricting access to information to the minimum level needed to perform activities. A diverse security scheme, such as one that uses redundant hardware from a variety of vendors, provides additional security. Obscuring information about security systems helps keep attackers off balance. Finally, simplicity involves using simple security defenses, because complex systems can be difficult to manage and tempt users to circumvent the security so it's easier for them to use the system.

KEY TERMS

asset — An entity that has value.

California Database Security Breach Act — A state act that requires disclosure to California residents if a breach of personal information has or is believed to have occurred.

Children's Online Privacy Protection Act (COPPA) — A federal act that requires operators of online services or Web sites directed at children under the age of 13 to obtain parental consent prior to the collection, use, disclosure, or display of a child's personal information.

cracker — A person who violates computer system security with a malicious intent.

cyberterrorism — An attack launched by a cyberterrorist that could cripple a nation's electronic and commercial infrastructure.

cyberterrorist — An attacker motivated by ideology to attack computers or infrastructure networks.

exploit — To take advantage of a vulnerability.

Gramm-Leach-Bliley Act (GLBA) — A federal act that requires private data to be protected by banks and other financial institutions.

hacker — 1) Anyone who illegally breaks into or attempts to break into a computer system. 2) A person who uses advanced computer skills to attack computers but not with a malicious intent.

Health Insurance Portability and Accountability Act (HIPAA) — A federal act that requires healthcare enterprises to guard protected health information.

information security — The tasks of guarding digital information.

patch — Software used to repair security flaws or other problems in an existing software program or operating system.

risk — The likelihood that a threat agent will exploit a vulnerability.

Sarbanes-Oxley Act (Sarbox) — A federal act that enforces reporting requirements and internal controls on electronic financial reporting systems.

script kiddie — An unskilled user who downloads automated attack software to attack computers.

spam — Unsolicited e-mail messages.

spy — A person who has been hired to break into a computer and steal information.

threat — An event or action that may defeat the security measures in place and result in a loss.

threat agent — A person or thing that has the power to carry out a threat.

USA Patriot Act — A federal act that broadens the surveillance of law enforcement agencies to enhance the detection and suppression of terrorism.

vulnerability — A weakness that allows a threat agent to bypass security.

zero day attack — An attack that occurs when an attacker discovers and exploits a previously unknown flaw, providing "zero days" of warning.

REVIEW QUESTIONS

1. Many attack methods can launch new attacks without any _____ , increasing the speed at which systems are attacked.
   a. human initiative
   b. cost
   c. network infrastructure
   d. Internet connection

2. Attackers now use common _____ tools, such as e-mail and Hypertext Transfer Protocol (HTTP), to send data or commands to attack computers, making it difficult to distinguish an attack from legitimate traffic.
   a. process qualifier
   b. Internet
   c. keyboard
   d. Disk Operating System

3. A _____ occurs when an attacker discovers and exploits a previously unknown flaw.
   a. hidden process attack (HPA)
   b. rogue implementation
   c. private key exploit
   d. zero day attack

4. A _____ is software that is used to repair security flaws or other problems in an existing software program or operating system.
   a. patch
   b. mesh
   c. coronet
   d. coverall

5. The term _____ is frequently used to describe the tasks of guarding information that is in a digital format.
   a. information security
   b. Resource Device Allocation (RDA)
   c. diversity
   d. Universal Protection Prevention (UPP)

6. Integrity ensures that the information is correct and that no unauthorized person or malicious software has altered that data. True or False?

7. Confidentiality ensures that only unauthorized parties can view the information. True or False?

8. Information security protects the confidentiality, integrity, and availability of information on the devices that store, manipulate, and transmit the information through products, people, and procedures. True or False?

9. An asset is defined as something that has a value. True or False?

10. Personnel hacking (PH) involves using someone's personal information, such as Social Security number, to establish bank or credit card accounts that are then left unpaid. True or False?

11. Under the _____ , healthcare enterprises must guard protected health information and implement policies and procedures to safeguard that information, whether it be in paper or electronic format.

12. _____ is a federal act that attempts to fight corporate corruption.

13. An attack launched by terrorists that could cripple a nation's electronic and commercial infrastructure is known as _____ .

14. The term _____ is often used in a generic sense to describe anyone who illegally breaks into or attempts to break into a computer system and is synonymous with "attacker."

15. A(n) _____ is sometimes used to refer to a person who violates system security with malicious intent.

16. Explain what script kiddies are and how they operate.

17. How can layering help protect information from attacks?

18. What is identity theft?

19. What is the purpose and scope of the USA Patriot Act?

20. What is cyberterrorism?

HANDS-ON PROJECTS

HANDS-ON PROJECTS

Project 1-1: Working With Microsoft Office Security

The Microsoft Office suite contains several tools that can enhance the security of its documents. In this project you will work with three security settings: setting a password, disabling macros, and creating metadata.

1. Start Microsoft Word 2003, and open a new, blank document.

2. Click **Tools** on the menu bar, and then click **Options**. The Options dialog box opens. Click the **Security** tab to see the options, as shown in Figure 1-3.

3. In the Password to open text box, type **ab1234cd**, and then click **OK**. The Confirm Password dialog box opens so you can verify the password. Type **ab1234cd** again and then click **OK**.

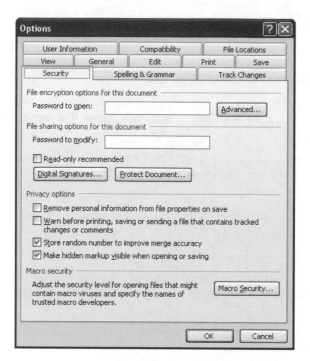

Figure 1-3   Security tab in the Options dialog box

4. Click **File** on the menu bar, and then click **Save**. Save the document as **Project 1–1**.

5. Close the document and Word by clicking **File** on the menu bar and then clicking **Exit**.

6. Start Microsoft Word again. Open the document by clicking **File** on the menu bar and then clicking **Open**. Locate and then double-click **Project 1-1.doc**. What happens when you try to open a password-protected document?

7. Enter the password **ab1234cd** when prompted to open the document, and then click **OK**.

8. Microsoft Office macros can be used to infect a computer with viruses and should be disabled unless you are absolutely sure that the macro is from a secure source. Click **Tools** on the menu bar, point to **Macro**, and then click **Security**. The Security dialog box opens, as shown in Figure 1-4.

9. Click the **Security Level** tab, if necessary. Then click the **High** option button if it is not already selected.

10. Click the **Trusted Publishers** tab.

11. Click to uncheck the **Trust all installed add-ins and templates** check box and the **Trust access to Visual Basic Project** check box as necessary.

12. Click **OK**.

Figure 1-4   Security dialog box

NOTE You can perform the same steps in Microsoft Excel and PowerPoint to disable macros. Disabling macros will protect you from viruses but may also prevent you from running a valid macro, such as one that is contained in a company payroll spreadsheet. In this case it may be necessary to change the security setting to Medium, which will ask you first for permission to load the file with the macros.

13. Microsoft Office products also add information about a document, such as the person who created the document, the date and time, and other information. This information, sometimes called "metadata," could be used by an unauthorized person to view personal information. Click **File** on the Word menu bar, and then click **Properties** to display the Properties dialog box, as shown in Figure 1-5.

    Enter the following information:

    Subject—**Metadata**

    Manager—The name of your instructor or supervisor

    Category—**Computer Security**

    Keywords—**Metadata**

    Comments—**Viewing metadata in Microsoft Word**

14. Click the **Statistics** tab and view the information it contains. How could an attacker use this metadata when examining this file?

15. Click the **Custom** tab, and in Name box click **Checked by**.

16. Click the **Type** list arrow, and then click **Yes or no**. The Value field now contains two option buttons: Yes and No.

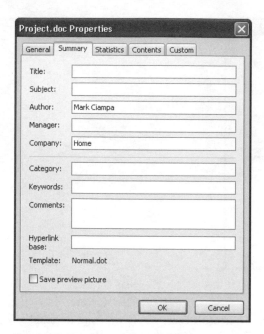

Figure 1-5   Properties dialog box

17. Click the **No** option button.

18. Click the **Add** button.

19. Click to select five other fields in the Name box. Match the type of data that will be entered in this field with the values in the Type field, as shown in Figure 1-6. Click **OK** to close the Properties dialog box when you are finished.

20. Save the file and close it. Close Microsoft Word.

**HANDS-ON
PROJECTS**

Project 1-2: Managing User Accounts

The principle of limiting access to information greatly reduces the threat against it. Only those individuals who must use the data or computer should have access to it. Making a computer secure involves properly managing user accounts and their privileges as well as disabling accounts that are not necessary. Each user should have an individual account and password. When a user no longer uses that account, it should be disabled. In this project, you will set up and delete user accounts. You should have administrator privileges to perform this assignment. If you are using a computer in a school's computer lab or a computer at work, talk to your network administrator before performing this project. You may need special permissions set to change these configuration settings.

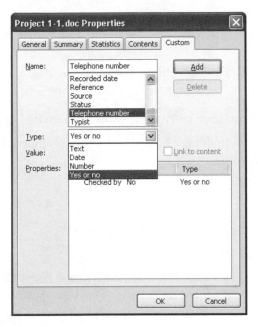

Figure 1-6   Value options

1. On a Windows XP computer, click **Start**, and then click **Control Panel**.

2. If the Control Panel opens in Category view, click **User Accounts**. If the Control panel opens in Classic view, double-click **User Accounts**. The User Accounts window opens.

3. Click **Change an account**.

4. Look at the Guest account. This account lets anyone use the computer without a user name and password. It should be disabled. (If the description for this account is "Guest account is on", click **Guest**. Then click **Turn off the guest account**.)

5. In the left pane of the User Accounts window, click **Create a new account**.

6. Type **USER1** in the Type a name for the new account text box, and then click **Next**. The Pick an account type step appears.

7. In the left pane, click **User account types** to learn about the difference between computer administrator and limited account types. Read the description, and then close the Learn About window.

8. In the right pane of the Pick an account type step, click the **Limited** option button.

9. Click **Create Account**. The account USER1 appears in the list of accounts.

10. Click **USER1** to display a set of options for changing this account.

11. Click **Create a password**. Follow the instructions on the screen to enter a password for this account. Click **Create Password** when you are finished, and then close all open windows.

12. Click **Start** and then click **Log Off**. The Log Off Windows dialog box opens.

13. Click **Log Off**.

14. At the logon window, click **USER1** and then enter the password you created in Step 11.

Now you can delete this account so it can no longer be used on your computer. To do so, you must log on to your previous administrative account.

1. Click **Start**, and then click **Log Off**.

2. Click **Log Off**.

3. At the logon window, log onto your account as you usually do.

4. Click **Start**, and then click **Control Panel**.

5. If the Control Panel opens in Category view, click **User Accounts**. If the Control panel opens in Classic view, double-click **User Accounts**. The User Accounts window opens.

6. Click **Change an account**. The Pick an account to change window opens.

7. Click **USER1**.

8. Click **Delete the account**.

9. Click **Delete Files**.

10. Click **Delete Account** and then close all open windows.

HANDS-ON PROJECTS

Project 1-3: Viewing Windows Auditing of User Accounts

Auditing is an important task that security personnel perform to help monitor computers and the network. Windows Server 2003 and Windows XP automatically create three event logs: Application, System, and Security. All users can view Application and System logs, but only administrators can access Security logs. The Application log contains events logged by applications or programs, while the System log contains events logged by the Windows system components (such as the failure of a driver or other system component to load during startup). The Security log can record security events such as valid and invalid logon attempts, as well as events related to resource use, such as creating, opening, or deleting files. An administrator can specify what events are recorded in the Security log.

There are five types of entries recorded in the Event logs:

❐ *Error*—a significant problem such as the loss of data or loss of functionality

❐ *Warning*—an event that is not necessarily significant but may indicate a possible future problem, such as low disk space

1

❏ *Information*—an event that describes the successful operation of an application, driver, or service

❏ *Success Audit*—an audited security access attempt that succeeds. For example, a user's successful attempt to log onto the system is listed as a Success Audit event.

❏ *Failure Audit*—an audited security access attempt that fails. For example, if a user tries to access a network drive and fails, the attempt is logged as a Failure Audit event.

In this project, you will view the security event log.

1. Log off of your computer, and then attempt to log on entering an incorrect password.

2. Log on again using your correct password.

> If you are using a computer that does not require a password, see your instructor or lab supervisor about setting up a temporary user account.

TIP

3. Click **Start**, and then click **Control Panel**.

4. If the Control Panel opens in Category view, click **Performance and Maintenance**, and then click **Administrative Tools**. If the Control Panel opens in Classic view, double-click **Administrative Tools**.

5. Double-click **Event Viewer**. The Event Viewer window opens.

6. In the console tree in the left pane, click **Security**.

7. In the right pane, double-click the most recent failure audit. View the information about the failed logon.

8. Click the **Type** column heading to sort the entries by type, with the Failure Audits appearing first.

9. Double-click several of the failures to determine why they occurred.

10. Close all open windows.

HANDS-ON PROJECTS

Project 1-4: Receiving Updated Security Information

It is important to know the latest security threats to keep your computer secure. Instead of making constant visits to security Web sites in which you scan the page looking for information, a new approach automates this process and makes it easier to have the information delivered to you. RSS (the name behind the acronym is in debate, though one agreed upon by many is Really Simple Syndication) is an eXtensible Markup Language (XML) format for automatically retrieving content from a Web page and delivering it to your browser. From within the browser, you can then quickly scan, sort, and scroll through headline and article summaries in one pane while viewing the corresponding Web page in the other pane. RSS feeds are available for financial information, news headlines, and security alerts. In this project, you install an RSS reader and link it to a security site.

1. Open your Web browser, and then go the Pluck Web site at **www.pluck.com/ download.aspx**. Click the **Download** button next to **Pluck Internet Explorer Edition** to retrieve the latest version of Pluck, an RSS reader.

2. When the download dialog box appears, choose to save the file, navigate to where you saved the file, and double-click it (or, if you are using Windows XP or Windows Server 2003, click **Run**).

3. Close your Web browser.

4. Use the Installation Wizard to install Pluck on your computer. When installation is complete, Pluck automatically starts your browser.

5. At the **Welcome to Pluck!** window, click **create an account** in the left pane. Enter the requested information and then click **Sign In**. A dialog box might open indicating that you are not registered with the Pluck server. Click **Register Now**. You will then be asked to set up an account to register. Enter the requested information and then retrieve the e-mail message. Click the link in the e-mail message to activate the account.

6. The Pluck **Getting Started** window appears. Click **Get feeds**.

7. Click the **Technology** check box and then click **Add**. Click the **Next Page** button.

8. On the **Import bookmarks** page, click **Read & manage feeds**.

9. Click **Finish**.

10. Click the **Start Page** link.

11. In the **Browse Feeds** pane, click **Technology**.

12. Scroll down and click **SecurityFocus News**, and then click the **Pluck** icon. Click the **Technology** folder in the left pane.

13. Click **Save Item** and then click **OK**, if necessary.

14. Click **Security Focus News** located in the left pane, as shown in Figure 1-7.

    Security advisories will be fed regularly to your Web browser, as shown in Figure 1-8.

15. Close all windows.

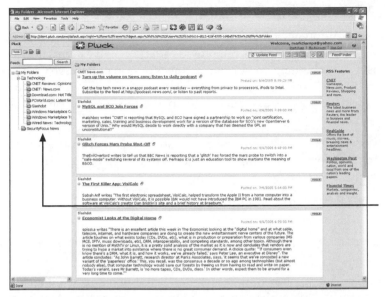

Figure 1-7   SecurityFocus News

Figure 1-8   Security Advisories

**HANDS-ON
PROJECTS**

Project 1-5: Viewing and Disabling Windows Services

Services are Microsoft Windows programs that the operating system uses to perform its functions. However, unnecessary services can provide attackers entry points into a computer. One of the first tasks in establishing a security baseline is to stop unnecessary services. Before stopping any services, you should know how to determine what services are running on a system. In this project, you explore several ways to see the services on a Windows XP computer.

If you are using a computer in a school's computer lab or a computer at work, talk to your network administrator before performing this project. You may need special permissions set before you can change these configuration settings.

1. On a Windows XP computer, click **Start** and then click **Run**. The Run dialog box opens.

2. Type **msconfig** and then press **Enter** to display the System Configuration Utility dialog box.

3. Click the **Services** tab, as shown in Figure 1-9. Scroll down to see which services are running or stopped. Note the extensive number of services that are running.

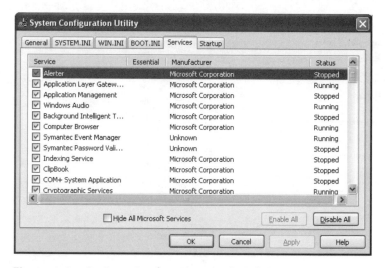

Figure 1-9   System Configuration Utility dialog box

4. Click **Cancel** to close the dialog box.

5. Click **Start** and then click **Run**. In the Run dialog box, type **Services.msc** and then press **Enter** to display the Services (Local) window, shown in Figure 1-10.

6. If necessary, expand the columns to read the description of the service. Then locate and click the **Secondary Logon** service. Notice that three options are displayed for this service: Stop, Pause, and Restart.

Figure 1-10   Services (Local) window

7. Double-click the **Secondary Logon** service to open the Secondary Logon Properties (Local Computer) dialog box, shown in Figure 1-11. Notice that it is here that a service can be stopped and started.

Figure 1-11   Secondary Logon Properties (Local Computer) dialog box

8. Click **Cancel** to close the dialog box. Then close the Services (Local) window.

9. Right-click a blank area of the taskbar, and then click **Task Manager** to open the Windows Task Manager dialog box.

10. Click the **Processes** tab. Scroll down to see the process names of the services.

11. You will now disable a service that is rarely used. Scroll down to see that the Clip-Book process (Clipsrv.exe) is not running. Then minimize the Windows Task Manager dialog box.

12. Click **Start** and then click **Run**. The Run dialog box opens.

13. Type **Services.msc** and then press **Enter** to display the Services (Local) window. If necessary, expand the columns to read the descriptions of the services.

14. Locate and then click the **ClipBook** service. Notice that only one option is displayed for this service: Start the service. This indicates that the service is currently not running.

15. Double-click the **ClipBook** service to open the ClipBook Properties (Local Computer) dialog box, shown in Figure 1-12.

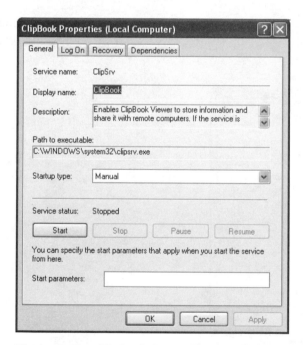

Figure 1-12   ClipBook Properties (Local Computer) dialog box

Notice that the startup mode is Manual, meaning that it is run only when needed. The service status is Stopped unless you have already used this service. Also notice that you can use a series of buttons to manage this service: Start, Stop, Pause, and Remove. Based on the current status of the service, some of the buttons may be unavailable.

16. Click the **Recovery** tab to display the recovery options, shown in Figure 1-13.

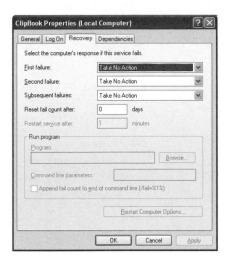

Figure 1-13   Recovery options for the ClipBook service

17. Click the **First failure** list arrow, and then click **Restart the Service**. This tells Windows that if the service is needed but is not running to start the service.

18. Click the **General** tab. Click the **Start** button to start this service.

19. Maximize the Windows Task Manager dialog box, and then click the **Image Name** column heading to sort the column. Locate clipserv.exe, shown in Figure 1-14.

20. Return to the ClipBook Properties (Local Computer) dialog box. (You may need to double-click **ClipBook** again in the Services (Local) window.) Click the **Stop** button.

21. Maximize the Windows Task Manager dialog box and note that Clipserv.exe is no longer running.

22. Return to the ClipBook Properties (Local Computer) dialog box. (You may need to double-click **ClipBook** again in the Services (Local) window.) Click the **Startup type** list arrow, and then click **Disabled**.

23. Click **Apply**. The ClipBook service now will not be loaded even if the service is needed.

24. Close all windows.

Figure 1-14 Clipserv.exe running

CASE PROJECTS

Case Project 1-1: Attack Experiences

Based on either your own personal experiences or those of someone you know (you may have to interview other students or a network administrator), write a paragraph regarding a computer attack that occurred. When did it happen? What was the attack? What type of damage did it inflict? How was the computer "fixed" after the attack? What could have prevented it?

Case Project 1-2: Helping Customers

As Susan waited at the electronics store, she overheard conversations by customers who thought their computers had been attacked by a worm. What could Susan have done to help these customers with their concerns? Make a list of the different options that Susan could have presented to these customers that would have given them more information about security. Are there short classes at a local college in your area that cover security from a user's perspective? Do computer stores have workshops on making computers more secure? Are there any magazine articles that explore home security that are easy to read and understand? What about Web sites that contain important information? Create a list of several different options for the area in which you live.

Case Project 1-3: Survey of Security

Survey a group of your classmates, friends, or acquaintances regarding security. First ask them how much they know about computer security. Then find out how secure their computers are: do they have good passwords and antivirus and antispyware software, for example. Have they ever tried to use someone else's computer without permission? Do they download music or copy photographs? Do they think that security is something they should be concerned about? Write a paragraph on what you find.

Case Project 1-4: Security Statistics Web Sites

The Internet is filled with Web sites that keep statistics on the latest attacks as well as summary data for the day, week, month, and year of the attacks. Using a search engine, locate several security statistics Web sites (try searching with the keywords "security statistics"). Narrow the list of sites down to the top three that you think contain good information. How could you use this type information?

Case Project 1-5: Baypoint Computer Consulting

Baypoint Computer Consulting (BCC) is a local information technology company that specializes in security. BCC often hires outside help to assist them with projects. A local chain of jewelry stores, Diamonds Are Forever, has recently been the victim of a security attack that caused their computers and network to be unavailable for several days. Diamonds Are Forever has contacted BCC for help.

BCC has contracted with you to create a presentation about security: the dangers of unprotected computer systems, who is responsible for launching attacks, and general principles regarding protecting a computer. Create a PowerPoint presentation of eight or more slides that covers this information. Because the audience does not have a strong technical background, your presentation should be more general in its tone and easily understood by those unfamiliar with computer security issues.

CHAPTER TWO

DESKTOP SECURITY

After completing this chapter you should be able to do the following:

➤ Describe the type of attacks that are launched against a desktop computer

➤ List the defenses that can be set up to protect a desktop computer

➤ Describe the steps for recovering from an attack

Security in Your World

"Guess what happened at work today," Lorenzo said to his new roommate, Brian. Lorenzo works at the home center store helping customers pick out door and window locks. "A man came in and said that he wanted to buy the most expensive deadbolt lock we had for his front door. He was going to be traveling in his new job and wanted to make sure the house was secure while he was gone. I showed to him a Secure Armor model 82605, which will stop a tank! He grabbed it right up."

"I then noticed in his shopping cart," Lorenzo continued, "that he had a cheap new garage door opener. I asked him if he was going to install that too, and he said he was. I pointed out to him that a thief can easily duplicate the code and open the door in a matter of seconds. His eyes lit right up! I then showed him another model that has over 3 billion codes so it's impossible to duplicate. It's funny that he was going to spend hundreds of dollars on a deadbolt door lock but leave the garage door unprotected!"

Brian closed his book. "I know just what you mean. In fact, we were talking about that in our computer class today." Lorenzo laughed and said, "You were talking about garage door openers in a computer class?" Brian smiled and said, "Well, not exactly. We were talking about computer security and about how people wrongly think that their computer is fully protected when they only have one kind of defensive software installed. The instructor said that it's like having a front door made out of armor but leaving the garage door or all the windows wide open."

Lorenzo sat down at his computer. "You mean there's more than one kind of software that I need? I have antivirus software installed on this computer. Isn't that enough?" Brian walked over to Lorenzo's computer. "No, not at all. Antivirus software stops only one type of problem from infecting your computer. There are a whole lot of other things that you need to defend against, too."

Lorenzo looked up from his computer. "What kinds of other things?"

Protecting your desktop computer has become a daunting challenge. Many different types of attacks can be launched against a personal computer, and each type of attack might have tens of thousands of variations. As attackers continue to create and modify attacks every day, users must be constantly vigilant to protect their desktop computers and the information on them.

One of the greatest challenges in security is that no single defense mechanism can adequately protect a desktop computer from all types of attacks. Whereas a single door lock can keep all types of threatening people from a house, the same is not true with a computer. Instead, specific defensive software must be installed and updated regularly—sometimes daily—to keep a computer secure. Unfortunately, knowing what to install, how to install it, and how to keep it regularly updated is challenging; this is one of the key reasons that attackers are so successful today.

In this chapter, we will examine desktop computer security. We will start by looking at the types of desktop computer attacks that occur today. Next, we will discuss what defenses must be in place to keep desktop information secure. Because it's not possible to guarantee that an attack will never be successful, we will conclude by looking at how to recover from an attack.

ATTACKS ON DESKTOP COMPUTERS

Although many types of attacks can affect a desktop computer, the major types can be classified into two categories. These categories are malicious software and basic desktop attacks.

"Desktop computers" can refer to either computers that sit on a user's desk or portable laptop computers.

NOTE

Malicious Software

Malicious software, also called **malware**, is the term used to describe computer programs designed to break into and create havoc on desktop computers. According to the security organization Sandvine, Internet service providers (ISPs) in North America spend more than $245 million annually to combat malware. The most common types of malware are viruses, worms, and logic bombs.

Viruses

A computer **virus** is a program that secretly attaches itself to a document or another program and executes when that document or program is opened. Like its biological equivalent, viruses require a host to carry them from one system to another. Although viruses once spread by exchanging infected floppy disks, today viruses spread primarily through CD-ROMs, Web sites, downloaded files, and e-mail attachments. After a computer is infected, the virus then seeks another computer to attack.

NOTE Modern viruses can be programmed to send themselves to all users listed in an e-mail address book. The recipients, seeing they have received a message from a friend or business contact, often unsuspectingly open the attachment, infect their own computer, and then unknowingly send the virus to their contacts.

2

A virus might do something as simple as display an annoying message, similar to the one shown in Figure 2-1.

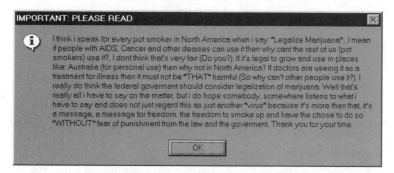

Figure 2-1   Annoying virus message

However, some viruses can be much more problematic. Viruses can:

- Cause a computer to continually crash
- Erase files from a hard drive
- Install hidden programs, such as stolen ("pirated") software, which is then secretly distributed or even sold to other users from the computer
- Make multiple copies of itself and consume all of the free space in a hard drive
- Reduce security settings and allow intruders to remotely access the computer
- Reformat the hard disk drive and erase its entire contents

NOTE The number of viruses is staggering. According to Sophos, an antivirus software vendor, more than 95,000 known viruses attack computers, and on average one new virus is written and released every hour.

In addition to e-mail, viruses can also be spread through **instant messaging (IM)**. IM is another method of online communication like e-mail, except that it is instantaneous. Using an IM program, such as MSN Messenger, AOL Instant Messenger, Yahoo Messenger, or others, users can receive messages almost immediately after they are sent. Like e-mail viruses, IM viruses are malicious or annoying programs that travel through IM. In most instances, IM viruses are spread when a user opens an infected file that was sent in an instant message.

The symptoms that indicate a virus has infected a computer include any of the following:

- An e-mail contact says that recently received e-mail messages from you contained unusual attachments.

- A program suddenly disappears from the computer.

- An e-mail message appears that has an unexpected attachment or the attachment has a double file extension, such as PICTURE.JPG.VPS or SUNSET.TIF.EXE. After opening the attachment, dialog boxes open or the computer slows significantly.

- New icons appear on the desktop that are not associated with any recently installed programs.

- New programs do not install properly.

- Out-of-memory error messages appear.

- Programs that used to function normally stop responding. If the software is removed and reinstalled, the problem continues.

- Sometimes the computer starts normally, but at other times it stops responding before the desktop icons and taskbar appear.

- Unusual dialog boxes or message boxes appear.

- Sounds or music plays from the speakers unexpectedly.

- The computer runs very slowly and takes a long time to start.

- There is a significant amount of modem activity.

- Windows restarts unexpectedly.

- Windows error messages appear listing "critical system files" that are missing and refuse to load.

Worms

Another type of malicious software is a **worm**. Although similar to viruses, worms are different in two regards. First, a virus must attach itself to a computer document, such as an e-mail message, and is spread by traveling along with the document. A worm, on the other hand, does not attach to a document to spread, but can instead travel by itself.

NOTE

Worms are most often distributed via e-mail attachments as separate executable programs. Although the worm does not depend on the e-mail message for its survival like a virus, but is self-contained within the separate program, it uses e-mail as a convenient means of distribution.

A second difference between a worm and a virus is that a virus needs the user to perform an action, such as starting a program or reading an e-mail message, to start the infection. A worm does not always require action by the computer user to begin its execution.

2

Because worms are self-executing, meaning they do not require any action on the part of the user, many users falsely believe they are safe from infection as long as they have not opened a suspicious e-mail message or started an infected program. However, because a worm can start on its own, a user's lack of activity does not affect the process.

Worms usually replicate themselves until they clog all available resources, such as the hard disk drive, computer memory, or the Internet network connection. The typical symptoms that indicate a worm has infected computer are that the computer suddenly runs slowly and sluggishly and may unexpectedly reboot, often several times in a row.

Logic Bombs

Logic bombs are another type of malicious code. A **logic bomb** is a computer program that lies dormant until it is triggered by a specific logical event, such as a certain date reached on the system calendar or a person's rank in an organization dropped below a previous level. Once triggered, the program can perform any number of malicious activities. An example of a logic bomb is one that was planted in a company's payroll system by an employee. This employee designed the program so that if the employee's name was removed from the payroll (meaning he quit or was fired), after three months the logic bomb would corrupt the entire computerized accounting system.

Logic bombs are extremely difficult to detect before they are triggered. This is because logic bombs are often embedded in large computer programs, some containing tens of thousands of lines of computer code. An attacker can easily insert three or four lines of computer code into a long program without anyone detecting the insertion.

Logic bombs have often been used to ensure payment for software. If a payment was not made by the due date, the logic bomb would activate and prevent the software from being used again. In some instances, the logic bomb even erased the software and all the accompanying payroll or customer files from the computer.

Basic Attacks

In addition to malicious software, other types of attacks are launched against desktop computers. These basic attacks include social engineering, password guessing, physical theft or lost data, and improper use of recycled computers.

Social Engineering

The easiest way to attack a computer system requires no technical ability and is highly successful. **Social engineering** relies on tricking and deceiving someone to access a system. Consider the following examples:

- Maria is a customer service representative who receives a telephone call from someone claiming to be a client. This person has a thick accent that makes his speech difficult to understand. Maria asks him to respond to a series of ID authentication questions to ensure that he is an approved client. However, when asked a question, the caller mumbles his response so that Maria cannot understand him. Too embarrassed to keep asking him to repeat his answer, Maria finally provides him with the password.

- The help desk at a large corporation is overwhelmed by the number of telephone calls it receives after a virus attacks. Ari is a help desk technician and receives a frantic call from a user who identifies himself as Frank, a company vice president. Frank says that an office assistant has been unable to complete and send him a critical report because of the virus and is now going home sick. Frank must have that office assistant's network password so he can finish the report, which is due by the end of the day. Because Ari is worn out from the virus attack and has more calls coming in, he looks up the password and gives it to Frank. Ari does not know that Frank is not an employee, but an outsider who now can easily access the company's computer system.

- Natasha, a contract programmer at a financial institution, drives past a security guard who recognizes her and waves her into the building. However, the guard does not realize that Natasha's contract was terminated the previous week. Once inside, Natasha pretends that she is performing an audit and questions a new employee, who willingly gives her the information she requests. Natasha then uses that information to transfer more than $10 million to her foreign bank account.

These examples are based on actual incidents and share a common characteristic: no technical skills or abilities were needed to break into the system. Social engineering relies on the friendliness, frustration, or helpfulness of a company employee to reveal the information necessary to access a system. Social engineering is a difficult security weakness to defend because it relies on human nature ("I just want to be helpful") and not on technology.

Social engineering is not limited to telephone calls or dated credentials. Another popular technique, called **dumpster diving**, involves digging through trash receptacles to find computer manuals, printouts, or password lists that have been thrown away.

NOTE

One of the most celebrated cases of social engineering occurred in 1978, when Stanley Mark Rifkin tricked the Security Pacific National Bank in Los Angeles to send more than $10 million to his private bank account in Switzerland. He was caught only after he tried to return to the U.S. with $8 million worth of diamonds that he had purchased. The bank was unaware of the theft until after his arrest.

Password Guessing

Before users can be given access to a computer and its data, they must prove that they are who they claim to be. That is, users must give proof that they are genuine, or authentic. This process of providing proof is known as **authentication**. Authentication can be performed based on what you have, what you know, or what you are.

Consider Lorenzo, who stops at the health club to exercise in the afternoon. After he locks his car doors, he walks into the club and is greeted by Sam, the clerk at the desk. Sam chats with Lorenzo and allows him to continue to the locker room. Once in the locker room, Lorenzo opens his locker using a combination lock that requires him to spin a dial to a series of numbers that he has memorized.

Lorenzo has used all three methods of authentication at the health club. First, by locking the doors of his car, its contents are protected by what he *has*, namely the car key. Next, access to the locker room is protected by what Lorenzo *is*. Sam recognized Lorenzo's unique characteristics (his hair color, his face, his body type, and his voice) before he allowed him to enter the locker room. Those characteristics serve to make Lorenzo who he is. Finally, the contents of Lorenzo's locker are protected by what he *knows*: the lock combination.

A **password** is a secret combination of letters and numbers that serves to validate or authenticate a user by what he knows. Along with usernames, passwords are provided to log on to a computer using a dialog box, such as the one shown in Figure 2-2. A username is a unique identifier, such as "Jbutterfield,""Traci_Li," or "Administrator."While anyone could type the person's username, only that person would know the secret password. Passwords are used to prove that the person entering it is authentic and not a fake.

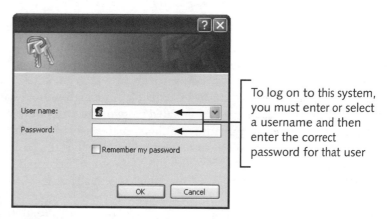

Figure 2-2   Username and password

Although passwords are the first and sometimes the only line of defense for a desktop computer, passwords actually provide weak security. This is because of what is known as the **password paradox**. For a password to remain secure and to prevent an attacker from discovering it, passwords should never be written down, but instead must be committed to memory. Passwords must also be of a sufficient length and complexity so that an attacker cannot easily guess the password. However, this creates the paradox: it is very difficult to memorize lengthy and complex passwords.

In addition, most users today have on average 20 or more different computers or accounts that require a password, such as computers at work, school, and home, e-mail accounts, banks, and Internet stores. The sheer number of passwords makes it impossible to remember all of them. Some passwords also expire after a set period of time, such as 60 days, and a new one must be created. In addition, some computer systems even prevent a previously used password from being recycled and used again, forcing the user to memorize an entirely new password again. This makes using passwords more difficult.

All of these factors cause most computer users to revert to using **weak passwords**, or those that compromise security. Characteristics of weak passwords include:

- *Passwords that are short (such as ABCD)*—Short passwords are easier to guess than long passwords.

- *A common word used as a password (such as Friday)*—Attackers can use an electronic dictionary of common words to match the password.

- *Personal information in a password (such as the name of a child)*—These passwords are easy to identify.

- *Using the same password for all accounts*—Once an attacker has one password, it is easy to gain access to any computer or account this person uses.

- *Writing the password down*—This serves as an open invitation to break into the account.

- *Not changing passwords unless forced to do so*—An attacker would have unlimited access to the user's account for the foreseeable future.

Attackers can exploit weak passwords by **password guessing**. Password-guessing attacks fall into three categories. The first type of attack is **brute force**, in which an attacker attempts to create every possible password combination by systematically changing one character at a time in a password, and then using each newly generated password to attempt to access the system. For example, if a password contains four numbers, such as 4983, the brute force attack would start with the combination 0000 and attempt to use that as the password. If it fails, the next attack is 0001, then 0002, and so on until the password is discovered. Although it seems that a brute force attack could take a long time, it actually might not. In this example, if a password consists of four digits, then there are $10*10*10*10$ or 10,000 possible combinations. A standard personal computer can easily create over 1,000,000 possible password combinations per second. Kiddie-script programs that use brute force for password guessing are readily available on the Internet.

Although most desktop computers can be set to lock out an attacker after a set number (typically three) of failed attempts at a password, it is not always possible to set this limitation on a pool of Web servers.

The second type of password guessing is a **dictionary attack**. Unlike a brute force attack in which all possible combinations are used, a dictionary attack takes each word from a dictionary and encodes it in the same way the computer encodes a user's password for protection. Attackers then compare the encoded dictionary words against those in the encoded password file. When attackers find a match, they know which dictionary word is the password. Figure 2-3 shows a dictionary attack.

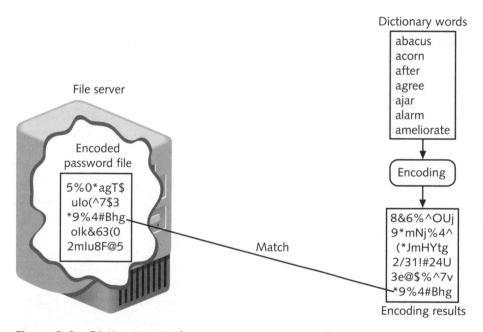

Figure 2-3   Dictionary attack

During World War II, British code-breakers used a dictionary attack to help decipher German coded messages.

Physical Theft or Lost Data

Whereas attackers can attempt to break into a computer to steal data, sometimes it is easier to steal the computer itself. Other times, the data is simply lost, and an attacker can try to locate the lost data or purchase it from someone who has located it. Consider the following list of thefts or lost data:

- *February 2005*—The Bank of America said that it lost computer backup tapes containing personal information on about 1.2 million charge card users.

- *May 2005*—Time Warner, Inc., which owns America Online (AOL) and other companies, reported that information on 600,000 current and former employees was missing.

- *June 2005*—The financial firm Citigroup announced that personal information on 3.9 million consumer lending customers of its CitiFinancial subsidiary was lost or stolen. This occurred while computer tapes were being transported by a package delivery system to a credit bureau in Texas. The tapes included Social Security numbers, names, account history, and loan information about customers.

Laptop computers are particularly vulnerable to theft. Within a three month period in early 2005, four major universities reported laptop computers containing personal information on over 181,000 students were stolen or misplaced. By some estimates, almost 60 percent of all stolen data is result of laptop computer theft.

Improperly Recycled Computers

Because of the difficulty in disposing of older computers, many organizations and individuals recycle older computers by giving them to schools, charities, or selling them online. However, information that should have been deleted from hard drives often is still available on recycled computers. This is because with many operating systems, such as Microsoft Windows, simply deleting a file (and even emptying the Recycle Bin folder) does not necessarily make the information irretrievable. When you create a file, such as by saving a Microsoft Word document, Windows enters information into a table with the name of the file and its location on the hard drive. When that file is deleted, only the name is removed from the table; as more files are saved, the disk space that was used by the first file can be reclaimed and used for other files. Thus, deleting a file means that the filename is removed from the table, but the information itself remains on the hard drive until it is overwritten by new files. This means that data can be retrieved from a hard drive by an attacker even after files have been deleted.

There are many examples of improperly recycled computers exposing sensitive information. Two people purchased 158 recycled computers or hard drives at secondhand computer stores and through online auctions. Of the 129 drives that functioned, 69 contained recoverable files and 49 contained "significant personal information," such as medical correspondence, love letters, and 5,000 credit card numbers. One computer contained an entire year's worth of transactions with account numbers from a cash machine in Illinois. Pennsylvania, Kentucky, and Nevada have all sold used state computers that turned out to contain information about state employees or individual health records.

NOTE

Even reformatting a drive, or preparing the hard drive to store files, may not fully erase all of the data on it. Fifty-one of the 129 working drives mentioned in the previous paragraph had been reformatted, yet 19 of them still contained recoverable data.

Desktop Defenses

Several tools and procedures should be implemented to provide desktop security. These include patch software, antivirus software, strong authentication methods, protection for laptop computers, cryptography, and proper disposal of old computers.

NOTE This list of desktop defenses is not intended to be all inclusive. Additional critical defenses, such as firewalls and antispyware, will be introduced in future chapters.

Patch Software

UPDATE DEFENSES **Patch software** is a general term used to describe software security updates that vendors provide for their programs and operating systems. Unlike version upgrades that provide enhanced functionality to the program, patch software is generally designed to fix a security vulnerability. The most frequently distributed patch software is for the Microsoft Windows operating system.

Prior to October 2003, Microsoft released Windows patches whenever a vulnerability was discovered. This often resulted in a new patch canceling out a previous patch or multiple patches being released within a few days. Due to user demand, Microsoft now releases patches to its operating systems on the second Tuesday of every month (sometimes called "Patch Tuesday"). Microsoft typically releases 5-15 software patches for download and installation. Each of the patches is given a unique number, which includes the year of the patch followed by a three-digit number indicating its release order. The first patch of 2005 was designated *MS05-001*, the second patch was *MS05-002*, and so on. The number of the patch corresponds to detailed information in the Microsoft Knowledge Base that explains the vulnerability and what the patch does in order to correct it, as shown in Figure 2-4.

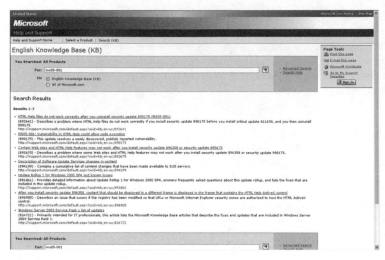

Figure 2-4   Microsoft patch information

NOTE   The Microsoft Knowledge Base can be accessed at *http://support. microsoft.com*.

Microsoft classifies patches based on level of vulnerability that the patch fixes:

- **Critical**—A critical vulnerability could freely allow a worm to infect a computer even when other defense mechanisms are in place.
- **Important**—An important vulnerability could result in the confidentiality, integrity, or availability of data or resources being compromised.
- **Moderate**—Moderate vulnerabilities are those that are difficult for an attacker to exploit because of current configurations.
- **Low**—Low vulnerability means that it would be very difficult for an attacker to take advantage of this weakness and whose impact would be minimal.

NOTE   If a critical vulnerability is exposed, Microsoft might also release a special patch prior to Patch Tuesday.

Desktop computers can be configured to automatically receive Windows patches. The four automatic update configuration options, as shown in Figure 2-5, are:

2

Figure 2-5   Windows automatic update options

- **Automatic**—This option checks the Microsoft Web site every day at a user-designated time and, if there are any patches, Windows automatically downloads and installs them onto the desktop computer.

- **Download**—The Download option automatically downloads the patches but does not install them, allowing the user to review and choose which patches to install.

- **Notify**—This option alerts the user that patches are available but does not download or install them. The user must go to the Microsoft Web site to review and install the patches.

- **Turn off**—The Turn off option disables automatic updates.

Keeping a system patch is one of the most important steps that a user can take to protect his or her desktop computer. After recent enhancements to Microsoft Windows, automatic updates are now easier to manage.

According to Microsoft, the highest number of patches released in one month was 12 (February 2005). During the first eight months of 2005, they released 24 critical patches and 13 important patches.

Antivirus Software

The best defense against viruses is **antivirus (AV) software**. This software can scan a computer for infections and isolate any file that contains a virus, as well as monitor computer activity and scan all new documents, such as e-mail attachments, that might contain a virus. The drawback of antivirus software is that it must be continuously updated to recognize new viruses. Known as **definition files** or **signature files**, these updates can be downloaded automatically through the Internet.

According to a survey conducted by the National Cyber Security Alliance, 67 percent of broadband users have no antivirus software or have outdated antivirus software on their desktop computers.

Antivirus software is generally configured to constantly monitor for viruses and automatically check for updated signature files. However, the entire hard drive should be scanned for viruses at least once a week. In addition, most antivirus software allows for manual signature updates. These features are illustrated in Figure 2-6.

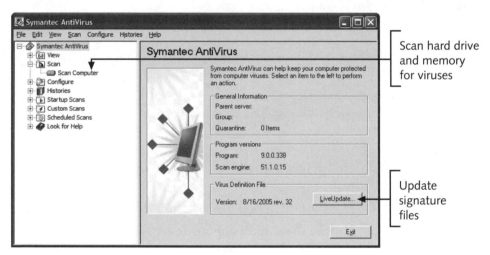

Figure 2-6   Antivirus software features

Although Microsoft Windows does not itself contain an antivirus software product, most antivirus software packages work with the Windows Security Center, which is a cental location in which some security tools can be managed. An advantage of this is that the Security Center can indicate to the user that antivirus software is not installed or is not

2

properly functioning, something the antivirus software cannot do if it is defective. This is illustrated in Figure 2-7.

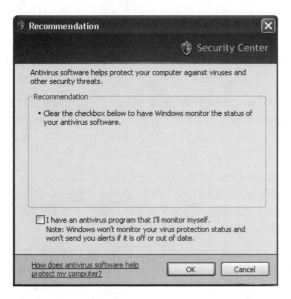

Figure 2-7 Windows monitoring AV software

Strong Authentication Methods

Because passwords are a fundamental means of desktop computer security, it is essential that **strong passwords** (passwords that are difficult to break) and strong authentication methods be used. Password-guessing attacks can be minimized by following basic rules for creating strong passwords:

- Passwords must have at least eight characters.

- Passwords must contain a combination of letters, numbers, and special characters. Passwords on Windows XP systems can be enhanced by using a space in the password or by using nonprintable characters. These special characters can be created by holding down the ALT key and entering the value on the numeric keypad.

- Passwords should be replaced at least every 30 days.

- Passwords should not be reused for 12 months.

- The same password should not be used on two or more systems or accounts.

To see a list of nonprintable characters, you can search the Internet for "nonprintable characters."

There are two techniques that can help make passwords easy to remember but hard to be broken.

First, think of a phrase or expression instead of a single word, such as an event in your life ("Today I passed my final exam"), a jingle from a commercial ("Yeah, we've got that"), or a famous line from a song or speech ("Four score and seven years ago"). This simple trick of using a long phrase instead of single word immediately makes the password more difficult for an attacker to break.

Next, replace the spaces between the words with a special character ("Today@I@passed@my@final@exam"), an alphanumeric character, ("1Yeah2we've3got4that5"), or a combination *("%Fourscore1and2seven3years4ago%")*. This makes it harder for an attacker to break the password by using the contents of an electronic dictionary.

Passwords can be made even more secure by substituting the first and last words of the phrase with their first letters ("T@I@passed@my@final@e" or "1Y2we've3got4t5") or replacing specific letters with numbers, such as using a 3 for an E or a 0 (zero) or an O ("%F0ursc0r31and2s3v3n3y3ars4ag0%").

However, any user who follows all of these rules and has more than a few passwords to remember will find it difficult to commit them to memory. As an alternative, you can record passwords in an electronic file and create a single strong password to open that file. The file can be a basic Microsoft Word or Adobe Acrobat document, as shown in Figure 2-8, or it can be a file created with a special program designed for safely storing passwords.

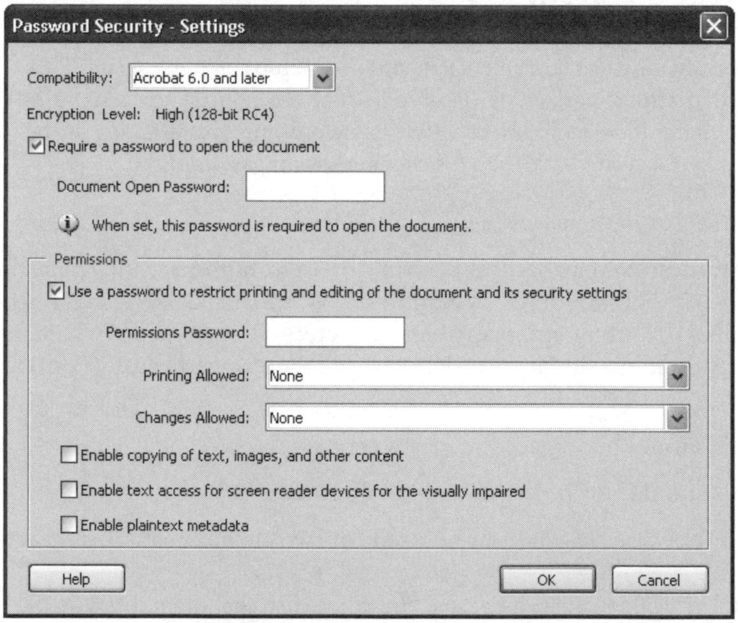

Figure 2-8   Password protected Adobe Acrobat file

If passwords are stored in a single file, the highest level of security must be applied to that file.

NOTE

As an alternative to passwords, some users are turning to using **biometrics** instead. Biometrics uses the unique human characteristics of a person for authentication. Some of the human characteristics that can be used for biometric identification include a fingerprint, face, hand, iris, retina, or voice.

The most common biometric device is a fingerprint scanner, shown in Figure 2-9. Every fingerprint consists of a number of ridges and valleys, with ridges being the upper skin layer segments and valleys the lower segments. In one method of fingerprint scanning, the scanner locates the point where these ridges end and split, converts them into a unique series of numbers, and then stores the information as a template. A second method creates a template from only selected locations on the finger. Although the cost of biometric devices once made them prohibitive except for the most secure environments, today the costs have dropped to under $40 for desktop fingerprint scanners. Companies have found that the cost of using many of the expensive biometrics is more than offset by the reduced number of telephone calls to the help desk about passwords that have been forgotten or must be reset.

Most inexpensive desktop fingerprint scanners allow you to use the fingerprint scanners for several different programs or Web sites that use a password. You can enter your username and password and it is then associated with your fingerprint, so anytime the password is required all you do is to touch the scanner with your finger. However, in some products these passwords are not saved in a secure format. This means that an attacker could steal this file and have a list of all of your passwords.

NOTE

Figure 2-9 Fingerprint scanner

Biometrics does have its weaknesses. Many high-end scanners are still relatively expensive, can be difficult to use, and can reject authorized users while accepting unauthorized users. These errors are mainly due to the many facial or hand characteristics that must be scanned and then compared. Also, it is possible to "steal" someone's characteristics by lifting a fingerprint from a glass, photographing an iris, or recording a voice and then use these to trick the scanner.

Protecting Laptop Computers

BLOCK ATTACKS

Although the data on a laptop computer must be protected like that on a desktop computer, with patch software, antivirus sofware, and strong authentication methods, the steps for protecting the laptop computers themselves are different from those for protecting desktop equipment. Portable equipment by definition normally does not remain behind locked doors. Instead, it is specifically designed to be moved from one location to another, which means that a new approach must be taken to protect the equipment from theft.

One of the most effective means of protecting a laptop computer is by securing it to a desk or another object. This can be done with a **device lock**, which consists of a steel cable and a lock. One end of the cable locks into a laptop's security slot, usually located on the back left or back right side of the laptop. The security slot allows a laptop device lock to attach and lock onto the computer case, as shown in Figure 2-10. The other end of the device lock is secured to a desk or chair. Device locks are economical, simple and quick to install, and are very portable.

Figure 2-10   Device lock

A more sophisticated security device for laptop computers is known as a stealth signal transmitter. A **stealth signal transmitter** is software installed on the laptop computer that cannot be detected. If the computer is stolen and connected to the Internet, the transmitter software sends a signal to a central monitoring center that can be traced. This center receives the signal and attempts to analyze the location of the stolen laptop. Working with police, telephone companies, and Internet service providers, the center can attempt to retrieve and return the stolen laptop.

NOTE

If the hard drive of a stolen laptop computer that is equipped with a stealth signal transmitter is removed and installed on another computer, it will send a signal from the new computer.

Cryptography

**SEND
SECURE
INFO**

Another means of protecting information on a desktop or laptop computer is to "scramble" it so that even if an attacker reaches the data, he or she cannot read it. This is a process known as **cryptography** (from Greek words meaning "hidden writing"). Cryptography is the science of transforming information so that it is secure while it is being transmitted or stored. Cryptography does not attempt to hide the existence of the data (that is steganography); instead, it scrambles the data so that it cannot be viewed by unauthorized users.

Cryptography's origins date back centuries. One of the most famous ancient cryptographers was Julius Caesar. Caesar shifted each letter of his messages to his generals three places down in the alphabet so that an A was replaced by a D, a B was replaced by an E, and so forth. Changing the original text to a secret message using cryptography was known as **encryption**. When Caesar's generals received his messages, they reversed the process (such as substituting a D for an A) to change the secret message back to its original form. This was called **decryption**.

A simple substitution like Caesar's is too simple to be used today. Instead, much more sophisticated methods are the basis for modern cryptography.

Public and Private Keys

Just as a key is used to lock and unlock a door, in cryptography a key is a mathematical value used to encrypt or decrypt a message. With a **private key system**, the same key is used to both encrypt and decrypt the message. For example, if Alice encrypts her message and sends it to Bob, he must also have the key to decrypt the message. This is illustrated in Figure 2-11. With a private key system, the key must remain secret by all users in order for the system to work. An outsider who discovers the key could read all of the messages being sent. Transporting a private key to multiple users and ensuring that it has not been copied can be difficult.

In the mid–1970s, two mathematicians introduced the concept of a public key system. With a **public key system**, two mathematically related keys are used: a public key and a private key. A user who wants to send an encrypted message can obtain the recipient's public key to encode the message. When the recipient receives the encrypted message, he or she can decrypt it with a matching private key, which no one else can access. The value of a public key system is that the public key (which encrypts data) does not have to be kept secret; it can be openly distributed to anyone because it can only encrypt data. Only the private key (which decrypts data) is kept confidential. This eliminates the need to securely transport keys. A public key system is illustrated in Figure 2-12.

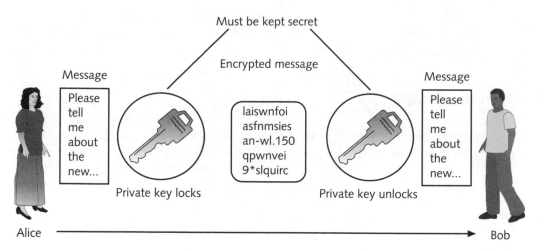

Figure 2-11   Private key system

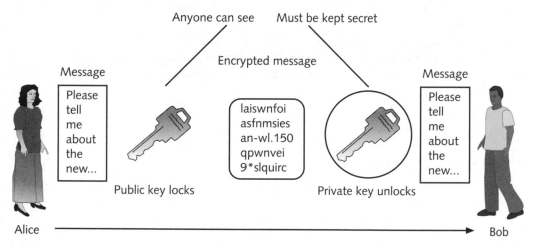

Figure 2-12   Public key system

Digital Signatures

The public key system can also be used to provide for multiple types of security functions. This is done through using a **digital signature**, which is a code attached to an electronic message that helps to prove that the person sending the message with a public key is not an imposter, that the message was not altered, and that it cannot be denied that the message was sent. A digital signature is an encrypted hash of a message that is transmitted along with the message. A **hash** creates encrypted text that is never intended to be decrypted; instead, it is used in a comparison for authentication purposes.

NOTE

Consider the number 12,345. If 12,345 is multiplied by 143, the result is 1,765,335. If you give someone the number 1,765,335 and ask what your original number was, it is almost impossible for the person to work backwards and derive the original number of 12,345. However, if you provide the correct multiplier (143), the original number is easy to determine. That is the principle behind a hash.

2

Consider again that Alice wants to send Bob a secure message. When using a digital signature, Alice, the sender, first creates her message. She then generates a hash value for that entire message. That hash value is then encrypted by the sender's private key. If the sender wants to encrypt the entire message, she would use the receiver's (Bob's) public key to do so. The encrypted message, along with the digital signature, is then combined and transmitted. Upon receiving the message, Bob uses Alice's public key to decrypt the digital signature and retrieve the hash value. He then, if necessary, decrypts the message with his private key and runs it through the same hash algorithm. If the two hash values match, then the receiver can be sure that the message came from the sender and was not altered in transmission.

In Figure 2-13, Alice creates a message for Bob. She generates a hash value and encrypts it with her private key. She also encrypts the message using Bob's public key. Figure 2-14 illustrates what happens when Bob receives the message. He decrypts the message using his private key and decrypts the digital signature with Alice's public key. Then Bob runs the decrypted message through the same hash function that Alice used and compares that hash value with the decrypted digital signature. If the two values match, Bob can assume that Alice actually sent the message.

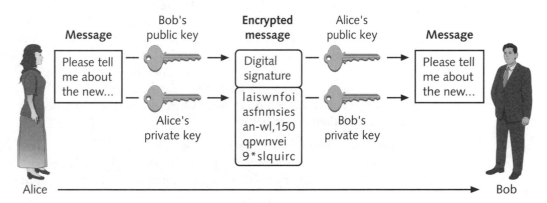

Figure 2-13   Alice creating digital signature

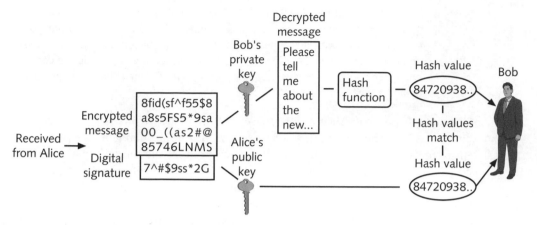

Figure 2-14   Bob comparing digital signatures

Digital Certificates

Public keys are an excellent means of sending messages so that unauthorized users cannot see them. However, one of the weaknesses of a public key system is that it does not prove that the senders are actually who they claim to be. Because public keys are easily accessible, how does the receiver know who actually sent the message? That is, Frankie could create a message using Bob's public key, but sign his name as Alice. How can Bob be sure that Alice actually sent the message?

The answer is a digital certificate. A **digital certificate** links or binds a specific person to a public key. Digital certificates are provided by a **certification authority (CA)**, which is an independent third-party organization. A user requesting a CA must provide personal information, such as name, former last name (if changed in last twelve months), home address, Social Security number, date of birth, driver's license number, e-mail address, and work/home phone numbers. In some instances, the CA may require that the person visit the CA office in order to verify the claimed identity. Once the person's identity is established, then the CA will issue a digital certificate.

A digital certificate is a public key that has been digitally signed by a recognized authority (the CA) attesting that the owner of the key is not an imposter. When Alice sends a message to Bob, her certificate will verify that she is the one using her public and private keys.

Properly Retiring Old Computers

BLOCK ATTACKS

When selling or donating an old computer, all personal data stored on the computer's hard drive must be removed. The files that should be removed include:

- E-mail contacts
- E-mail messages

- All personal documents
- All files in the operating system recycle bin or trash folder
- Internet files
- All nontransferable software (most software is transferable if you have the original disks and product key)

Remember from earlier that deleting computer files by using the operating system means the files can still be recovered. To properly remove files from the computer, special disk-cleaning software packages should be used. This software will overwrite any deleted data so that the original data cannot be recovered. If the data is extremely sensitive, the hard drive from the computer should be removed and taken to a local reputable computer supplier, where the files can be safely overwritten.

NOTE

The cost for cleaning up a computer by a computer supplier averages about $250.

SECURITY IN YOUR WORLD

"That should do it!" proclaimed Lorenzo as he and Brian finished installing antivirus software and patching his Windows operating system. "Attackers, give me your best shot! You won't get through to me!"

Brian leaned back in his chair. "Well, I'm not sure that I would go that far. Chances are that before you graduate from here, there will be at least one attack that will get through this and mess up your computer."

Lorenzo looked surprised. "How?" he asked. "We just finished installing some of the latest software out there."

"I know," said Brian. "But remember that these attackers never sleep. Even right now they are working on attacks that take advantage of security holes in software that we don't even know are there."

"So what should I do now?" asked Lorenzo.

"My instructor says that it is not a matter of *if* you will be attacked but rather *when* you will be attacked. That means you have to be prepared for when that attack gets through," said Brian. "Here, let me show you what you can do to be ready."

RECOVERING FROM ATTACKS

In spite of the best defenses, sooner or later an attack will break through and corrupt any desktop computer. Just as homeowners cannot be certain that their houses will never be broken into despite strong door locks, the same is true with computer security. Because it is only a matter of time before an attack occurs, the best defense is to be prepared for the inevitable and "hope for the best but prepare for the worst." Recovering from attacks involves both preparing for the attack and restoring the computer after the attack.

Preparing For an Attack

There are two major steps to take when preparing for an attack that will breach the security defenses. Those two steps are backing up your data and backing up system information.

Generating Data Backups

MINIMIZE LOSSES

Most of the possessions that we own can be divided into two categories: those that can be replaced and those that cannot be replaced. An example of an item that can be replaced is a chair that is damaged by water or a backpack that is stolen. Items that cannot be replaced include photographs or momentos of deceased relatives. Items in this latter category are usually protected by being kept in a safe place, such as a safe deposit box at a bank.

This same approach should be applied to information stored on a personal desktop computer. Some information, such as statistics gathered from a Web site, can usually be restored easily. Other information, such as photos taken with a digital camera or personal checking account data, either cannot be replaced or would be difficult to recreate. Items in this latter category should be protected by a **data backup**. Creating a data backup involves copying data onto digital media and storing it in a secure location.

When creating a data backup, answer the following five basic questions:

1. *What information should be backed up?* The type of information to back up should be information that cannot be easily or quickly recreated. Programs installed on the computer, such as a word processor, should not be backed up because the program can be reinstalled easily from the installation CD-ROM or, if necessary, from a new copy. However, documents that you created using various programs, such as the manuscript for a book created using a word processor, should be backed up because this document could not be easily or quickly recreated. Digital photos, personal financial information, and other similar information should be backed up because it cannot be easily or quickly replaced.

2. *How often should it be backed up?* The best approach is to back up a document every time it changes. However, most users find that is not practical. Instead, follow a regular backup schedule, such as once a day or once a week.

3. *What media should be used?* Temporary storage media, such as floppy disks or Universal Serial Bus (USB) flash drives, should not be used for long-term storage. Instead, permanent storage such as Compact Disc – Recordable (CD-R) or Digital Versatile Disc (DVD) should be used, in addition to the following alternatives:

- **Portable USB hard drives**—These devices connect to the USB port of a computer and provide backup capabilities that are fast and portable, and they can store large amounts of data. A portable USB hard drive is shown in Figure 2-15.

Figure 2-15 Portable USB hard drive

- **Network Attached Storage (NAS)**—A **network attached storage (NAS)** device is similar to a portable USB hard drive, except it has additional "intelligence" that allows all devices connected to the computer network to access it (instead of unplugging it a computer and moving it from computer to computer). NAS devices are increasing in popularity among home network users.

- **Internet services**—Fee-based Internet services are available that allow users to back up documents over the Internet to a centralized backup server computer. Some of these services provide "transparent access" to the backups, in that they look like another hard drive attached to a desktop computer.

- **Tape backup**—Once the only means of backing up data, tape backups today are usually found only on large networked file servers.

4. *Where should the backup be stored?* Backups should be stored in a different location away from the device that contains the information. This protects the data if a fire or storm destroys the computer. If it is not possible to store the backups in another location, then they should be clearly labeled and stored in another room of the house or apartment, preferably in a fireproof safe.

5. *How should the backup be performed?* All operating systems today come with features that make it easy to perform automated backups. In addition, third-party software is available that provides additional functionality.

An old adage well describes the importance of backups: "There are two types of people in the world: those who do backups and those who should!"

Saving Automated System Recovery (ASR) Data

Much like backing up personal data, it is also important to back up system data as well. The Windows XP **Automated System Recovery (ASR)** is a system that includes an ASR backup and ASR restore. The ASR backup records the system state, system services, and all disks associated with the operating system components. It also creates a file containing information about the backup, the disk configurations (including basic and dynamic volumes), and how to accomplish a restore. Only those system files necessary for starting up a computer are backed up by ASR. An ASR backup set should be created on a regular basis, just like a data backup, as part of an overall plan for system recovery in case of an attack.

If a computer is so corrupted that it cannot restart, it may be necessary to boot the computer from a floppy disk to try to diagnose the problem or recover critical documents. An emergency repair disk (ERD) can boot the computer from a floppy drive. ERD bootable floppies can be created for Microsoft Windows Server 2003, Windows 2000, and Windows NT. However, users cannot create ERD disks for Windows XP.

Restoring the Computer

Because individual attacks are unique, it is difficult to prescribe exactly what actions to take to restore an infected computer. There are, however, three major steps to perform: boot the computer, clean up the infection, and restore data files.

Boot the Computer

After an attack, boot the computer so repair work can take place. The first step is to unplug the computer from the network or modem to prevent the infection from reaching other computers. Next, reboot the system to Windows.

If an attack changes the operating system so that the computer will not reboot, an ASR backup may be used. However, ASR is the last resort after all other recovery methods have failed. ASR will read the disk configurations from the file that it created on the floppy disk and restore all of the disk signatures, volumes and partitions on, at a minimum, the disks required to start the computer. ASR then installs a simple installation of Windows and automatically starts a restoration using the ASR backup data.

To recover from an attack using ASR:

1. Insert the original operating system installation CD into the CD drive.

2. Restart the computer. If prompted to press a key in order to start the computer from CD, press the appropriate key.

3. Press the F2 key when prompted during the text–only mode section of Setup.

4. Insert the ASR floppy disk when prompted.

5. Follow the remaining directions on the screen.

ASR does not restore any data files.

Clean up the Attack

After the computer is booted, it is then necessary to clean up from the attack by removing the virus or worm. Both Microsoft and antivirus vendors offer removal tools.

The Microsoft Windows Malicious Software Removal Tool for Windows XP, Windows 2000, and Windows Server 2003 helps remove infections by specific malware. When the detection and removal process is complete, the tool displays a report describing the outcome, including which, if any, malicious software was detected and removed. Microsoft releases an updated version of the tool on Patch Tuesday of each month. New versions are also available on the Microsoft Web site.

Software removal tools are not a replacement for antivirus software.

Antivirus vendors likewise offer removal tools, as shown in Figure 2-16. These tools provide information regarding the impact of the attack and how to remove it.

Figure 2-16   AV vendor software removal tool

Restore Data from Backups

Once you've booted the computer and removed the malicious software, the final step is to restore the backup data. This varies depending on the software used to create the data backups. Most vendors provide an automated wizard that guides the user through the process of restoring the files.

After any successful attack, it is vital to analyze why the attack got through the defenses. Was the antivirus software missing or out of date? Were weak passwords used? Spend time determining why it happened and what can be done to prevent it from occurring again.

CHAPTER SUMMARY

❏ Malicious software, also called malware, is the term used to describe computer programs designed to break into desktop computers or to create havoc on computers. One type of malicious software is a computer virus. A computer virus is a program that secretly attaches itself to a document or another program and executes when that document or program is opened. A computer virus requires a host to carry it from one computer to another. Computer viruses can display a message, cause a computer crash, or even erase files from the hard drive. Another type of malware, a worm, does not attach itself to a document to spread; nor is it necessarily started by the user. A third type of malware, a logic bomb, is a computer program that lies dormant until it is triggered by a specific logical event.

2

❏ Social engineering relies on trickery and deceit and is considered a basic attack. A password is a secret combination of letters and numbers that serves to authenticate a user. Because it is difficult for users to remember complex and lengthy passwords, many users implement weak passwords (those that are easy to break). Attackers can exploit weak passwords by password guessing, either by a brute force attack or a dictionary attack. Many times the attacker can simply steal a computer or look for lost data. Because improperly recycled computers may still contain valuable information, attackers often seek these out.

❏ Patch software is a general term used to describe software security updates that vendors provide for their programs. The Microsoft Windows operating system release patch is on the second Tuesday of each month. Antivirus software can scan the computer for infections and isolate any file that may contain a virus. Antivirus software must be continuously updated in order to recognize new viruses.

❏ Strong passwords (those that are difficult break) are an important defense mechanism against attackers. As an alternative to passwords, some users are turning to biometrics, which uses the unique human characteristics of a person for authentication. Cryptography is the science of transforming information so that it is secure while it is being transmitted or stored. A private key system uses the same key to both encrypt and decrypt a message. A public key system uses two mathematically related keys, a public key and a private key, to encrypt and decrypt messages. A digital signature is an encrypted hash of a message that is transmitted along with the message itself. A digital certificate links a specific person to a key.

❏ Because an attack can break through a security breach, it is important to perform data backups on a regular basis. System data should also be backed up using the Automated System Recovery software that comes with Windows XP.

❏ If a computer becomes infected with malware, first remove the computer from the network and then try to reboot the computer. If the computer does not reboot, you may need to use the Automated System Recovery (ASR) disk. Antivirus software vendors and Microsoft provide malicious software removal tools to disinfect the computer from a worm or a virus. The final step in recovering from an attack is to restore the data backups to the hard drive.

Key Terms

antivirus (AV) software — Software that can scan a computer for infections, isolate any file that contains a virus, and continuously monitor computer activity.

authentication — The process of providing proof of an individual's identity.

Automated System Recovery (ASR) — A Windows XP program that records the system state, system services, and all disks associated with the operating system components.

biometrics — The process of using the unique human characteristics of a person for authentication.

brute force — A password guessing attack in which an attacker attempts to create every possible password combination by systematically changing one character at a time.

certification authority (CA) — An independent third-party organization that verifies digital certificates.

cryptography — The science of transforming information so that it is secure while it is being transmitted or stored.

data backup — The process of copying data onto another media and storing it in a secure location.

decryption — Changing encrypted text back to original text.

definition files — Files that are used by antivirus software to identify viruses.

device lock — A steel cable and a lock used to secure a laptop computer.

dictionary attack — A password guessing attack in which each word from a dictionary is encoded in the same way the computer encodes a word and then compared with a possible password.

digital certificate — A technology that links or binds a specific person to a public key.

digital signature — An encrypted hash of a message that is transmitted along with the message.

dumpster diving — A social engineering technique that involves digging through trash receptacles to find computer manuals, printouts, or password lists that have been thrown away.

encryption — Changing original text to a secret message using cryptography.

hash — Encrypted text that is never intended to be decrypted but instead is used in a comparison for authentication purposes.

instant messaging (IM) — A method of instantaneous online communication.

key — A mathematical value used to encrypt or decrypt a message.

logic bomb — A computer program that lies dormant until it is triggered by a specific logical event.

malicious software (malware) — Computer programs designed to break into desktop computers or to create havoc on computers.

network attached storage (NAS) — A storage device that allows all devices connected to the computer network to access it.

password — A secret combination of letters and numbers that serves to validate or authenticate a user.

password guessing — An attempt by attackers to guess passwords.

password paradox — The problem that lengthy and complex passwords are secure when they are not recorded on paper, yet that makes them very difficult to memorize and use.

patch software — A general term used to describe software security updates that vendors provide for their programs and operating systems.

private key system — Using the same key to encrypt and decrypt a message.

public key system — Two mathematically related keys are used for encrypting and decrypting, a public key and a private key.

signature files — Files that are used by antivirus software to identify viruses.

social engineering — A technique that relies on tricking and deceiving someone to give information that enables an attacker to access a system.

stealth signal transmitter — Software installed on a laptop computer that cannot be detected but can track stolen laptop computers.

2

strong passwords — Passwords that are difficult to break.

virus — A program that secretly attaches itself to a document or another program and executes when that document or program is opened.

weak password — Passwords that compromise security because they are short, use a common word, or contain personal information.

worm — Malicious software that does not attach to a document to spread but can travel by itself and does not always require action by the computer user to begin its execution.

REVIEW QUESTIONS

1. _____ is the term used to describe computer programs like worms and viruses that are designed to break into or create havoc on computers.
   a. Malicious software
   b. Badware
   c. Hackerware
   d. Targetware

2. _____ require(s) a host to carry them from one computer to another.
   a. Worms
   b. Viruses
   c. Worms and viruses
   d. Windows

3. Each of the following may be a symptom of a virus except:
   a. The computer continually crashes.
   b. Files disappear from the hard drive.
   c. E-mail no longer accepts small attachments.
   d. Security settings are adjusted.

4. A(n) _____ does not always require an action by the user in order for it to begin executing.
   a. virus
   b. worm
   c. attachment
   d. ASR

5. A(n) _____ is a computer program that lies dormant until it is triggered by a specific logical event.
   a. worm
   b. logic bomb
   c. vulnerability
   d. exploit

6. Social engineering relies on tricking and deceiving someone into giving information than enables an attacker to access a system. True or False?

7. A username is used to authenticate a person and prove that he or she is genuine. True or False?

8. A strong password is normally longer than a weak password. True or False?

9. Common dictionary words should be used as passwords in order to confuse attackers. True or False?

10. In a brute force password guessing attack, an attacker will use a dictionary in order to guess the user's password. True or False?

11. _____ is a general term used to describe software security updates that vendors provide for their programs and operating systems.

12. The day on which Microsoft releases its Windows updates is known as _____ .

13. Another name for an antivirus definition file is a(n) _____ file.

14. _____ uses the unique human characteristics of a person for authentication.

15. A(n) _____ consists of a steel cable and lock and is used to secure a laptop computer.

16. What is the password paradox?

17. What happens when you delete a file in Microsoft Windows?

18. What is a stealth signal transmitter?

19. How does public key cryptography work?

20. What is a digital signature and how does it work?

HANDS-ON PROJECTS

Project 2-1: Backing Up Data

It is essential that data and system information be backed up regularly in order to recover from an attack. In this project, you use the Windows XP Professional Backup utility to back up data on a personal computer to a floppy disk. Note that you usually back up much more data than you will in this project, and you would usually use a CD, tape, hard disk, or other high-capacity storage device on which to store the backup file. However, the procedure you follow is the same as the following procedure.

If you are using a Windows XP Home system, you may need to install the Backup utility from the setup CD.

NOTE

1. Insert a blank formatted floppy disk into the floppy disk drive.

2. Click **Start**, point to **All Programs**, point to **Accessories**, point to **System Tools**, and then click **Backup**. The Backup or Restore Wizard starts, as shown in Figure 2-17. Click **Next**.

Figure 2-17   Backup or Restore Wizard

If the Backup program starts in Advanced mode, click the **Wizard Mode** link to use the wizard, and then click **Next**.

3. The Backup or Restore Wizard dialog box is displayed with the question, "What do you want to do?" Click the **Back up files and settings** option button, if necessary, and then click **Next**.

4. The What to Back Up dialog box is displayed with the question, "What do you want to back up?" Click the **Let me choose what to back up** option button, as shown in Figure 2-18. Click **Next**.

NOTE

If you wanted to back up all of the important documents on the computer that you had saved, you would click the My documents and settings option button.

5. The Items to Back Up step is displayed, where you select the drives, folders, or files that you want to back up. For this project, select one small file on the hard drive. In the left pane of the dialog box, click the **plus sign (+)** in front of My Computer to expand the file listing, and then click **Local Disk (C:)**. (Do not check the drive C check box.) The contents of drive C are listed in the right pane.

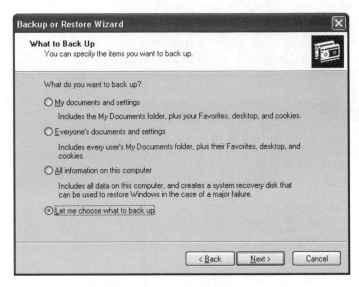

Figure 2-18   What to Back Up dialog box

6. Scroll the right pane to locate the file **AUTOEXEC.BAT**, and then click the check box in front of it. A check mark also appears in the left pane in front of Local Disk (C:), as shown in Figure 2-19. (The list of files on your drive C will be different.) Click **Next**.

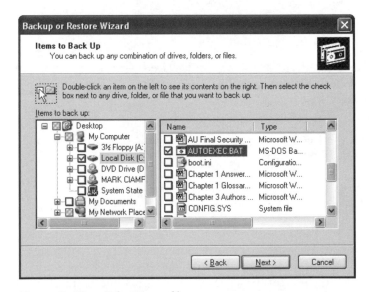

Figure 2-19   Selecting a file

7. The Backup Type, Destination, and Name step is displayed, in which you select where you want to save the backup. For this project, be sure that **3½ Floppy (A:)** is selected. Type **backup**, if necessary, as the name for this backup file. Click **Next**.

    If you were backing up to a device such as a tape, USB flash drive, or CD, you could click Browse and select that device here.

8. In the Completing the Backup or Restore Wizard step, click the **Advanced** button to examine additional backup options.

9. The Type of Backup step is displayed, where you can choose the type of backup that fits your needs. Make sure that Normal appears in the Select the type of backup text box. Click **Next**.

10. The How to Back Up dialog box is displayed with the different backup options and explanations, as shown in Figure 2-20. Because you are backing up one small file in this project, none of the options are necessary. Click **Next**.

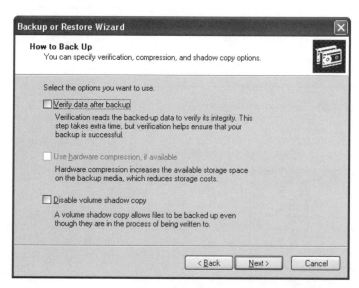

Figure 2-20   How to Back Up dialog box

11. The Backup Options step is displayed, where you can append the new backup to an existing one or replace the existing backup. Because this is the first backup on the floppy disk, either option will work. Click **Next**.

12. The When to Back Up dialog step is displayed, where you specify when to back up the selected files. Click the **Now** option button, if necessary, and then click **Next**.

NOTE   If you wanted this backup to run unattended at a later time, you could indicate that here by clicking **Later**. The Schedule Entry dialog box would be available with the current date and time. Clicking the **Set Schedule** button would allow you to set when the backup should start.

13. The final step displays all of the options selected, as shown in Figure 2-21. To start the backup, click **Finish**. The Backup Progress window is displayed as the backup progresses.

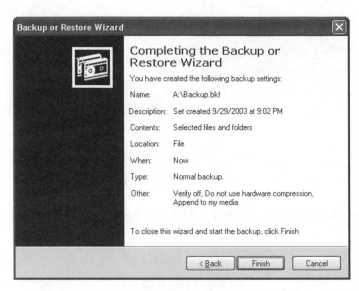

Figure 2-21   Completing the Backup or Restore Wizard dialog box

14. When the backup is complete, a summary appears, as in Figure 2-22. Click **Close**.

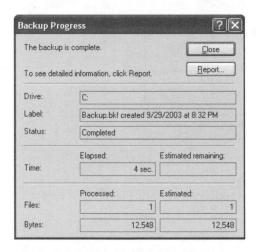

Figure 2-22   Backup summary

If files need to be restored from the backup, start the Backup or Restore Wizard and click Restore files or settings.

NOTE

Project 2-2: Installing and Managing Microsoft Windows Updates

HANDS-ON PROJECTS

One of the most important tasks in keeping a desktop computer secure is to install patches for the operating system. In this project, you will install the latest Windows updates on your computer and then set up your computer to automatically download the updates. You should be using a computer running Windows XP that is connected to the Internet. If you are using a computer in a school's computer lab or another computer that is not your own, you should first talk to the lab manager or network administrator. You may need special permissions set to complete this project.

1. On a Windows XP computer, click **Start**, point to **All Programs**, and then click **Windows Update**. Internet Explorer (or the default browser) starts and connects you to the Microsoft Windows Update Web site, shown in Figure 2-23.

Figure 2-23   Microsoft Windows Update Web site

2. Click **Express**. Windows Update checks your computer's operating system to determine if the latest patches have been installed.

3. If there are any high priority updates to install, Windows will list those. If there are updates available, click **Download and Install Now**.

4. In the left pane, click **Review your update history** to see a list of all the updates installed on this computer.

5. Close your browser.

6. Now you will set the update options on your computer to automatically receive patches. Click **Start**, click **Control Panel**, and then double-click **Security Center**.

7. Scroll down and click **Automatic Updates** under Manage security settings for:. This will display the Windows Automatic Updates options, shown in Figure 2-24.

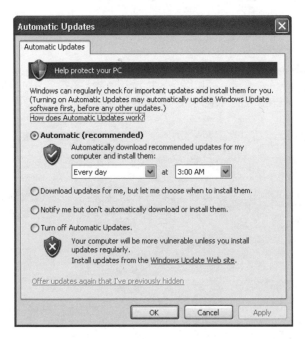

Figure 2-24   Windows Automatic Updates options

8. Click **Notify me but don't automatically download or install them**. When updates are available, you will receive a balloon message on your taskbar that you can click to download the updates. Click **OK**.

9. Close all windows.

Project 2-3: Testing Antivirus Software

Because antivirus software is so important, one recommended procedure is to test the antivirus software to ensure that it is functioning as intended. In this project, you download a virus test file. This file is not a virus but is designed to appear as a virus to an antivirus scanner. You need to have antivirus software installed on your computer to perform this project.

1. Check the antivirus settings on your computer. Click **Start**, click **Control Panel**, and then click **Security Center**.

2. The Virus Protection setting should be **On**. If it is not, click the **Recommendations** button and indicate that you want Windows to monitor the AV software.

3. Close all windows.

4. Use your Web browser (such as Internet Explorer) to go to the eicar – Anti-Virus test file Web site at **www.eicar.org/anti_virus_test_file.htm**. Read the "Anti-Virus test file" information.

5. Click the file **eicar.com**, which contains a fake virus. A dialog box opens that asks if you want to download the file. Wait to see what happens. Your antivirus software should catch the file even before you start to download, as shown in Figure 2-25. Close your antivirus pop-up message and click **Cancel** to stop the download procedure.

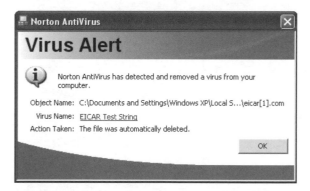

Figure 2-25   Antivirus software stopped eicar.com

6. At the eicar – Anti-Virus test file Web site, click **eicar_com.zip**. This file contains a fake virus inside a compressed (ZIP) file. What happened? Most AV software cannot scan a compressed file for a virus.

7. If your antivirus software did not prevent you from accessing the eicar_com.zip file, click **Save** to save it to your computer.

8. Click **Save** again, and when the download is complete, click **Close**, if necessary.

9. Right-click the **Start** button, and then click **Explore**.

10. In Windows Explorer, navigate to the folder that contains the eicar_com.zip file.

11. Right-click **eicar_com.zip**, and then click **Scan for viruses** on the shortcut menu (your menu command may be slightly different). What happened now?

12. Delete **eicar_com.zip** from your hard drive.

13. Close all windows.

Project 2-4: Password Guessing

Password guessing is a technique used to attempt to break easy passwords. In this project you will use a password recovery tool to perform different types of password guessing techniques.

1. Start Microsoft Word and open a new, blank document.

2. Click **Tools** on the menu bar, and then click **Options**. The Options dialog box opens. Click the **Security** tab to see the options, shown in Figure 2-26.

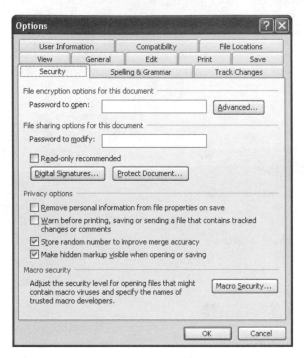

Figure 2-26   Security tab in the Options dialog box

3. In the Password to open text box, type **1234**, and then click **OK**. The Confirm Password dialog box opens so you can verify the password. Type **1234** again and click **OK**.

4. In the new Word document, type **Weak**. Save this document as **Weak** in the Chap02 folder of your work folder for this book, and then close the document.

5. Use your Web browser (such as Internet Explorer) to go to **www.elcomsoft.com/aopr.html**. Click **Download the free trial version of AOPR**. Click **Save** to download the file and then click **Save** again to accept the default download filename. After the download is complete you may need to click **Close**. Navigate to the directory in which you saved the file and double-click the file. Click **Extract all files** and use the Extraction Wizard to uncompress the files. Double-click **setup.exe** and follow the default instructions to install the program on your computer.

6. Start the program to display the opening window, shown in Figure 2-27.

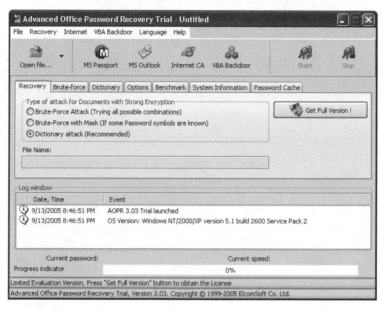

Figure 2-27   AOPR window

7. Be sure that **Dictionary attack (Recommended)** is selected.

8. Click the **Open file** button and select the file **Weak.doc**. AOPR will unlock and display the password under **Word File Opening Password.** Click **OK**.

9. Note the lower part of the window shows how the password **1234** was encrypted (under **Current Password**).

10. Next to **Current Speed**, observe how many passwords per second the program checks in order to crack this password.

11. How quickly could an attacker crack any short or simple passwords that you use? How quickly should you change these weak passwords to strong passwords?

12. Close the AOPR program.

HANDS-ON PROJECTS

Project 2-5: Wiping Data from a Floppy Disk

Many security breaches have occurred because data was left on the hard drive of a computer that was sold or donated to charity. Deleting files in Windows does not physically remove the data, meaning it can still be retrieved. A recommendation is to use a third-party product to perform a true erase of the data. In this project, you download a product to wipe data from a floppy disk.

1. Use your Web browser (such as Internet Explorer) to go to the r-tools technology Web site at **www.r-wipe.com**, click the **Download Page** button, and then click the **Download Now** button.

2. When the Download dialog box opens, click **Save**, and then click **Save** again. After the file has downloaded, click **Close**. Navigate to where you saved the file, and then double-click the file (or, click the file and then click **Run**).

3. When the Setup dialog box opens, click **Yes**.

4. Use the Install Wizard to install the software on your computer.

5. Copy one or two files onto a floppy disk.

6. Start the R-Wipe&Clean program. (You can use the trial version of this program for 15 days.) Click **Try It!**

7. Click **Tools** on the menu bar, and then click **Settings**.

8. Click the **Disks and Files** tab, if necessary.

9. Under File Options, click the **Wiping Algorithm** list arrow, and then click each algorithm to select it. An explanation appears under the algorithm. Select what you think will be the most secure method.

10. Click **Apply** and then click **OK**.

Now you are ready to thoroughly delete all the files from the floppy disk.

1. Right-click **Start**, and then click **Explore**.

2. Use Windows Explorer to navigate to the floppy drive (A:).

3. Right-click a file on the floppy disk to open the shortcut menu, as shown in Figure 2-28.

4. Click **Delete and Wipe!**.

5. When the Confirm deleting and wiping dialog box opens, click **Yes**.

6. The file is now completely removed. How long did it take to wipe one file?

7. Close all windows.

Project 2-6: Store Passwords in Safe Document

HANDS-ON PROJECTS

Because of the difficulty in remembering strong passwords, you can store all passwords in a single "strong" document. In this project, you will download and use a Windows utility that encrypts passwords in one document.

1. Use your Web browser to go to **http://passwordsafe.sourceforge.net**.

2. Click **Latest version** and then click **available for download**.

3. Click **Download pwsafe-x.xx-exe** where "x.xx" is the latest version number.

4. You may be redirected to another site. Follow the instructions to locate the file. When the **File Download** dialog box opens, click **Save**.

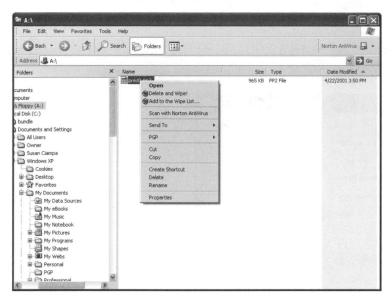

Figure 2-28   Wiping a file

5. When the file is finished downloading, click **Run**. Follow the instructions to install this program on your computer.

6. Double-click the desktop icon to start Password Safe, shown in Figure 2-29.

Figure 2-29   Password Safe

7. Click **Create new database**.

8. Enter a strong password for **Safe Combination**. The password must have upper and lowercase letters and at least one digit or character of punctuation. Re-enter it under **Verify**. Click **OK**.

9. Click **File** and **Save** and enter the filename **Password**. Click **Save**.

10. Now you can add your passwords to the database. Click **Edit** and **Add entry**, as shown in Figure 2-30. Fill in the blanks for an account, password, and title you use regularly. **Group** and **Notes** are optional entries. Note that the password will appear in clear text when you enter it. Click **OK**.

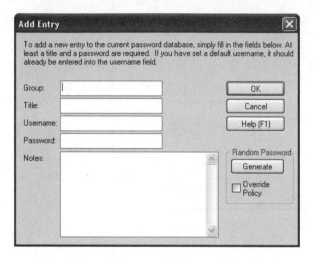

Figure 2-30   Enter passwords

11. Click **File** and then click **Exit**. Be sure to save the file before exiting.

12. Start **Password Safe**. Enter your safe combination.

13. Double-click the entry. Your password is now added to the Windows Clipboard. You can paste the password into the **Password** line whenever you access the account to which it corresponds. The password will be cleared from the Clipboard when Password Safe is closed.

14. Close Password Safe.

HANDS-ON
PROJECTS

Project 2-7: Run Software Removal Tool

In this project, you will install and run the Microsoft software removal tool to scan for any malware and then remove it from your computer.

1. Use your Web browser to go to **www.microsoft.com/security/ malwareremove/default.mspx#run**.

2. Although the tool can be run directly from the Web, browser settings often interfere with it. Click **try downloading the tool directly from the Microsoft.com Download Center**.

3. Click **Download** and then **Save**, and then click **Save** again.

4. When the file has finished downloading, locate the file and then click **Run**.

5. Follow the instructions to install the program on your computer. When it has finished installing, click Next to start the program, as shown in Figure 2-31. Click **Finished**.

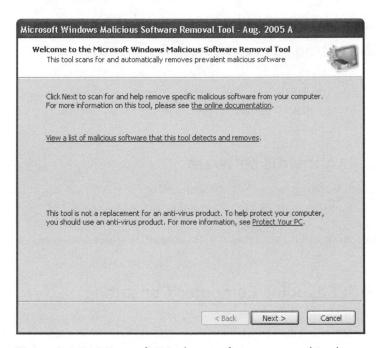

Figure 2-31   Microsoft Windows software removal tool

6. The tool will scan your computer for specific worms and viruses, remove them, and then report any that it found and removed.

7. Close all windows.

CASE PROJECTS

Case Project 2-1: Virus and Worm Update

What are the most recent virus and worm attacks? How much damage did they inflict? How much time was there between when the vulnerability was exposed and the malware was released? Write a one- to two-paragraph description of these viruses and worms and the harm that they caused.

Case Project 2-2: Famous Logic Bombs or Social Engineering Attacks

Using the Internet or print sources, research logic bombs or social engineering attacks and find the one that is most fascinating to you. What was the attack? Was the culprit ever caught? Write a one- to two-paragraph summary of your findings.

Case Project 2-3: Strong versus Weak Passwords

Create a list of five to seven characteristics of a strong password. Next, write down at least five passwords that you commonly use. On a scale of A–F, grade the strengths of each password. For any password that does not receive a grade of A, change the password to something stronger.

Case Project 2-4: Antivirus software

Select one brand of antivirus software. What features does it have that are different from other vendors' products? What are its strengths? What are its weaknesses? How much does it cost to be able to update the signature files? How expensive is it compared with competing products? Would you recommend this product to others? Write a one-page summary of your findings.

Case Project 2-5: Baypoint Computer Consulting

Baypoint Computer Consulting (BCC) has once again asked you to assist them with a client. A community college in the area has asked for someone to come speak to a computer class about security, particularly what students should do to protect their computers.

1. Create a PowerPoint presentation of eight or more slides that covers this information. Because the audience does not have a strong technical background, your presentation should be general in tone.

2. Your presentation went so well they have asked you to return and this time talk about what steps students should take if their computers become infected this semester. Again using PowerPoint, create a presentation of eight or more slides that outlines the steps students should follow in preparing for an attack and then recovering from it.

CHAPTER THREE

INTERNET SECURITY

After completing this chapter you should be able to do the following:	
➤ Explain how the World Wide Web and e-mail work	➤ Describe how to set Web defenses using a browser
➤ List the types of Web and e-mail attacks	➤ Identify the type of defenses that can be implemented in order to protect e-mail

Security in Your World

"This is really frustrating!" said Josh as he clicked the mouse. Kathy looked up from her textbook. "What's the matter?" she asked. "I get so aggravated at this," he said. "Every time I try to download a file from this Web site I keep getting a message that something is blocked. You know, it didn't used to be this way in here." Josh and Kathy were sitting in one of the student computer labs located in the school's technology building. "Ever since they did something last semester to these computers I keep getting messages that something is blocked. What did they do?"

"I think they changed the security settings on the Web browsers," said Kathy. "Is that because they don't want us downloading music anymore?" asked Josh. "No, that's not it," said Kathy. "It has to do with security. They don't want these computers to get infected with all that bad stuff from attackers on the Internet."

"But I can't get those files that I need," complained Josh. "What am I supposed to do?" Kathy slid her chair over to Josh's computer. "All you have to do is click right here and then click OK to download the file. See?"

"Oh, I didn't know that," said Josh. "Well, they don't need to block everything. I just use these computers to read my e-mail through a Web browser. And I know that if you do it that way the computer can't get infected. That's how I do it in my dorm room and my computer's never been infected."

"I'm afraid not," replied Kathy. "Just because you read your e-mail through a Web browser doesn't mean that you are protected. You still have to set your security on your Web browser to keep the destructive stuff out."

Josh looked over at Kathy. "How do you set it?"

The impact of the Internet upon our world has been truly astonishing. With more than one billion people connected to the Internet worldwide, it has had a revolutionary impact on how people learn, interact, and communicate. Some experts even claim that the Internet is creating a collective force of unprecedented power. For the first time in human history, mass cooperation across space and time is now possible, which creates a fundamental shift in power and communication.

What is equally remarkable is the speed at which the Internet has become a core tool of our society. Ever since the Internet entered the consumer computer world in the early 1990s, it has penetrated all parts of our lives almost overnight. Whereas other technological advances have taken years to be accepted (for example, almost 30 years passed before the telephone changed communication and 20 years passed before the automobile changed transportation), the Internet has changed how we access information in less than ten years. To imagine a world today without the Internet is almost impossible.

Yet for all of the benefits that the Internet has provided, it also has drawbacks. The Internet has opened the door for malicious attacks to be unleashed on any computer that is connected to it, leading to continuous software attacks that cause widespread harm. Unfortunately, there appears to be no end in sight for these attacks.

In this chapter, we will explore how the Internet works and identify the types of attacks that can occur. Then we'll examine the defenses that can be set up to make using the Web a more enjoyable and productive experience.

How the Internet Works

The **Internet** is a worldwide set of interconnected computers, servers, and networks. The Internet is not owned or regulated by any organization or government entity. Instead, computers and networks that are operated by industry, government, schools, and private parties all loosely cooperate to make the Internet a global information resource. Understanding how some of the basic Internet tools work helps to provide the foundation for establishing Internet security. The two main Internet tools that are used today are the World Wide Web and e-mail, and it is through these tools that the majority of the Internet attacks occur.

The World Wide Web

The **World Wide Web (WWW)**, better known as the Web, is composed of Internet server computers that provide online information in a specific format. The format is based on the **Hypertext Markup Language (HTML)**. HTML allows Web authors to combine into a single document text, graphic images, audio, video, and **hyperlinks**, which users click to jump from one area on the Web to another. A sample of HTML code is shown in Figure 3-1. Instructions written in HTML specify how a Web browser should display the words, pictures, and other elements on a user's screen, as shown in Figure 3-2.

NOTE

You can view the HTML code for any Web page. For example, using Microsoft Internet Explorer, click View on the menu bar and then click Source.

3

```
<!DOCTYPE HTML PUBLIC "-//W3C//DTD HTML 4.0 Transitional//EN" >

<html dir="ltr" lang="en">
<head>
<META http-equiv="Content-Type" content="text/html; charset=utf-8" >
<!--TOOLBAR_EXEMPT-->
<meta http-equiv="PICS-Label" content="(PICS-1.1 &quot;http://www.rsac.org/ratingsv01.html&quot; l gen
true r (n 0 s 0 v 0 l 0))" >
<meta name="KEYWORDS" content="products; headlines; downloads; news; web site; what's new; solutions;
services; software; contests; corporate news;" >
<meta name="DESCRIPTION" content="The entry page to Microsoft's Web site. Find software, solutions,
answers, support, and Microsoft news." >
<meta name="MS.LOCALE" content="EN-US" >
<meta name="CATEGORY" content="home page" >
<title>Microsoft Corporation</title>
<base href="http://g.msn.com/mh_mshp/98765" >
<style type="text/css" media="all">
@import "http://i.microsoft.com/h/en-us/r/hp.css";
</style>
<script type="text/javascript" src="http://i2.microsoft.com/h/all/s/hp.js"></script>
<script type="text/javascript" src="http://i.microsoft.com/h/en-
us/r/SiteRecruit_PageConfiguration_HomePage_Page.js"></script>
</head>
<body>
<script type="text/javascript">
<!--
var isw;isw=
(document&&document.body.clientWidth&&document.body.clientWidth>=895&&document.getElementById);
//-->
</script>
<a href="http://207.46.225.60/default.aspx#cArea" class="hide">Click here to jump to main page
content</a>
<div id="dPage" class="page">
<table cellpadding="0" width="100%"><tr><td colspan="2">
<table cellpadding="0" width="100%" style="height: 22px"><tr>
<td width="50%" style="filter:progid:DXImageTransform.Microsoft.Gradient(startColorStr='#4B92D9',
```

Figure 3-1   Hypertext Markup Language (HTML)

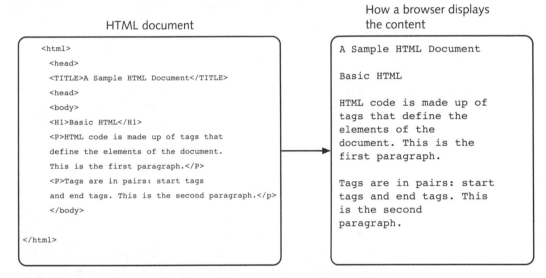

HTML document

How a browser displays the content

```
<html>

  <head>

  <TITLE>A Sample HTML Document</TITLE>

  <head>

  <body>

  <H1>Basic HTML</H1>

  <P>HTML code is made up of tags that

  define the elements of the document.

  This is the first paragraph.</P>

  <P>Tags are in pairs: start tags

  and end tags. This is the second paragraph.</p>

  </body>

</html>
```

A Sample HTML Document

Basic HTML

HTML code is made up of tags that define the elements of the document. This is the first paragraph.

Tags are in pairs: start tags and end tags. This is the second paragraph.

Figure 3-2   How a browser displays HTML

Web servers distribute HTML documents based on a set of standards, or **protocols**, known as the **Hypertext Transport Protocol (HTTP)**. HTTP is a subset of a larger set of standards for Internet transmission known as the **Transmission Control Protocol/ Internet Protocol (TCP/IP)**.

NOTE   The word *protocol* comes from two Greek words for "first" and "glue," and originally referred to the first sheet glued onto a manuscript on which the table of contents was written. The term later evolved to mean an "official account of a diplomatic document" and was used in France to refer to a formula of diplomatic etiquette.

Most Internet transmissions are based on **port numbers**, which identify what program or service on the receiving computer is being requested. For example, a Web browser on a user's computer may send a message to a Web server and specify port 80, which is the standard port for HTTP transmissions. The Web server immediately knows that the request is for an HTML document and responds by sending the entire HTML document (again using HTTP), which is stored on the user's local computer. The Web browser then displays the document. This process is illustrated in Figure 3-3.

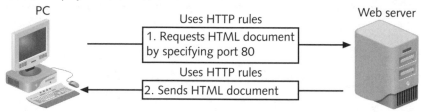

4. Browser reads and displays HTML document

PC

Uses HTTP rules

1. Requests HTML document by specifying port 80

Uses HTTP rules

2. Sends HTML document

Web server

3. HTML document stored on computer

Figure 3-3   HTML documents sent to browser

The local computer does not view the HTML document on the Web server; instead the entire document is transferred and then stored on the local computer before the browser displays it. This transfer-and-store process creates opportunities for sending different types of malicious code to the user's local computer, and it makes Web browsing a risky security experience if not done correctly.

E-Mail

Since developer Ray Tomlinson sent the first e-mail message in 1971, e-mail has become an essential part of everyday life. The number of daily e-mails will exceed 30 billion in 2005. According to Jupiter Research, the average user in an organization receives 81 e-mails and sends 30 e-mails daily. E-mail has replaced the fax machine as the primary communication tool for businesses.

NOTE   Although Ray Tomlinson developed the first e-mail system, he is more often remembered for selecting the @ symbol for use in all e-mail addresses, such as *administrator@course.com*. Ray said that his inspiration came from commercial transactions used to indicate a unit price, such as 5 items @ $2.95 apiece.

E-mail systems can use two TCP/IP protocols to send and receive messages. The **Simple Mail Transfer Protocol (SMTP)** handles outgoing mail, while the **Post Office Protocol** (**POP**, more commonly known as **POP3** for the current version) is responsible for incoming mail. The SMTP server "listens" for requests on port 25, while POP3 "listens" on port 110. E-mail, as illustrated in Figure 3-4, works as described in the steps below.

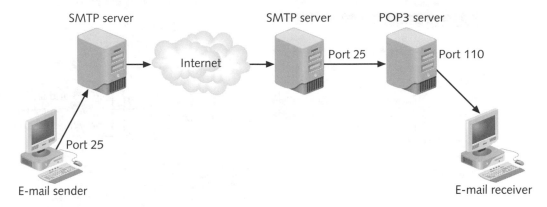

Figure 3-4   E-mail functions

1. The sender (*sender@source.com*) uses an e-mail program such as Microsoft Outlook to address the message to the receiver (*receiver@destination.com*), enter the body of the message, and then send it.

2. Outlook uses port 25 to connect to the user's local SMTP server at *mail.source. com*, and passes the message.

3. The SMTP server divides the "To" address into two parts: the recipient name (*receiver*) and the name of where it is going (*destination.com*).

4. The SMTP server at *source.com* connects through the Internet with the SMTP server at *destination.com* using port 25, and passes the e-mail message.

5. The SMTP server at *destination.com* hands the message to the POP3 server for *destination.com*, which in turn puts the message in receiver's mailbox.

NOTE If the SMTP server at *source.com* cannot connect with the SMTP server at *destination.com*, the message goes into a waiting queue at *source.com*, and the SMTP server periodically tries to resend the message in its queue, normally about every 15 minutes. After four hours, it sends an e-mail message to the sender indicating a problem. After five days, most servers stop attempting to send the message.

When configuring an e-mail program such as Microsoft Outlook, the addresses of the SMTP and POP3 servers must be provided, as shown in Figure 3-5. POP3 is a basic protocol that allows users to retrieve messages sent to the server by using an e-mail client to connect to the POP3 server and download the messages onto the local computer. After the messages are downloaded, they are generally erased from the POP3 server. **IMAP (Internet Mail Access Protocol**, or **IMAP4)** is a more advanced mail protocol. With IMAP, the e-mail remains on the e-mail server and is not sent to the user's local computer. Mail can be organized into folders on the mail server and read from any computer.

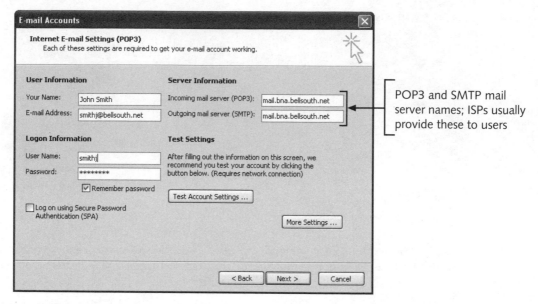

Figure 3-5   Configuring an e-mail client

NOTE

IMAP users can work with e-mail while offline. This is accomplished by downloading e-mail onto the local computer without erasing the e-mail on the IMAP server. A user can read and reply to e-mail offline. The next time a connection is established, the new messages are sent and any new e-mail is downloaded.

E-mail attachments are documents in a binary (nontext) format, such as word processing documents, spreadsheets, sound files, or pictures. These nontext documents must be converted into a text format before they can be transmitted.

INTERNET ATTACKS

Many of the attacks through the Internet are brute force attacks in which malicious software tries to invade a user's computer. However, other attacks actually "piggyback" onto legitimate Internet activities and sneak in while users are performing normal activities. Two of the most common types of these attacks are Web attacks and e-mail.

3

Web Attacks

Attackers use many different techniques to launch attacks through the Web. These Web attacks include repurposed programming, cookies, Trojan horses, redirected Web traffic, and search engine scanning.

Repurposed Programming

One beachhead for Web attacks is Web programming tools. In the early days of the Web, users viewed only static content (information that does not change) such as text and pictures. As the Internet increased in popularity, the demand rose for content that can change, such as animated images or information that is customized based on who is viewing it or the time of day. This dynamic content called for more sophisticated programming tools than basic HTML code.

Although dynamic content is widely used on the Web to create dynamic pages, it can also be used by attackers. This is sometimes known as **repurposed programming**, or using programming tools in ways more harmful than for what they were originally intended. Three of the most common repurposed programming tools are JavaScript, Java applets, and ActiveX.

JavaScript   One popular technology used to make dynamic content is known as **JavaScript**. Based on the programming language Java, JavaScript is special program code embedded into an HTML document. When a Web site that uses JavaScript is accessed, the HTML document with the JavaScript code is downloaded onto the user's computer. The Web browser then executes that code within the browser using the **Virtual Machine (VM)**, which is a Java interpreter. JavaScript is illustrated in Figure 3-6.

Because visiting a Web site that automatically downloads a program to run on the local computer introduces obvious security concerns, several defense mechanisms are intended to prevent JavaScript programs from causing serious harm. First, JavaScript does not support certain capabilities. For example, JavaScript running on a local computer cannot read, write, create, delete, or even list the files on that computer. This prevents a JavaScript program from

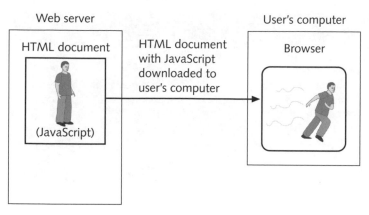

Figure 3-6   JavaScript in an HTML document

deleting data or placing a virus on the user's computer. In addition, JavaScript has no networking capabilities so that it cannot establish a direct connection to any other computers on the network. This prevents a JavaScript program from using a local computer to launch attacks on other network computers.

However, other security concerns still remain with JavaScript. JavaScript programs can capture and send user information without the user's knowledge or authorization. For example, a JavaScript program could capture and send the user's e-mail address to a source or even send a malicious e-mail from the user's e-mail account.

Usually the browser restricts what a JavaScript program can do if it is downloaded from the Web, but provides additional functionality if the program is loaded from the computer's hard drive. The assumption is that a user running a local JavaScript program wrote the program himself or accepted it from a trusted source. However, security vulnerabilities in browsers have allowed malicious JavaScript programs to perform harmful activities without the user's knowledge.

 If the default Web page on your browser changes without your permission, that was probably the result of a malicious JavaScript program.

NOTE

Java Applet   Another popular Web programming tool that can be repurposed is a **Java applet**. Unlike JavaScript, which is embedded in an HTML document, a Java applet is a separate program. Java applets are stored on the Web server and then downloaded onto the user's computer along with the HTML code. Java applets can perform interactive animations, immediate calculations, or other simple tasks very quickly because the user's request does not have to be sent to the Web server for processing and then returned with the answer. All of the processing is done on the local computer by the Java applet. Java applets are illustrated in Figure 3-7.

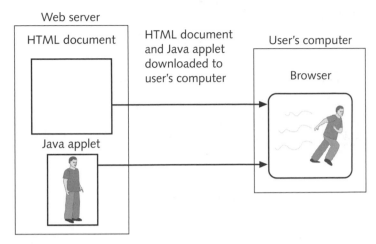

Figure 3-7   Java applet

Java applets can also be changed into hostile attack programs. The defense against a hostile Java applet is a sandbox. Downloaded Java applet programs are supposed to run within a security **sandbox**, which is like a fence that surrounds the program and keeps it away from private data and other resources on a local computer. Unfortunately, breakdowns in the Java sandbox have occurred, allowing a hostile Java applet to access data and passwords stored on the hard drive.

Two types of Java applets are defined by their relation to sandboxes. An **unsigned Java applet** is a program that does not come from a trusted source. A **signed Java applet** has a digital signature that proves the program is from a trusted source and has not been altered. Unsigned Java applets by default run in the sandbox and are restricted regarding what they can do, while signed Java applets are not restricted. Unsigned Java applets that attempt to do something outside of the sandbox automatically generate a warning message to the user. However, these messages are not always clear to users. Figure 3-8 shows a Java applet dialog box that is the work of an attacker attempting to obtain a password by making it appear like a legitimate request. As a warning, the browser displays a message at the bottom of the dialog box (*Warning: Applet Window*) that is intended to alert the user that this is an unsigned Java applet. Unfortunately, many users don't know what this warning means and provide the password anyway.

ActiveX   **ActiveX** is a set of technologies developed by Microsoft. ActiveX is not a programming language but a set of rules for how programs should share information. **ActiveX controls** represent a specific way of implementing ActiveX.

Programmers can develop ActiveX controls in a variety of computer programming languages (C, C++, Visual Basic, and Java). ActiveX controls can also be invoked from Web pages through the use of a scripting language or directly with an HTML command.

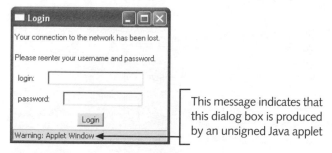

This message indicates that this dialog box is produced by an unsigned Java applet

Figure 3-8   Unsigned Java applet

NOTE

If an ActiveX control is not installed locally, the Web page can specify an address where the control can be obtained. Once a connection is made to where the ActiveX control is located, the control installs itself.

An ActiveX control is similar to a Java applet in that it can perform many of the same functions. Unlike Java applets, however, ActiveX controls do not run in a sandbox, but have full access to the Windows operating system. An ActiveX control can do anything a user can do, such as deleting files or reformatting a hard drive. To control this free-reign risk, Microsoft developed a registration system so that browsers can identify and authenticate an ActiveX control before downloading it. ActiveX controls can be signed or unsigned. A signed control provides a high degree of verification that the control was produced by the signer and has not been modified. However, signing does not guarantee the trustworthiness of the signer; it only provides assurance that the control originated from the signer.

ActiveX poses a number of security concerns:

- The user's decision to allow installation of an ActiveX control is based on the *source* of the ActiveX control and not on the ActiveX control itself. The person who signed the control may not have properly assessed the control's safety and may have left open security vulnerabilities.

- A control is registered only once per computer. If a computer is shared by multiple users, any user can download a control, making it available to all users on the machine. This means that a malicious ActiveX control can affect all users of that computer.

- Nearly all ActiveX control security mechanisms are set in Internet Explorer. However, ActiveX controls do not rely exclusively on Internet Explorer, but can be installed and executed independently. Third-party programs that use ActiveX technology may not provide the security mechanisms available in Internet Explorer.

- When an ActiveX control is executed, it usually executes with the privileges of the current user. It is not possible to externally restrict the privileges of a control.

- Because each ActiveX control decides when it can be run and what it can do, it is impossible for users to accurately determine the behavior of a control.

Cookies

A **cookie** is a small text file that a Web server stores on a user's hard disk and that contains user-specific information. Cookies allow that Web site to store information on a user's machine and later retrieve it when the user revisits the site. The need for cookies is based on HTTP. The rules of HTTP make it impossible for a Web site to track whether a user has previously visited that site. Any information that was entered on a previous visit, such as name or address, is lost. Instead of the Web server asking the user for this information each time he visits that site, the Web server can store that personal information in a file on the local computer. This file is called a cookie. The contents of a cookie might look similar to the following text:

RMID

449aa21d3f873a20

realmedia.com/

1024

3567004032

30124358

886173696

29593474

*

Cookies by themselves are not dangerous. A cookie cannot contain a virus nor steal personal information you have created and stored on a hard drive. It only contains information that can be used by a Web server.

Yet cookies can pose a security risk. Because cookies can contain sensitive information such as usernames and other private information, attackers often target cookies. A **first-party cookie** is created from the Web site that a user is currently viewing. For example, when viewing the Web site *www.123.org*, the cookie 123-ORG would be saved on the computer's hard drive. Whenever the user returns to this site, that cookie would be used by *www.123.org* to see the user's preferences. However, some Web sites attempt to access cookies they did not create. If a user went to *www.456.org*, that site might attempt to retrieve the cookie 123-ORG from the hard drive. The cookie is now known as a **third-party cookie** because it was not created by the Web site that attempts to access the cookie. The most common purpose of third-party cookies is for Web marketers to try to track preferences and the types of Web sites users like to visit.

NOTE
Cookies can also be used to determine which Web sites have been visited. Each time your browser goes to a Web site, it leaves some information about you behind, such as the name and address of your computer, the address of the Web page you accessed, and the address of the Web page you were last viewing. With cookies, the trail of where you have been can be more easily traced. Cookies are often examined by law enforcement personnel when they are attempting to identify the Web sites that a criminal suspect has been viewing.

Trojan Horse

A **Trojan horse** attack is another type of Web attack. According to ancient legend, the Greeks won the Trojan War by hiding in a large, hollow, wooden horse that was presented as a gift to the city of Troy. Once the horse was wheeled into the fortified city, the soldiers crept out of the horse during the night and attacked the unsuspecting defenders. A computer Trojan horse is a malicious program disguised as a legitimate program. For example, a user may download what appears to be a music file, yet when it is opened, a malicious program runs that erases the hard disk or steals the user's passwords and sends them to the attacker.

Trojan horse programs are **executable programs**, or programs that perform an action when the file is opened (or clicked). Filenames in Microsoft Windows programs typically have a three-character **file extension** preceded by a period, such as "Filename.*doc*". Although newer versions of the Windows software allow longer file extensions, to maintain backward compatibility with previous versions, the three-character file extension is still generally used. Windows executable programs have file extensions such as .exe, .vbs, .com., or .bat.

A Trojan horse may disguise itself by using a valid filename and extension. For example, you could download a free calendar program from the Internet with a file named Setup.exe, which would normally be the program to install the software. However, the file Setup.exe may actually be a program that reformats the hard drive when it is launched. Another technique commonly used is to make the program appear as though it is not an executable program, but only contains data or information. For example, the file Discount-Coupons.doc.exe at first glance may appear to be a nonexecutable Microsoft Word document (because it looks like the file extension is .doc); however, it is actually an executable program (because its true file extension is .exe) that steals the user's password.

Redirecting Web Traffic

Users make a variety of mistakes when typing a Web address into a browser. These mistakes include:

- *Misspelling the address*—Typing *www.corse.com* instead of *www.course.com*
- *Omitting the dot*—Typing *grocerycom* instead of *grocery.com*
- *Omitting a word*—Typing only *grocery* instead of *grocery.com*
- *Using inappropriate punctuation*—Typing *tool's.com* instead of *tools.com*

Usually these mistakes result in an error message like that shown in Figure 3-9.

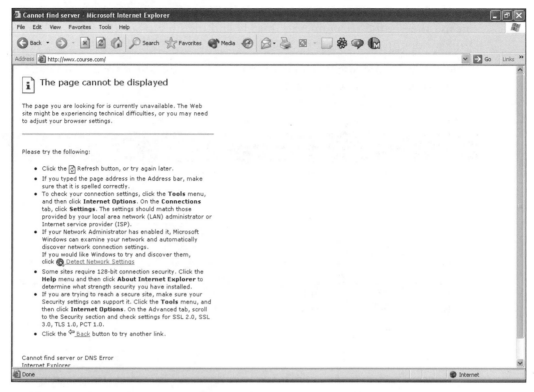

Figure 3-9   Browser error message

Hackers can exploit a misaddressed Web name and steal information from unsuspecting users through social engineering. Attackers may register the names of similar-sounding Web sites, such as *corse.com, courrse.com, cuorse.com* and *course.org*. When users attempt to enter *course.com* but make a typing error and enter *corse.com* instead, they are taken to the hacker's Web site. This site looks identical to the genuine site, but users are again tricked into entering personal information that is then stolen.

NOTE   Redirecting Web traffic is not limited to attackers. Several well-known Internet service providers (ISPs) automatically funnel misspelled addresses into their own Web sites that contain a search feature to help users find the sites they originally wanted.

Search Engine Scanning

Search engines, such as Google, are important tools for locating information on the Internet. However, attackers now also use these same search tools to assess the security of Web servers before launching an attack. Although most users simply type the word or phrase that they want to search for, Google and other search engines also have advanced search tools that can narrow criteria for more specific information. For example, entering *site:www.course.com security* would provide every Web page at that site that contains the word *security*. Attackers can use these same techniques to quickly and invisibly scour the Internet for information that can identify computers to attack.

Table 3-1 lists some search engine scanning techniques. These are used by attackers to locate information that can be used in an attack.

Table 3-1   Search engine scanning techniques

Search Operator	Description	Example	Why Used By Attackers
site	Searches a specific Web site for a certain term	*site:www.microsoft. com microsoft*	Provides a listing of every Web page on the site that has information about security
filetype	Searches for specific types of documents that contain a certain term	*filetype:pdf security*	Returns a listing of documents that contain security-related information
intitle	Searches Web sites that contain a certain term in the title of the page	*intitle:index of "parent directory"*	Provides a list of files and directories on a Web page that can be used to identify desired information and how the Web server is organized

E-mail Attacks

As with Web attacks, e-mail attackers also use different techniques to access personal computers. These attacks included malicious attachments and spam.

Malicious Attachments

The preferred method of distributing viruses and worms is through e-mail attachments, or files that are sent with an e-mail message. E-mail-distributed viruses typically use social engineering to trick recipients into opening the document and thereby infecting their own computers. After infecting a computer, many viruses and worms replicate by sending themselves in an e-mail message to all of the contacts in an e-mail address book. The unsuspecting users, seeing that an e-mail and attachment arrived from a "friend" and typically includes an interesting subject line, open the attachment and thereby infect their computers.

If a file attached to an e-mail message contains a virus, it is often launched when the file attachment is opened. This is usually done by double-clicking the attachment icon.

Spam

The amount of **spam**, or unsolicited e-mail, that flows across the Internet is difficult to judge. According to a Pew Memorial Trust survey, of the approximately 30 billion daily e-mail messages, almost half are spam. This survey also reports that spam has a negative effect on users:

- 25 percent of e-mail users say the ever-increasing volume of spam has reduced their overall use of e-mail.

- 52 percent indicate that spam has made them less trusting of e-mail in general.

- 70 percent say spam has made being online unpleasant or annoying.

- 5 percent (about six million users) report that they ordered a product or service as a result of receiving a spam message.

Spam also reduces work productivity. More than 11 percent of workers receive about 50 spam messages each day and spend more than half an hour deleting it. Nucleus Research reports that spam e-mail, on average, costs U.S. organizations $874 per person annually in lost productivity.

NOTE Spammers often build their own lists of e-mail addresses using special software that rapidly generates millions of random e-mail addresses from well-known ISPs, such as Yahoo! and others, and then sends messages to these addresses. Because an invalid e-mail account returns the message to the sender, the software can automatically delete the invalid accounts, leaving a list of valid e-mail addresses to send the actual spam. Spammers often swap or buy lists of valid e-mail addresses from other spammers as well.

The reason so many spam messages advertise drugs, cheap mortgage rates, or items for sale is that sending spam is a lucrative business. It costs spammers next to nothing to send millions of spam e-mail messages. Even if they receive only a very small percentage of responses, the spammers make a tremendous profit. Consider the following costs involved for spamming:

- *Equipment and Internet connection for launching spam*—Spammers typically purchase an inexpensive laptop computer ($500) and rent a motel room with a high-speed Internet connection ($85 per day) as a base for launching attacks. Sometimes spammers actually lease time from other attackers to use a network of 10,000 to 100,000 infected computers to launch an attack ($40 per hour).

- *E-mail addresses*—If a spammer wants to save time by purchasing a list of valid e-mail addresses to spam, the cost is relatively inexpensive ($100 for 10 million addresses).

The profit from spamming can be significant. If a spammer sent out spam to six million users for a product with a sale price of $50 that cost only $5 to make, and if 0.001 percent of the recipients responded and bought the product (a typical response rate), the spammer would make over $270,000 in profit.

Approximately 60 percent of all spam originates in the US, according to CipherTrust. South Korea ranks second with 10.4 percent.

NOTE

Beyond being annoying and disruptive, spam can also be dangerous. Spammers can overwhelm users with offers to buy merchandise or trick them into giving money away. It is not unusual for spammers to pretend to be a legitimate charity, particularly in times of a natural disaster such as an earthquake or hurricane. Spammers can also distribute viruses and worms through the e-mail messages.

The first known spam was sent in May of 1978 by a salesperson for the Digital Equipment Corporation to 320 individuals who were connected to the Arpanet, which later became the Internet.

NOTE

The U.S. Congress passed a law in late 2003 entitled the **Controlling the Assault of Non-Solicited Pornography and Marketing Act of 2003 (CAN-SPAM)**. The provisions of that bill are summarized in Table 3-2.

Table 3-2 CAN-SPAM law

Provisions of Bill	Description
Who is affected	• Spammers and those who procure their services • Organizations or individuals who know (or should know) that the promotion of their services or goods is prohibited
What is legal	• E-mail that contains a transaction or relationship message, such as order processing or product update information • Unsolicited commercial e-mail that contains accurate contact information for the sender
What is illegal	• Fraudulent or deceptive subject lines, headers, or e-mail addresses • Sending e-mail to addresses that have been harvested from Web sites or that were randomly generated • Sending sexually oriented e-mail without an identifying subject line • Not maintaining a functioning unsubscribe system for at least 30 days from the mailing • Registering for e-mail addresses under a false identity • Not removing an e-mail address in a timely fashion after receiving a request from a recipient

Table 3-2   CAN-SPAM law (continued)

Provisions of Bill	Description
Who may bring litigation	• Federal Trade Commission (FTC) • State Attorneys General • Internet service providers (Individual e-mail recipients are not eligible to bring litigation.)
What are the penalties	• State Attorneys General may sue for $250 per spam message, up to $2 million • Internet service providers may sue for $100 per spam message, up to $1 million • Three to five years imprisonment

Most security experts note that although the CAN-SPAM law was initially slow to affect spammers, recent successful convictions may begin to stem the tide of spam. Table 3-3 lists some of the 2005 legal victories over spammers.

Table 3-3   Legal victories using CAN-SPAM

Date	Spammer	Plaintiff	Judgment
June 2005	The Timeshare Spammer	U.S. Attorney, Northern District of Georgia	One of the first criminal convictions under CAN-SPAM
July 2005	Four spammers of X-rated material	Federal Trade Commission (FTC)	$1.2 million settlement with a promise to stop sending spam
August 2005	The Spam King	Microsoft	$7 million settlement with a promise to stop sending spam
August 2005	New Hampshire spam gang	America Online (AOL)	$13 million settlement

NOTE

AOL is offering to share with its members the confiscated property of spammers it has prosecuted. In the summer of 2005, AOL announced a sweepstakes in which it will give away $100,000 in cash, gold bars, and a fully loaded Hummer as a reward to its members who have reported spam that they have received.

WEB DEFENSES THROUGH BROWSER SETTINGS

The first line of defense against Internet attack is properly configuring the security settings on your Web browser. Modern Web browsers are highly customizable and allow the user to tailor the settings based on personal preferences. Beyond basic settings such as the color and the size of displayed characters, you can also customize browser security and privacy.

When using Microsoft Internet Explorer (IE), the configuration of Web browser settings is performed through selecting security options to be turned on or off. IE groups settings into the units General, Security, Privacy, Content, and Advanced. These Web browser defenses can be divided into three categories: advanced security settings, security zones, and privacy settings.

Advanced Security Settings

IE offers more than 60 configuration settings, many related to security. Figure 3-10 illustrates some of the basic settings that should be turned on, which are described in the following list.

BLOCK ATTACKS

- *Do not save encrypted pages to disk*—When a Web site is viewed, the actual HTML documents are sent from the Web server to the local computer and saved on the hard drive for the browser to display. A secure Web site may transmit sensitive information in an encrypted form that prevents attackers from seeing the information while in transit. However, after the HTML document is saved on the hard drive, an attacker could gain access to the computer and see it. This option prevents sensitive encrypted Web pages from being permanently saved on the hard drive.

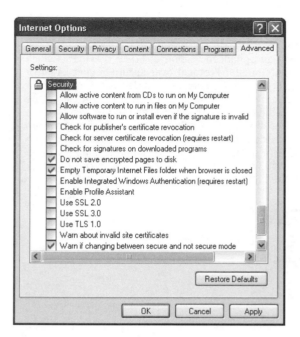

Figure 3-10   Basic IE security settings

BLOCK ATTACKS

■ *Empty Temporary Internet Files folder when browser is closed*—To speed up processing, a Web browser will check the storage area on the hard drive in which the HTML documents are stored when they are received from the Web server. This is called the **cache**. If the requested document is already on the cache, a Web browser only has to redisplay it and not request it again from the Web server. The cache could contain information an attacker may use. This basic browser security option empties the cache whenever the browser is closed.

SEND SECURE INFO

- *Warn if changing between secure and not secure mode*—Although Web sites use the HTTP protocol for sending data through the Internet, this protocol is not secure and an attacker could view the contents. However, an enhanced version of HTTP is **HTTPS**, which stands for **Hypertext Transfer Protocol over Secure Socket Layer** or sometimes HTTP Secure. HTTPS encrypts and decrypts the data sent between the client browser and the Web server so that it cannot be viewed by others. If this option is on, the IE Web browser will alert the user with a warning message when the Web server changes from HTTPS to HTTP and vice versa. This message appears like that shown in Figure 3-11; a similar message is shown when it changes back. Another indication that HTTPS is being used is a small closed padlock at the bottom of the browser screen, as seen in Figure 3-12.

Figure 3-11   HTTPS warning message

Closed padlock

Figure 3-12   HTTPS closed padlock

NOTE

HTTPS can only be turned on and off by the Web server; you cannot force all of your transmissions to use the more secure HTTPS through your browser settings.

3

BLOCK ATTACKS

Other advanced security settings restrict repurposed programming. Figure 3-13 illustrates the settings for controlling JavaScript. This is accomplished by regulating the VM, which is a Java interpreter for the Web browser.

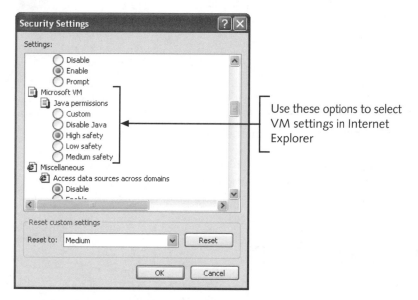

Figure 3-13   VM settings for JavaScript in Internet Explorer

BLOCK ATTACKS

Figure 3-14 shows the settings that relate to Java applets. The options are to Disable, Enable, or Prompt the user before a Java applet runs.

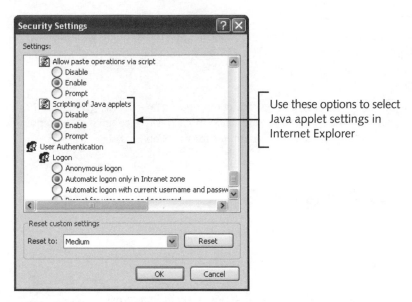

Figure 3-14   Java applet settings in Internet Explorer

ActiveX settings, shown in Figure 3-15, likewise allow the user to Disable, Enable, or Prompt before the ActiveX is downloaded. However, this setting can vary depending on whether the control is signed or unsigned.

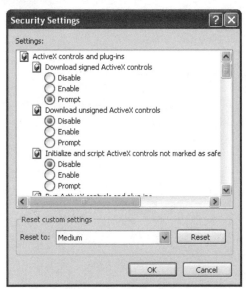

Figure 3-15   ActiveX settings in Internet Explorer

Security Zones

BLOCK ATTACKS
One of the drawbacks of the security settings in Web browsers is that the same settings may not need to be applied to all Web sites that are visited. For example, a school Web site may require specific settings to access an online course management system. A user who sets standard security settings to block other sites would have to change the settings or answer a series of questions when the school site is visited.

With most Web browsers, you can classify zones, set customized security for these zones, and then assign specific Web sites to a zone. Internet Explorer divides the Internet into four security zones, each of which can have a predefined level of security (High, Medium, Medium-low, and Low) or a customized security level, as shown in Figure 3-16.

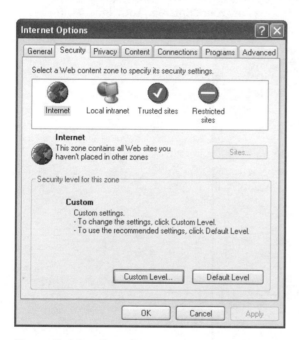

Figure 3-16   Security zones

- *Internet*—This zone contains all of the Web sites that have not been placed in any other zone. The default security level is Medium.

- *Local Intranet*—Web pages from an organization's internal Web site can be added to this zone. The default security level is Medium-Low.

- *Trusted Sites*—Web sites that are trusted not to pose any harm to a computer can be placed here. The default security level is Low.

- *Restricted Sites*—A Web site that is considered to be potentially harmful can be placed in the Restricted Sizes zone. The default security level is High.

You can assign Web sites to one of these four zones. When that site is accessed, the security level for that zone is automatically invoked. This makes it easier to set browser viewing security levels for different Web sites.

When a Web site that has been placed in one of the security zones is viewed, an icon representing that zone is displayed on the right side of the status bar in Internet Explorer.

NOTE

Restricting Cookies

BLOCK ATTACKS

You can restrict how cookies are created and used by configuring your Web browser. In IE you do this by adjusting privacy settings. Privacy levels can be established for each of the four security zones (Internet, Local Intranet, Trusted Sites, and Restricted Sites), as shown in Figure 3-17.

Figure 3-17   Privacy zones

The privacy levels are:

- Block All Cookies
- High
- Medium High
- Medium

3

- Low
- Accept All Cookies

Each privacy level can have custom settings configured by the user .

SECURITY IN YOUR WORLD

"That's great! Thanks for helping me, Kathy," said Josh. "You're right, it really isn't that hard to set everything up." "But just remember," said Kathy, "that using the technology is only part of the battle. The other part is using common sense sometimes."

"Common sense?" said Josh. "About what?" Kathy leaned over his shoulder. "E-mail is a great example of using both technology and common sense to protect yourself. Let me show you how."

E-Mail Defenses

Creating a defense mechanism regarding e-mail generally requires two separate solutions. The first solution is technology-based defenses, while the second is understanding and following sound procedures when using e-mail.

Technology-Based Defenses

Besides installing and running updated antivirus and antispyware software, the best technology defense against malicious e-mail attachments is to configure the client e-mail software to block spam or potentially harmful attachments. E-mail programs such as Microsoft Outlook contain several features to block e-mail, as shown in Figure 3-18.

- *Level of junk e-mail protection*—You can select the level of protection that is the most appropriate for your situation. The highest level of protection will accept e-mail messages only from a list of preapproved senders.

- *Blocked senders*—A list of senders can be entered here from which the user does not want to receive any e-mail; this is also known as a **blacklist**. Any message received from one of the senders is sent to the junk e-mail folder.

- *Blocked top level domain list*—E-mail from entire countries or regions can also be blocked and treated as junk e-mail, as shown in Figure 3-19.

Figure 3-18   Outlook settings to block e-mail

Figure 3-19   Blocked top level domain listing

NOTE   Several databases of blacklists are available on the Internet that include known spammers and others who distribute malicious content. Some of these allow users to download the lists and automatically add them to their e-mail server. The most common sites are *www.spamhaus.org/sbl*, *www.ahbl.org*, *spamcop. net/bl.shtml*, and *sspbl.tripod.com*.

Figure 3-20 illustrates the function to create a **whitelist**, or names/addresses of those individuals from whom an e-mail message will be accepted. Options include the ability to import a list of approved senders, to automatically add to the whitelist anyone in the contacts list, and to automatically add to the whitelist anyone to whom an e-mail message is sent.

Figure 3-20   E-mail whitelist

NOTE Microsoft Outlook automatically blocks 71 different types of file attachments that may contain viruses or worms, such as .exe, .bat, and .com. Your Inbox displays a paper clip icon in the Attachment column to let you know that the message has an attachment, and it lists the blocked attachment files at the top of the message. The complete list of blocked "Level 1" file types is provided at *http://office.microsoft.com/en-us/assistance/HP030850041033.aspx*.

If these built-in filters do not trap enough spam, users can install separate filtering software that works with the e-mail client software. Sophisticated e-mail filters use a technique known as **Bayesian filtering**. The user divides e-mail messages that have been received into two piles: spam and not spam. The filter then analyzes every word in each e-mail and determines how frequently a word occurs in the spam pile compared to the not spam pile. A word such as "the" would occur equally in both piles and be given a neutral 50 percent ranking. A word such as "report" may occur frequently in nonspam messages and would receive a 99 percent probability of being a nonspam word, while a word like "sex" may receive a 100 probability of being a spam word. Whenever e-mail arrives, the filter looks for the 15 words with the highest probabilities to calculate the message's overall spam probability rating. Although Bayesian filters are not perfect, they do trap a much higher percentage of spam than other techniques.

NOTE

Most organizations automatically check for worms and viruses in attachments as e-mails reach the POP3 and SMTP mail servers. However, when e-mail is read using a Web browser instead of an e-mail client such as Outlook, it may be possible for the attachments to bypass these mail server defenses. That makes it even more important to have good antivirus software running on each local computer.

Procedures

BLOCK ATTACKS

Using common-sense procedures to protect against harmful e-mail is also helpful. For example, when you receive an e-mail with an attachment, consider the following questions:

- Is the e-mail from someone that you know?
- Have you received e-mail from this sender before?
- Were you expecting an attachment from this sender?
- Does e-mail from the sender with the contents as described in the Subject line and the name of the attachment make sense? For example, would a college professor send an e-mail message with the Subject line "Dude, Check This Out" that contains an attachment such as AnnaKournikova.jpg.vbs?

Other good e-mail procedures include:

- Remember that e-mail is the most popular method for infecting computers and you should therefore treat it cautiously.
- Never open an unexpected attachment, even if it is sent from someone you know, until you've contacted the person by phone if necessary to help determine that the attachment is safe.
- Never reply via e-mail to answer an e-mail request for personal information. Pick up the phone and call the company that requested it, using the number found in the telephone book and not in the e-mail message.

CHAPTER SUMMARY

- The World Wide Web (WWW), better known as the Web, is composed of Internet server computers that provide online information in a specific format. The format is based on the Hypertext Markup Language (HTML). HTML allows Web authors to combine text, graphic images, audio, video, and hyperlinks into a single document. Instructions written in HTML specify how a Web browser should display the words, pictures, and other elements on a user's screen. Web servers distribute HTML documents based on a set of standards, or protocols, known as the Hypertext Transport Protocol (HTTP).

❑ E-mail systems can use two TCP/IP protocols to send and receive messages. The Simple Mail Transfer Protocol (SMTP) handles outgoing mail, while the Post Office Protocol (POP, more commonly known as POP3 for the current version) is responsible for incoming mail. The SMTP server uses port 25, while POP3 uses port 110. E-mail attachments are documents in a binary (nontext) format, such as word processing documents, spreadsheets, sound files, or pictures.

❑ Repurposed programming is using programming tools in ways more harmful than for what they were intended. Three of the most common repurposed programming tools are JavaScript, Java applets, and ActiveX. JavaScript is a special program code embedded in an HTML document. A Java applet, unlike JavaScript, is a separate program. Java applets are stored on the Web server and then downloaded onto the user's computer along with the HTML code. ActiveX is a set of technologies developed by Microsoft. ActiveX is not a programming language but a set of rules for how programs should share information. ActiveX controls represent a specific way of implementing ActiveX.

❑ A cookie is a computer file that contains user-specific information. A Trojan horse is a malicious program that is disguised as a legitimate program.

❑ Spam, or unsolicited e-mail, has a negative effect on work productivity and may also be potentially dangerous. Spammers can overwhelm users with offers to buy merchandise or trick them into simply giving money away. It is not unusual for spammers to pretend to be a legitimate charity. Spammers can also distribute viruses and worms through e-mail messages.

❑ The first line of defense against an Internet attack is properly configuring the security settings on your Web browser. Modern Web browsers are highly customizable, allowing the user to set security and privacy settings. Web browsers also provide the ability to classify zones, set customized security for these zones, and then assign specific Web sites to the zones.

❑ The best technology defense against malicious e-mail attachments is to configure the client e-mail software to block spam or potentially harmful attachments. Using common sense procedures to protect against harmful e-mail is also helpful.

KEY TERMS

ActiveX — A set of technologies developed by Microsoft for creating special features in an HTML document.

ActiveX controls — A specific way of implementing ActiveX.

Bayesian filtering — A sophisticated e-mail filtering technique.

blacklist — A list of senders from whom the user does not want to receive any e-mail.

cache — A special area on a hard drive that holds downloaded HTML documents.

Controlling the Assault of Non-Solicited Pornography and Marketing Act of 2003 (CAN-SPAM) — A federal law intended to regulate spam.

cookie — A computer file that contains user-specific information.

e-mail attachments — Documents in a binary (nontext) format, such as word processing documents, spreadsheets, sound files, or pictures that are attached to an e-mail message.

executable program — A program that performs an action when the file is opened.

file extension — A three-character file designator.

first-party cookie — A cookie created from the Web site that a user is currently viewing.

hyperlinks — A notation in an HTML document that allows the user to jump from one area to another.

Hypertext Markup Language (HTML) — A language that allows text, graphic images, audio, video, and hyperlinks to be combined into a single document.

Hypertext Transfer Protocol over Secure Socket Layer (HTTPS) — A protocol that encrypts and decrypts the data sent between the client browser and the Web server so that it cannot be viewed by others.

Hypertext Transport Protocol (HTTP) — A set of standards for transmitting HTML documents.

IMAP (Internet Mail Access Protocol, or IMAP4) — An advanced e-mail protocol.

Internet — A worldwide, interconnected set of computers, servers, and networks.

Java applet — A program for creating special features in an HTML document.

JavaScript — A programming language for creating special features in an HTML document.

port numbers — A number that identifies what program or service on the receiving computer is being requested.

Post Office Protocol (POP or POP3) — A protocol that handles incoming e-mail.

protocol — A set of standards.

repurposed programming — Using programming tools in ways more harmful than for what they were intended.

sandbox — A restrictive area that surrounds a program and keeps it away from private data and other resources on a local computer.

signed Java applet — A program with a digital signature that proves the program is from a trusted source and has not been altered.

Simple Mail Transfer Protocol (SMTP) — A protocol that handles outgoing e-mail.

spam — Unsolicited e-mail

third-party cookie — A cookie that was not created by the Web site that attempts to access the cookie.

Transmission Control Protocol/Internet Protocol (TCP/IP) — A set of standards for Internet transmissions.

Trojan horse — A malicious program that is disguised as a legitimate program.

unsigned Java applet — A program that is not proven to come from a trusted source.

Virtual Machine (VM) — A Java interpreter that displays JavaScript.

whitelist — A list of senders from whom a user does want to receive e-mail messages.

World Wide Web (WWW) — A system of Internet server computers that provides online information in a specific format.

REVIEW QUESTIONS

1. The _____ is a worldwide, interconnected set of computers, servers, and networks.
   a. World Wide Web
   b. Internet
   c. ARANET
   d. HTTPS

2. _____ is used to combine text, graphic images, audio, and video into a single document.
   a. Hypertext Transport Protocol (HTTP)
   b. Secure HTTP
   c. Transmission Control Protocol/Internet Protocol (TCP/IP)
   d. Hypertext Markup Language (HTML)

3. A(n) _____ identifies what program or service on the receiving computer is being requested.
   a. port number
   b. HPTP code
   c. TPC/PPT designation
   d. Web Server Resource Indicator (WSRI)

4. The _____ handles outgoing mail.
   a. Transmission Hypertext Mail System (THMS)
   b. IMAPI
   c. Post Office Protocol (POP3)
   d. Simple Mail Transfer Protocol (SMTP)

5. Each of the following is a programming tool that can be used in a malicious way except _____ .
   a. ActiveX
   b. Windows
   c. Java applet
   d. JavaScript

6. Unlike JavaScript, which is embedded in an HTML document, a Java applet is a separate program. True or False?

7. Downloaded Java applets are supposed to run within a security sandbox, which is like a fence that surrounds the program and keeps it away from private data and other resources on a local computer. True or False?

8. A first-party cookie is created from the Web site that a user is currently viewing. True or False?

9. A signed Java applet is a program that does not come from a trusted source. True or False?

10. A computer Trojan horse is a malicious program that is disguised as a legitimate program. True or False?

11. _____ is unsolicited e-mail.

12. The federal law Controlling the Assault of Non-Solicited Pornography and Marketing Act of 2003 is also known as _____ .

13. The storage area on the hard drive in which HTML documents are stored when they are received from the Web server is called the _____ .

14. A list of senders for which the user does not want to receive any e-mail is known as a(n) _____ .

15. _____ allow a user to jump from one area to another with a click of the mouse button in an HTML document.

16. How does Bayesian filtering work?

17. What are port numbers and how do they function?

18. What is the difference between a signed Java applet and an unsigned Java applet?

19. What is the difference between a first-party cookie and a third-party cookie?

20. What does the Web browser setting *Do not save encrypted pages to disk* do?

HANDS-ON PROJECTS

HANDS-ON PROJECTS

Project 3-1: Setting Web Browser Security

Setting browser security is essential to keep a computer secure. In this project, you use the Windows Internet Explorer (IE) Version 6 Web browser with Windows XP Service Pack 2 installed.

1. Start Internet Explorer.

2. Click **Tools** on the menu bar, and then click **Internet Options** to display the Internet Options dialog box, as shown in Figure 3-21. Click the **General** tab, if necessary.

3. First, you want to remove all of the HTML documents and cookies that are in the cache on the computer. Before erasing the files, look at what is stored in the cache that an attacker could access and use. Click the **Settings** button and then click the **View Files** button to see all of the files. If necessary, maximize the window that displays the files.

Figure 3-21 Security options in the Internet Options dialog box

4. Click the **Last Checked** column heading to see how long this information has been on the computer. Next, select a cookie by locating one in the **Name** column (it will be something like *Cookie: windows_xp@microsoft.com*). Double-click the name of the cookie to open it. If you receive a Windows warning message, click **Yes**. What information does this cookie provide? Close the cookie file and open several other cookies. Do some cookies contain more information than others?

5. Close the window listing the cookie files to return to the **Settings** dialog box. Click the **Cancel** button.

6. Now remove the files in your cache. In the Internet Options dialog box, click the **Delete Cookies** button to remove all cookies from your computer. Click **OK** when asked "Delete all cookies in the Temporary Internet Files folder?".

7. Click the **Delete Files** button to remove the HTML documents. Depending on the last time this action was performed, it may take up to a minute or more to remove all of the files. Click **OK** when the delete files warning message appears.

8. Click the **Clear History** button to remove a record of the sites that you have visited. Click **Yes** when asked "Are you sure you want Windows to delete your history of visited Web sites?". Change the Days to keep pages in history to **1** so that these will be removed automatically.

9. Click the **Advanced** tab to view the advanced settings. Scroll down to Security. Be sure that the following boxes are checked: **Do not save encrypted pages to disk**, **Empty Temporary Internet Files folder when browser is closed**, and **Warn if changing between secure and not secure mode**. Click **Apply**.

10. Click the **Security** tab to display the security options. Click the **Internet** icon if necessary. This is the zone in which all Web sites that are not in another zone are placed. Click **Default level** and look at the settings. Is this sufficient security? Drag the slider up and down to see the other security options.

11. Click **Custom level** and scroll through the security settings. Which settings do you recognize? Click **OK**.

12. Now place a Web site in **Restricted** zone. Click **OK** and return to your Web browser. Go to **www.bad.com** and view the information on that site. Notice that the status bar displays an Internet icon, indicating that this Web site is in the Internet zone. Click your **Home** button.

13. Click **Tools** on the menu bar and then click **Internet Options** to display the Internet Options dialog box again. Click the **Security** tab and then click **Restricted sites**. Click **Sites** and enter **www.bad.com**, click **Add**, and then click **OK** twice. Now return to that site again. What happens this time? Why?

14. Click **Tools** and then click **Internet Options** to see the **Privacy** tab option. Click the **Privacy** tab. Drag the slider up and down to view the different privacy settings regarding cookies. Which one should you choose? Click **Apply** and then click **OK**.

15. Windows XP Service Pack 2 includes a pop-up blocker. Click **Tools** on the menu bar and point to **Pop-up Blocker**. If **Turn On Pop-up Blocker** appears, click it to turn the feature on and then click **Tools** on the menu bar and point to **Pop-up Blocker**. Then click **Pop-up Blocker Settings**. Note that you can add sites to allow pop-ups to appear. Be sure that the Filter Level is set to Medium or High and that **Block Popups** is turned on.

16. Click **Close**. Close your browser.

HANDS-ON PROJECTS

Project 3-2: Setting Client E-mail Security

In addition to Web browser security, client e-mail security is very important. In this project, you will configure Outlook 2003 security.

1. Start Microsoft Outlook 2003.

2. Click **Tools** on the menu bar and then click **Options**. The Options dialog box opens.

3. Click **Junk E-mail** to display the Junk E-mail dialog box.

4. Click **Safe Lists Only**.

5. Click the **Block Senders** tab and then click **Add**. Enter the e-mail address of a partner in the class, as shown in Figure 3-22. Click **OK**.

Figure 3-22   Partner added to blacklist

6. Click the **Safe Senders** tab. Check the boxes **Also trust e-mail from my Contacts** and **Automatically add people I e-mail to the Safe Senders List**.

7. Click **OK**. Close the Options dialog box.

8. Ask your partner to send you an e-mail message. What happens when it arrives? Where does Outlook put the message? Why?

9. Create an e-mail message and send it to a third party who is not in your contacts list. Now look at your Safe Senders list again. Is that person added?

10. Close Microsoft Outlook.

HANDS-ON
PROJECTS

Project 3-3: Installing and Using Outlook Backup Utility

E-mail is used for communication and as a means to record those communications by saving and filing e-mail messages. Unfortunately, a frequently overlooked protection is to backup e-mail files on a regular basis. A utility that facilitates backing up Outlook e-mail is available as a download from Microsoft. In this project, you will download and install that utility.

1. Use your Web browser to go to **www.microsoft.com**, and then click **Downloads**.

2. In the Search for a download section, type **Backup** under Keywords and select **Outlook** under Product/Technology. Click **Go**.

3. Select **Outlook 2003 Add-in: Personal Folders Backup**.

4. Click **Download**.

5. Click **Run** and follow the instructions to install the program.

6. Start Outlook 2003.

7. Click **File** on the menu bar. Note that the File menu includes a new command named Backup, as shown in Figure 3-23.

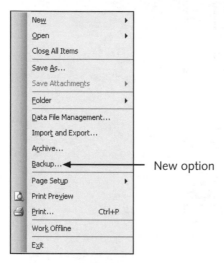

Figure 3-23   Outlook Backup option

8. Click **Backup**.

9. When the Outlook Personal Folders Backup dialog box opens, click **Options**.

10. Under Remind me to backup every _____ days, select the number **7** to be reminded once per week. You can adjust that number if you feel that you need to back up your e-mail more or less frequently.

11. Under Backup these personal folder files, click **Personal Folders**. (If you do not have any personal folders this option will not be available.)

12. Under Backup the file selected above to this location, click **Browse** and select the folder where you want to store the backup file. Your files should be backed up on an external device (the backup will not fit on a floppy disk); if this is not available, back up the files to your hard drive. Click **OK**.

13. Click **Save backup**. A message appears indicating that when you exit Outlook your files will be backed up. Click **OK**.

14. Before you close Outlook, perform some basic clean-up procedures to make your backup file as small as possible. Right-click the **Deleted Items** folder and then click **Empty "Deleted Items" folder** on the shortcut menu. Click **Yes** when asked to confirm this action.

15. Close Outlook. Your saved e-mail messages will now be backed up for protection.

Project 3-4: Installing Digital Certificate

You can verify the sender of an e-mail message by installing a digital certificate, sometimes called a digital ID. In this project, you install and use a digital ID with Microsoft Office Outlook.

1. Start Microsoft Office Outlook 2003.

2. Click **Tools** on the menu bar, and then click **Options**. The Options dialog box opens.

3. Click the **Security** tab.

4. Click the **Get a Digital ID** button. Outlook opens your Web browser to a page where you can download digital IDs.

5. In the list of available IDs, click the **VeriSign Web site** link. The VeriSign Digital ID Center Web page opens.

6. Click the **Click here** link to download a 60-day trial.

7. Enter the requested information. Do not change the Cryptographic Service Provider. Check the box to protect your private key. Click **Accept**.

8. Follow the prompts on the screen. Information about the digital ID will be sent to the e-mail address you entered. Close the Options dialog box. When the e-mail arrives, click **Continue**.

9. Click **INSTALL**. Click **Yes** when asked if you want to add the certificate and then click **Yes** again.

Now that you have installed the digital ID, you can use it to secure an outgoing e-mail message.

1. Start Microsoft Office Outlook 2003, if necessary.

2. Click **Tools** on the menu bar, and then click **Options**. The Options dialog box opens.

3. Click the **Security** tab.

4. Click the **Add digital signature to outgoing message** check box, and then click **OK**.

5. Compose and send an e-mail message to yourself. When you click **Send**, you may be asked to approve using the certificate. Click **OK**.

6. Open the e-mail message from yourself. Click the digital signature icon on the right of the message, and then click **Details**. The sender of the message is displayed in the dialog box, verifying that the sender is not posing as someone else.

7. Close the message and Microsoft Office Outlook.

Now you can verify that you have a personal digital signature on this computer.

1. Start Internet Explorer.

2. Click **Tools** on the menu bar, and then click **Internet Options**.

3. Click the **Content** tab.

4. Click the **Certificates** button. The Certificates dialog box opens.

5. Click the **Personal** tab, if necessary. The certificate that you installed appears in the list of certificates.

6. Close all windows.

CASE PROJECTS

Case Project 3-1: Using Cookies

Using the Internet and other sources, research recent attacks that have taken advantage of third-party cookies. What type of information was obtained? How many potential users were affected? How could these attacks have been prevented?

Case Project 3-2: Your E-mail Settings

How secure is your personal e-mail account? Using the information contained in this chapter and other Internet or print sources, create a list of e-mail security settings. Next, rank them in order of importance, with the most important receiving the highest number and the least important the lowest number. Finally, view your personal e-mail settings and give yourself a score. Then apply that same list to a friend's or other student's e-mail settings. What suggestions would you make to improve your e-mail settings? Write a one-page paper on your results.

Case Project 3-3: By-Passing Outlook Attachment Filtering

Although Microsoft Outlook does not allow attachments that contain a certain file extension, there are ways around this limitation. Using the Internet, research how to get around this without compromising security (Microsoft's Web site itself contains information about it). Do you think this information should be widely circulated? What implications are there if these limitations are avoided? Write a one- to two-paragraph summary of your findings.

Case Project 3-4: State Antispamming Laws

In addition to CAN-SPAM, several states are now passing or attempting to pass state antispamming laws. Research several of these laws and select the strongest points from each one. Then, create your own antispamming law. Write a one-page document describing your new law and why it is an improvement over CAN-SPAM.

Case Project 3-5: Calculate the Cost of Spam

The cost of spam can be staggering to an organization. Use your Web browser to go to the following Web site for an online calculator that estimates the cost of spam:

www.commtouch.com/site/ResearchLab/calculator.asp

3

Enter the requested values based on estimates for your school (you may want to ask your network administrator or instructor for some figures). What is the approximate cost of spam to your organization? In your opinion, how much should it be willing to spend in order to fight spam?

Case Project 3-5: Baypoint Computer Consulting

You have been asked by the president of Baypoint Computer Consulting (BCC) to assist the company with a special project. A local civic group has asked him to hire a speaker to address security at their luncheon next Friday, and the BCC president has offered the opportunity to you.

Create a PowerPoint presentation of eight or more slides that outlines e-mail attacks and the types of defenses that should be implemented. This audience may not have a strong technical background, so your presentation should be general enough for the average computer user.

As a follow-up to your presentation, the president has asked you to prepare a document to give the participants who heard your last presentation that outlines the steps to take if you receive an attachment you are unsure about. Create a short checklist that provides these steps.

PERSONAL SECURITY

Security in Your World

Lisa squeezed through the door just as the instructor was starting to close it and quickly walked over to an empty seat. "Whew, I made it!" she said. "Glad you could join us today for class," laughed Amy, who was sitting next to her. "Did you have trouble finding a parking place again?"

"No," said Lisa, "I just parked in the faculty lot. I was so busy posting on the wall that I forgot what time it was." "Posting on the wall?" asked Amy. "What's that?" Lisa opened her book and lowered her voice as the instructor started to talk. "Haven't you joined MyFaceBook.com yet? You really have to; it's so cool." "Oh, I remember now," said Amy. Lisa had told her last week about MyFaceBook.com, a "social net" for college students. Students can submit profiles about themselves, including birthdays, previous employers, blogs, and even photo albums. "And the wall is just this big forum where you can post anything you want to," said Lisa. "Are you going to join?"

Amy turned the page in her book. "No, I don't think so. I'm really concerned about identify theft." "What do you mean?" asked Lisa. "Well, with all of that personal information about me out there somebody could steal it and then use it to impersonate me and open up credit cards in my name. Remember I told you that happened to my aunt last fall when somebody faked her identity and bought a car under her name. It was awful."

"But Amy," said Lisa, "You don't have to give your street address or anything like that. And they say that everything is all locked up and nobody can steal your information." "Yes," said Amy, "But I've heard that online thieves are now using your cell phone numbers to actually tap into your personal data. Besides, I keep reading in the newspapers that online databases are getting hacked everyday and personal data is stolen. I just think it's asking for trouble to post all of my personal info in a place like that."

Lisa opened her notebook as the instructor wrote on the board. Maybe Amy's right, she thought. She promised herself she'd learn more about identify theft and reconsider her membership in MyFaceBook.com.

Many of the types of attacks discussed so far are malicious, designed to harm a computer or its data. Viruses are designed to corrupt computer data, worms are intended to "clog" a computer and slow it to a crawl, and logic bombs are written to explode and erase critical company data. These types of attacks are similar to vandalism, where the goal is to deface or destroy something.

Another type of attack has been rapidly proliferating in recent years and is now one of the most feared types. Instead of destroying *data* on the computer, these new attacks are designed to harm the *user*. For example, attackers might install software that monitors the Web sites a user visits in an effort to violate a user's *privacy*. Or, unwanted advertisements may continuously be displayed and affect a user's *productivity*. These attackers may even trick a user into revealing personal information in order to steal that person's identity, and destroy the person's *integrity*. Instead of vandalizing the computer and data, these new attacks are directly aimed at the user.

This chapter explores attacks directed at users and their personal security. It begins by describing what these attacks are and why they are so very dangerous. Next, it identifies some of the attack tools used. Finally, it examines how to defend against them.

WHAT IS SPYWARE?

Spyware is a general term used for describing software that violates a user's personal security. The Antispyware Coalition defines spyware as technologies that are implemented in ways that impair a user's control over:

- The use of system resources, including what programs are installed on a user's computer

- The collection, use, and distribution of personal or otherwise sensitive information

- Material changes that affect the user's experience, privacy, or system security

Spyware usually performs one of the following functions on a user's computer: advertising, collecting personal information, or changing computer configurations.

NOTE   The Antispyware Coalition is composed of antispyware software companies, hardware vendors, academic institutions, and consumer groups such as Microsoft, Dell, Symantec, and AOL. Their Web site is *www.antispywarecoalition.org*.

Two characteristics of spyware make it even more dangerous than viruses and worms, according to some security experts. First, unlike the creators of viruses, who generally focus on gaining personal notoriety through the malicious software that they create, spyware creators are instead motivated by money. Their goal is to generate income through spyware advertisements or by acquiring personal information that they can use to make illegitmate purchases, take out loans, and so on. Because of this heightened motivation, spyware is often more intrusive than viruses, harder to detect, and harder to remove.

A second characteristic is that harmful spyware is not always easy to identify. This is because not all software that performs one of the three functions listed earlier is necessarily spyware. With the proper notice, consent, and control, some of these same technologies can provide valuable benefits. For example, monitoring tools can help parents keep track of the online activities of their children, and remote-control features allow support technicians to diagnose computer problems without being physically located at the computer. Organizations that distribute software that performs these functions are legitimate businesses. By the same token, organizations that cause pop-up advertisements to appear on Web pages consider themselves to be legitimate. Whereas there is no question that someone who creates a virus performs a malicous act, it is not so easy to distinguish between legitimate businesses using spyware-like technology and other people using spyware technology for malicious purposes. This makes it difficult to pinpoint who the perpetrators of spyware are and how to defend against them.

NOTE Some industry experts state that the primary difference between a legitimate business that uses spyware-like technology and malicious spyware is that malicious spyware performs functions without appropriately obtaining the users' consent.

The number of spyware attacks is growing significantly. Recent studies reveal the following statistics:

- According to Webroot, approximately 116,386 Web pages distributed spyware during April 2005, a 151 percent increase over the previous month.

- The average computer has 25 pieces of spyware installed on the hard drive.

- Computer manufacturer Dell Inc. says that 12 percent of the calls made to its help desk are the result of spyware-infected computers.

- The spyware industry earns over $2 billion annually.

- According to Webroot, a 1,000-person organization with a spyware infection rate of only 10 percent per month spends $163,480 annually to remove spyware and return the computers to working condition.

- According to the National Cyber Security Alliance, over 74 percent of broadband users have some type of spyware on their computers.

Beyond being a "nuisance" to computer users, spyware attackers gather personal information about users, which can result in far more than just a nuisance. According to the Privacy Rights Clearinghouse, more than 50 million Americans had their personal information exposed in the first six months of 2005. Table 4-1 lists several of the security breaches that exposed personal information, some of which were caused by spyware.

Table 4-1 Security breaches that exposed personal information

Company	Number of People Affected
CardSystems Solutions	40,000,000
Citigroup	3,900,000
DSW Shoe Warehouse	1,400,000
Bank of America	1,200,000
Commerce Bank, PNC Bank, Bank of America	700,000

Table 4-1   Security breaches that exposed personal information (continued)

Company	Number of People Affected
Time Warner	600,000
LexisNexis	310,000
Ameritrade	200,000
Polo Ralph Lauren	180,000

After attackers have obtained personal information, they can perform identity theft.
Identity theft occurs when an individual uses the personal information of someone else
(such as a Social Security number, a credit card number, or other identifying information) to
impersonate that individual with the intent to commit fraud or other crimes. Once identity
thieves have obtained personal information they can:

- Change the mailing address on a credit card account. The thief then charges
  purchases to the account. Because the bills are being sent to the new address, the
  real person does not know that there is a problem.

- Produce counterfeit checks or debit cards and then empty the owner's bank
  accounts.

- Establish phone or wireless service in the person's name.

- File for bankruptcy under the person's name to avoid paying debts they have
  incurred, or to avoid eviction.

- Provide the name of the real person to police or other law enforcement officers
  during an arrest. When the suspect doesn't appear for a court date, an arrest
  warrant is issued in the name of the identity-theft victim.

- Use fraudulently obtained credit and debit card account numbers to buy expensive
  items and then either keep the items or sell them.

- Open a bank account in the person's name and write bad checks on that account.

- Open a new credit card account, using the name, date of birth, and Social Security
  number of the identity-theft victim. When the thief does not pay the bills, the
  delinquent account is included in the victim's credit report.

- Obtain loans for expensive items such as vehicles and even homes.

Identity theft becomes a serious problem for the victims. People whose identities have been
stolen can spend months or even years and thousands of dollars restoring their good name
and credit record. In the meantime, they may lose job opportunities, be refused loans,
education, or housing, or even get arrested for crimes they didn't commit.

NOTE

According to the Federal Trade Commission, 4.6 percent of Americans reported
being victims of identity theft in 2004. The FBI reports that in 2004 the privacy
of more than 10 million U.S. citizens had been compromised, resulting in losses
estimated to be $50 billion.

Some of the following characteristics indicate that a computer might be infected with spyware:

- Pop-up advertisements appear even when the user is not on the Web.

- The Web browser home page (the page that a browser first opens) or browser settings have changed without the user's consent.

- A new toolbar unexpectedly appears in a Web browser and is difficult to remove.

- The computer takes longer than usual to complete common tasks.

- The computer crashes frequently.

4

SECURITY IN YOUR WORLD

"Why can't I log on to this crazy system? How do they expect me to register for classes next semester?" asked Lisa. She was sitting at a computer outside of the registrar's office trying to register online for her classes. "What's the matter?" asked Amy, as she studied Lisa's computer screen. "Oh, it won't let me log on so I can register," said Lisa. "I know my Social Security number. I keep typing it in under 'Username' like I always do but it says I don't exist!"

"Lisa, you're not supposed to use your Social Security number anymore, remember?" said Amy. "They gave us those new student ID numbers last semester that we're supposed to use instead." Lisa started rummaging through her backpack. "Yes, I remember now. Why did they change that? Now I have something else that I have to remember. Why can't we use our Social Security numbers? At least I have mine memorized."

"I read in the student newspaper that it's for security reasons. Once somebody gets your Social Security number, they can open up bogus credit card accounts or get fake drivers licenses in your name," said Amy. "Well, I don't have a bank account or a credit card, so I don't have to worry about it," Lisa said. "Actually, you probably do," Amy replied. "If you don't have a credit card, then you probably won't think about checking your credit report to see if somebody has opened up a phony card under your name. Didn't you hear about Besim? Somebody stole his identity and opened up fake credit cards under his name and charged all sorts of stuff to him. His credit got so messed up that he lost his tuition assistance. That's why he couldn't enroll this semester."

Lisa stopped searching her backpack and looked up at Amy. "They can do all of that with just my Social Security number? How do they steal it in the first place?"

Spyware Tools

Attackers use a host of spyware tools, including adware, phishing, keyloggers, configuration changers, dialers, and backdoors.

Adware

Adware is software that delivers advertising content in a manner or context that is unexpected and unwanted by the user. Adware typically displays advertising banners or pop-up ads, as shown in Figure 4-1, and is frequently encountered while visiting Web sites with a browser. Most users frown on adware for the following reasons:

- Unwanted advertisements can be a nuisance.

- Repeated pop-up ads can impair productivity.

- Adware may display objectionable content.

- Advertisements can slow a computer down or cause crashes and the loss of data.

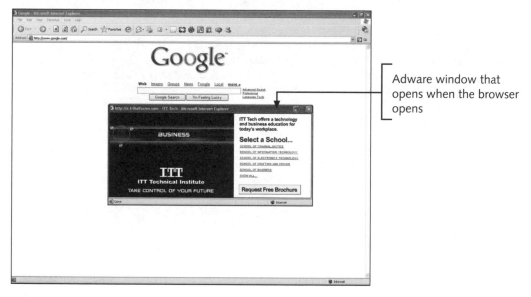

Adware window that opens when the browser opens

Figure 4-1   Pop-up adware

NOTE

The justification for adware is that it helps recover programming development expenses and thus helps to hold down costs for the user.

Beyond being a nuisance, adware can also be a security risk. Many adware programs perform a tracking function, which monitors and tracks a user's activities and then sends a log of these activities to third parties without the user's authorization or knowledge. For example, a user who visits online automobile sites to view specific types of cars can be tracked by adware and classified as someone interested in buying a new car. Based on the order of the sites visited and the types of Web sites, the adware can also determine whether the surfers' behavior suggests they are close to making a purchase or are also looking at competitor's cars. This information is gathered and sold to automobile advertisers, who then send the users pop-up ads about their cars.

NOTE One adware company's database had records of more than 1.3 million computer users who recently visited automotive Web sites.

Phishing

Phishing (pronounced "fishing") involves sending an e-mail or displaying a Web announcement that falsely claims to be from a legitimate enterprise and that attempts to trick a user into surrendering private information. The users are often directed to visit a Web site where they are asked to update personal information, such as passwords, credit card numbers, Social Security numbers, bank account numbers, or other information for which the legitimate organization already has a record. However, the Web site is actually a fake and is set up to steal the users' information.

NOTE The word *phishing* is a variation on actual fishing, the idea being that "bait" is thrown out, knowing that while most will ignore it, some will be tempted into "biting" it.

One of the problems with phishing is that both the e-mails and the fake Web sites appear legitimate. Figures 4-2 through 4-4 illustrate Web site announcements and e-mail messages that were used in phishing. Because these messages contain the actual logos, color schemes, and similar wording used by the real site, it is difficult to determine whether they are fraudulent or not.

Because of the difficulty in distinguishing between legitimate and fraudulent messages and Web sites, the number of phishing sites (Web sites that imitate the legitimate Web sites but instead fraudulently capture a user's information) and successful e-mail attacks is increasing at an alarming rate.

- In July 2005, there were 14,135 phishing Web sites, which represents a 4,000 percent increase in one year. In January 2004, there were only 198 phishing sites, according to data from the Anti-Phishing Working Group.

- More than 2.3 billion phishing messages worldwide were sent in March 2005, or a 500 percent increase in six months. As much as five percent of all e-mail is now believed to be phishing attempts, according to Brightmail, a company that tracks spam and scam e-mail.

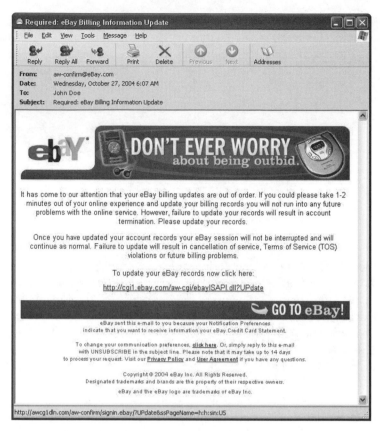

Figure 4-2   e-Bay phishing Web message

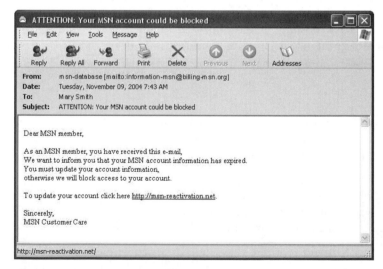

Figure 4-3   MSN phishing e-mail message

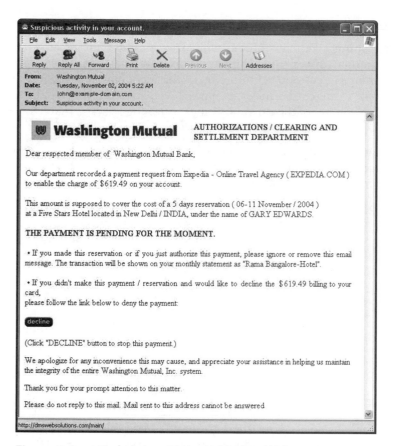

Figure 4-4   Washington Mutual phishing Web message

- It is estimated that consumers lost $500 million to phishing in 2004. A survey of 1,335 people reported that 70 percent of them had visited a fake phishing Web site, and 15 percent said they entered their private data at such sites, according to the Ponemon Institute.

- More than half of the consumers surveyed by Cyota, a fraud-prevention service, said that they were afraid to do online commerce because of phishing concerns. Another study by Symantec showed that one third of respondents said they would not conduct online banking transactions because of phishing.

Most phishing sites function for only three to five days to prevent law enforcement agencies from tracking the attackers. In that short period, a phishing attack can net over $50,000.

NOTE

Following are variations on phishing attacks:

- **Spear phishing**—Whereas phishing involves sending millions of generic e-mail messages to users, **spear phishing** targets only specific users. The e-mails used in spear phishing are customized to the recipient, including their name and personal information, to make the message appear even more legitimate than phishing. Because the volume of the e-mail in a spear phishing attack is much lower than in a regular phishing attack, spear phishing scams are more difficult to detect.

- **Pharming**—Instead of asking the user to visit a fraudulent Web site, **pharming** (pronounced "farming") automatically redirects the user to the fake site. This is accomplished by attackers penetrating the servers that direct traffic on the Internet.

- **Google phishing**—Named after the famous search engine, **Google phishing** involves phishers setting up their own search engines to direct traffic to illegitimate sites. For example, unsuspecting users who access a Google phishing search engine and search for "Amazon" are sent to a fake site that looks like Amazon but is actually a phishing site.

Despite heightened publicity regarding the dangers of phishing, many computer users still fall victim to attacks. A mock phishing attack conducted by the New York State Office of Cyber Security and Critical Information Coordination (CSCIC) sent phishing e-mails to more than 10,000 employees, trying to trick users into giving their passwords to a phishing site. More than 75 percent of the recipients opened the e-mail, and 17 percent clicked the embedded link in the message that directed them to the phishing site. However, because some users experienced difficulty in following the embedded link, three percent of the employees manually entered the Web address in the browser. Once at the phishing site, 15 percent, or 1,500 users, tried to enter their passwords. After all of the users attended a required training session regarding phishing, the same attack was conducted again two months later. This time over 800 users still opened and read the phishing e-mail.

Keyloggers

A **keylogger**, sometimes called a **keystroke logger**, is either a hardware device or a small program that monitors each keystroke a user types on the computer's keyboard. As the user types, the device records each keystroke and saves it as text. An attacker can retrieve this information, or the information can be silently transmitted to a remote location. The attacker then acquires all of the information that was entered, including passwords, credit card numbers, and personal information.

As a hardware device, a keylogger is a small plug located between the keyboard connector and computer keyboard port, as shown in Figure 4-5. Because the device resembles an ordinary keyboard plug, and because the keyboard port is on the back of the computer, someone can secretly attach a keylogger to a computer without the user noticing its presence. At a later point in time, the person who installed the keylogger returns and removes the device in order to access the information the device has gathered.

Figure 4-5   Hardware keylogger

Software keyloggers are programs that silently capture what a user types, including passwords and sensitive information. Figure 4-6 illustrates the keystrokes that a keylogger software program can acquire. Software keyloggers do not require physical access to the users' computer, but instead are unknowingly downloaded and installed as a Trojan horse or by a virus.

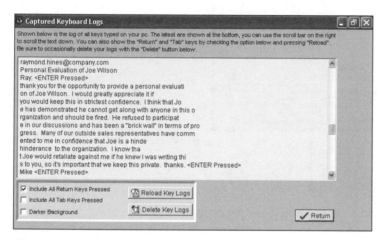

Figure 4-6   Software keylogger

NOTE

A software keylogger program typically consists of only two files that are installed in the same directory on the hard drive: a file that does all the recording, and an executable (.exe) file that installs the keylogger and triggers it to work.

Software keylogger programs also hide themselves so that they cannot be easily detected even if a user is searching for them. Operating systems contain a function that allows a user to observe the programs that are currently running. In Microsoft Windows, this is called the **Windows Task Manager**, which you can start by pressing the Ctrl, Alt, and Delete keys simultaneously. However, keyloggers can elude detection by the Windows Task Manager. Figure 4-7 shows the Windows Task Manager failing to list the software key logger as one of the running programs, even though the keylogger is running.

Although keylogger programs are often promoted for useful purposes such as allowing parents to monitor their children's activities on the Internet, the potential for abuse is staggering. Most privacy advocates agree that legislation should be enacted to make the unauthorized use of keyloggers a criminal offense.

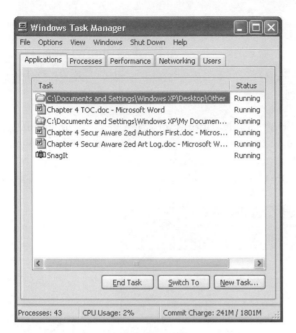

Figure 4-7   Invisible software keylogger

Configuration Changers

Users expect that they are the only ones who can change the configuration (or settings) on their personal computers. These settings are used to resist attacks and to keep computers personalized to meet user needs. However, **configuration changers** are a type of spyware that change the settings on a computer without the user's knowledge or permission. Configuration changers can do the following:

- Change operating system or software security settings, such as security settings for a Web browser
- Disable antivirus or other security software
- Initiate an outbound Internet connection
- Change startup procedures or security settings
- Run the computer in a mode that hides information from the user or from systems tools

Dialers

A **dialer** is a program that changes the settings of a computer that uses a dial-up telephone line to connect to the Internet. Typically a user who connects to the Internet using a dial-up modem configures the modem to dial a local telephone number to make connection, thus preventing unnecessary long-distance charges. Premium-rate numbers, such as 900 numbers, are a popular method for paying for a telephone service. However, users can be charged up to $4.00 or more per minute using one of these numbers. Dialer programs secretly change the dial-up connection setting so that instead of calling a local telephone number, the modem dials a premium-rate number or an international phone number, from which the attackers receive a portion of the fees. Because dial-up modems are inherently slow, the expense can accumulate quickly. In addition, most users do not know they are the victims of dialers until they receive their telephone bills a month later.

NOTE For the attackers, the cost of setting up such a premium-rate service is relatively low. Only 10 percent of the charge covers expenses, meaning attackers can keep 90 percent of the cost of a premium rate call.

Users with broadband connections such as cable modems or digital subscriber lines (DSL) are usually not affected by dialers. This is because these connections do not require dialing a telephone number to make an Internet connection.

NOTE Dialers can attack anyone. The vice president of European security for Microsoft was the victim of a dialer attack during the summer of 2005, when his dial-up number was changed and he accumulated over $872 in long-distance charges.

Backdoors

A **backdoor** provides an unauthorized way of gaining access to a program or to an entire computer system. Backdoors bypass the normal requirements of entering a username and password to access a computer or program. Once the attacker has gained access through the backdoor, he or she can remain hidden from casual inspection while remotely controlling almost any function of the computer. Backdoors enable the remote malicious user to perform the following activities:

- Upload files to the computer
- Start programs
- View a list of programs and processes that are currently running and terminate any program or process
- Collect information (including passwords) and other confidential data that a user enters with the keyboard
- Reboot the computer
- Send and receive files, as well as delete, copy, and rename files
- Log off the current user
- Prevent the computer from performing a specific function

- Display message boxes
- Play sounds through the speakers

NOTE

A backdoor can be either a program installed by a Trojan horse or it can be a modification to a legitimate program. One of the most famous backdoor programs was called Back Orifice.

SECURITY IN YOUR WORLD

Lisa walked over to her bed and sat down. "I can't believe it," she said to Amy. Amy had just spent the last half hour helping Lisa scan her computer for spyware. They found nine programs that were tagged as spyware. "I just bought this computer before the semester started, and it's already been infected?"

Amy moved her chair away from the desk. "I read somewhere that a new computer without any protection that's connected to the Internet will be infected in less than 20 minutes. You're probably lucky it's no worse than this." "I don't know what to do," Lisa sighed. "They've stolen everything I had on that computer."

"No, I don't think so," said Amy. "From what I can tell, this spyware wasn't all that bad. I think everything will be OK."

"Well, I'm really mad now," said Lisa. "I feel like somebody has broken into my room and stolen my property and even put up secret microphones to listen to me." Amy smiled. "You know, that's a pretty good definition of this spyware stuff."

"Amy," said Lisa as she stood up, "Show me what I need to do to protect myself. I don't want this to happen again."

PERSONAL SECURITY DEFENSES

It is clearly important to defend against spyware attack tools, such as adware, phishing, keyloggers, configuration changers, dialers, and backdoors. Fortunately, there are special tools you can use and practices you can implement to ward off attacks. These include installing antispyware software, recognizing phishing, and encouraging antispyware legislation and procedures.

Antispyware Software

BLOCK ATTACKS

Just as antivirus software is one of the best defenses against viruses, another class of defensive software known as **antispyware software** helps prevent computers from becoming infected by different types of spyware. Antivirus software and antispyware software share many similarities. First, antispyware software must be regularly updated to defend against the most recent spyware attacks, as shown in Figure 4-8. Secondly, antispyware can be set to provide both continuous real-time monitoring as well as to perform a complete scan of the entire computer system, as seen in Figure 4-9. And like antivirus software, antispyware provides good visual tools regarding the system scan. Figure 4-10 shows a scan taking place.

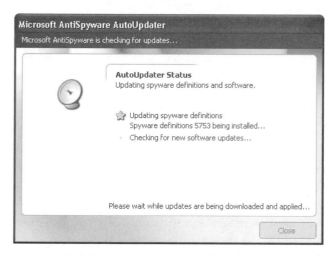

Figure 4-8   Antispyware updates

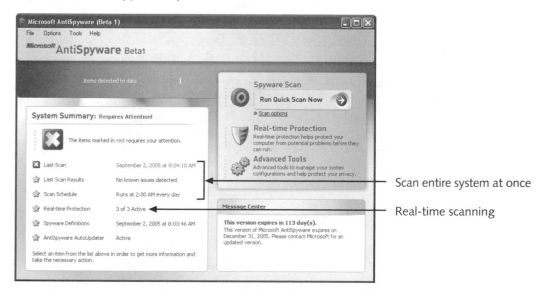

Figure 4-9   Real-time antispyware monitoring and scan capabilities

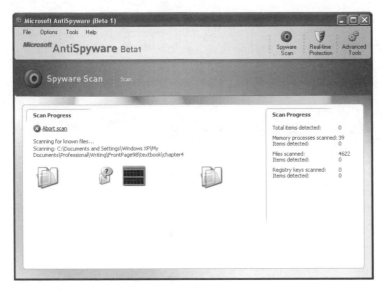

Figure 4-10   Antispyware scan

However, unlike most antivirus software programs, antispyware often provides more detailed information when it locates spyware. As shown in Figure 4-11, the antispyware program displays the name of the spyware, a threat level, a description of the spyware, and recommended action regarding how to handle it.

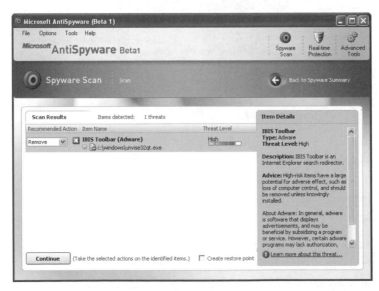

Figure 4-11   Antispyware detailed information

The default advice regarding how to handle spyware when detected by anti-spyware software is almost always *Remove*. Other typical options include *Ignore*, *Quarantine*, and *Always Ignore*.

Many antispyware products provide the following additional tools:

- *System explorers*—These tools expose configuration information that are normally difficult to access. Figure 4-12 shows the downloaded ActiveX controls revealed through the system explorer.

- *Tracks Eraser*—This tool automatically removes cookies, browser history, a record of which programs have been recently opened, and other information that attackers could benefit from.

- *Browser Restore*—The Browser Restore tool allows the user to restore specific browser settings if spyware infects the Web browser. The tool resets user-defined settings instead of the browser's default settings.

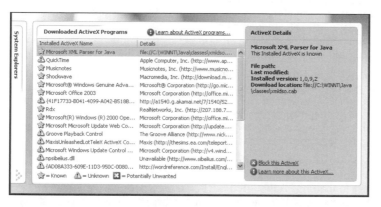

Figure 4-12   System explorer

Several good antispyware products are freely available on the Internet, as are several reasonably priced commercial packages. Some security experts recommend that you install at least two antispyware programs on a computer, because one product may not always detect all of the spyware.

Recognize Phishing

BLOCK ATTACKS

Because phishing involves social engineering to trick users into visiting a fake Web site, one of the first lines of defense is to recognize e-mails and Web messages that could be phishing attacks. Some of the common elements in these messages include:

- **Deceptive Web links**—A link to a Web site embedded in an e-mail should not have an @ sign in the middle of the address. Also, phishers like to use variations of a legitimate address, such as *www.ebay_secure.com, www.e--bay.com,* or *www.e-baynet.com.* Never log on to a Web site from a link in an e-mail; instead, open a new browser window and type the legitimate address.

- **E-mails that look like Web sites**—Phishers often include the logo of the vendor and otherwise try to make the e-mail look like the vendor's Web site as a way to convince the recipient that the message is genuine.

- **Fake sender's address**—Because sender addresses can be easily forged, an e-mail message should not be trusted simply because the sender's e-mail address appears to be valid (such as *tech_support@ebay.com*). Also, an @ in the sender's address is a technique used to hide the real address.

- **Generic greeting**—Many fishing e-mails begin with a general opening such as "Dear e-Bay Member" and do not include a valid account number. If an e-mail from an online vendor does not contain the user's name, it should be considered suspect. However, because spear phishing sends customized e-mail messages, the inclusion of a user name does not mean that the e-mail is legitimate.

- **Poor grammar, formatting, or misspellings**—Phishing e-mails often contain misspelled words, poor grammar and punctuation, and incorrect formatting. Although this is sometimes because the e-mail originated overseas from a phisher with subpar English language skills, often these mistakes are intentional. These errors help the e-mail avoid a spam filter.

- **Pop-up boxes and attachments**—Legitimate e-mails from vendors never contain a pop-up box or an attachment, since these are tools often used by phishers.

- **Unsafe Web sites**—Any Web site in which the user is asked to enter personal information should start with *https* instead of *http*, and it should also include a padlock in browser status bar. (Some phishers insert a fake padlock in the body of the message or Web page; however, for the padlock to be valid, it must be on the browser status bar.) Users should not enter data unless they see these two indicators.

- **Urgent request**—Many phishing e-mails try to encourage the recipient to act immediately or threaten that the recipients' accounts will be deactivated without a quick response.

Three examples of these phishing characteristics are shown in actual phishing e-mails in Figures 4-13 through 4-15. (Note that the graphic quality of the original e-mails is low, which is reflected in the following figures.)

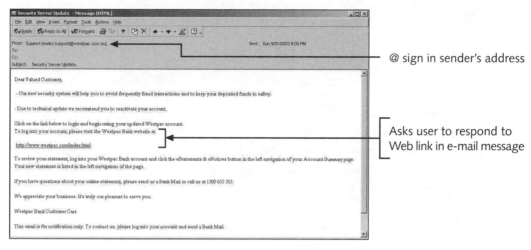

@ sign in sender's address

Asks user to respond to Web link in e-mail message

Figure 4-13 Phishing e-mail 1

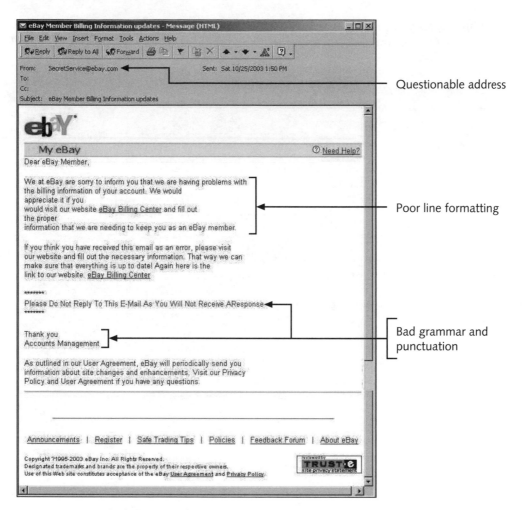

Questionable address

Poor line formatting

Bad grammar and punctuation

Figure 4-14   Phishing e-mail 2

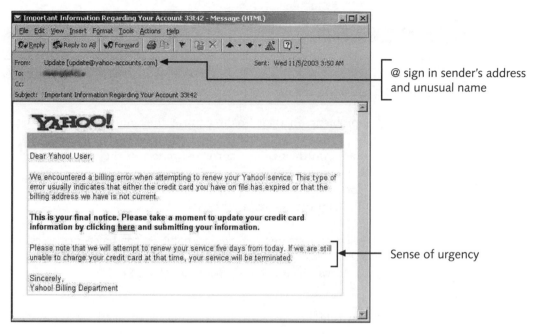

@ sign in sender's address and unusual name

Sense of urgency

Figure 4-15   Phishing e-mail 3

Legislation and Procedures

BLOCK ATTACKS

Because identity theft is such a potentially dangerous threat, state and federal legislatures have passed laws to protect consumers. Although many of these laws do not focus on stopping the attackers, they do provide some protection to mitigate identity theft.

Fair and Accurate Credit Transactions Act (FACTA) of 2003

The **Fair and Accurate Credit Transactions Act (FACTA) of 2003** contains two significant rules regarding consumer privacy. First, FACTA grants consumers the right to request one free credit report from each of the three national credit-reporting firms every twelve months. Access to the free reports were first offered to residents in 13 Western states in December of 2004 and was expanded to include all states by September 2005. Security experts recommend that consumers receive a copy of their credit report at least once per year and check it for accuracy. Table 4-2 lists the three credit-reporting agencies and their contact information.

NOTE

Because a credit report can be ordered only once per year from each of the credit agencies, most security experts recommend that you order one report every four months from one of the three credit agencies. That way you can see your credit report three times a year without being charged for it.

Table 4-2   Credit-reporting agency contact information

Credit Agency	Telephone Number	Web Site
Equifax	800-685-1111	*www.equifax.com*
Experian	888-397-3742	*www.experian.com*
TransUnion	800-916-8800	*www.transunion.com*

If consumers find a problem on their credit reports, they must first send a letter to the credit-reporting agency. Under federal law, the agency has 30 days to investigate and respond to the alleged inaccuracy and then issue a corrected report. If the claim is upheld, all three credit-reporting agencies must be notified of the inaccuracies so they can correct their files. If the investigation does not resolve the problem, a statement from the consumer can be placed in the file and in any future credit reports.

NOTE

While the credit reports are free, the law does not grant consumers free access to their credit score, which is a numerical measurement used by lenders to assess a consumer's creditworthiness. Those reports cost about $10.

The second significant rule, enacted on June 1, 2005 by the Federal Trade Commission, regards the proper destruction of data relating to personal information (such as names, addresses, and Social Security numbers). The **FACTA Disposal Rule** extends to employers, landlords, automobile dealers, private investigators, debt collectors, and anyone who obtains credit reports on prospective contractors. According to the new FACTA rules, if an organization possesses personal data within the workplace, it must make every effort to do the following:

- Burn, pulverize, or shred papers containing credit report information so that the information cannot be read or reconstructed.

- Destroy or erase electronic files or media containing credit report information so that the information cannot be read or reconstructed.

- Conduct due diligence and hire a document destruction contractor to dispose of material specifically identified as credit report information consistent with the rule.

NOTE

Failure to comply with the new regulations can result in civil and state penalties up to $1,000 per violation. Federal penalties can be as high as $2,500 for each incident. Violators also may open themselves up to class-action suits.

Payment Card Industry Data Security Standard (PCI-DSS)

Credit card giants Visa and Mastercard jointly established the **Payment Card Industry Data Security Standard (PCI-DSS)** to safeguard cardholder data and prevent identity theft based on stolen credit card information. PCI-DSS, which went into effect on June 30,

2005, is a voluntary standard that the payment card industry has chosen to impose on its affiliated merchants as a condition for participation in credit card programs. Merchants participating in card programs must state their compliance with this standard validated on an ongoing basis. Participating merchants who fail to comply can be assessed monetary penalties and can lose their ability to participate in card programs.

NOTE The PCI-DSS for the first time aligns the security requirements and standards for all card types into one standard.

The PCI-DSS is composed of 12 discrete requirements that force merchants to develop a secure network and to continually take steps to ensure that the security of the network remains intact. All retailers, online merchants, data processors, and other businesses that handle credit card data must meet these requirements. The PCI-DSS also sets technology mandates, including requirements that merchants use data encryption, control end-user access, and put activity monitoring and logging systems in place. PCI even includes procedural mandates, such as one requiring the implementation of formal security policies and vulnerability management programs.

Failure to comply can result in permanent prohibition of the merchant's or service provider's participation in credit card processing programs and a fine of up to $500,000 per incident. Furthermore, liability for illegitimate charges will shift from the card associations to the merchants, and payouts for fraud from the card associations will be limited if compliance is not met.

NOTE While many banks claim they reimburse customers for any unauthorized withdrawals from their accounts, that may not always be the case. A Miami businessman discovered a mysterious transfer of more than $90,000 from his account to an overseas bank. He immediately notified his bank, which in turn alerted the U.S. Secret Service. An examination of the businessman's computer revealed that it had been infected with a Trojan horse that helped attackers find his password. The bank has refused to reimburse the businessman, arguing that he was at fault for not using antivirus software strong enough to detect the Trojan horse.

Proposed Federal Legislation

Several bills have been proposed in the U.S. Congress to address spyware and identity theft. These include increasing criminal penalties for identity theft involving electronic personal data; requiring firms that maintain personal information to protect that data; and notifying people of any security breach that compromises sensitive data. The bills face opposition from retailers and banks that profit from the flow of personal information.

However, spyware attackers still can be prosecuted by other existing laws. Microsoft has teamed up with the FBI and has brought charges against over 100 suspected phishers, accusing them of wire fraud. In one case an alleged phisher was charged with 75 counts of wire fraud as he tried for 18 months to trick Microsoft MSN users into sending credit card information through his fake Web site. The messages were addressed "Dear MSN Customer" and appeared to be from *billing@msn.com*.

NOTE

This phisher was caught when he sent one such e-mail to the mother-in-law of a Microsoft employee, who passed it on to the company's attorneys.

Chapter Summary

- Spyware is a general term used to describe software that violates a user's personal security. Spyware software usually performs one of the following functions on a user's computer: advertising, collecting personal information, or changing computer configurations. Beyond being a nuisance to computer users, spyware is one of the tools attackers employ to gather personal information about users. Once attackers have obtained this personal information, they can perform identity theft. Identity theft occurs when an individual uses the personal information of someone else to impersonate that individual with the intent to commit fraud or other crimes.

- Adware is a software program that delivers advertising content in a manner or context that is unexpected and unwanted by the user. Adware typically displays advertising banners or pop-up ads. Adware can also pose a security risk. Many adware programs perform a tracking function, which monitors and tracks a user's activities and then sends a log of these activities to third parties without the user's authorization or knowledge.

- Phishing involves sending an e-mail or displaying a Web announcement that falsely claims to be from a legitimate enterprise. The objective is to trick the user into entering private information on a fake Web site established to steal the user's information. There are different variations to phishing, including spear phishing, pharming, and Google phishing.

- Besides adware and phishing, other spyware attack tools are frequently used. A keylogger, or keystroke logger, is either a hardware device or a small program that monitors and collects each keystroke a user types. This information can then be retrieved or silently transmitted to a remote location. Configuration changers are a type of spyware that change the settings on a computer without the user's knowledge or permission. A dialer is a program that changes the settings of a computer that uses a dial-up telephone line to connect to the Internet. A backdoor provides an unauthorized way of gaining access to a program or to an entire computer system.

- One of the best defenses against spyware is to install an antispyware program on your computer. Another defense is to recognize phishing e-mails and know how to avoid the traps it sets.

- There is significant legislation that addresses protection of personal data. The Fair and Accurate Credit Transactions Act (FACTA) of 2003 grants consumers the right to request one free credit report from each of the three national credit-reporting firms every twelve months. The FACTA Disposal Rule of 2005 regulates how credit reports are to be destroyed. The Payment Card Industry Data Security Standard (PCI-DSS), while not legislation, is a set of self-imposed rules set up by the payment card industry, intended to safeguard cardholder data and prevent identity-theft based on stolen credit card information.

4

KEY TERMS

adware — A software program that delivers advertising content in a manner or context that is unexpected and unwanted by the user.

antispyware software — Software that helps prevent computers from becoming infected by different types of spyware.

backdoor — A type of spyware that provides an unauthorized way of gaining access to a program or to an entire computer system.

configuration changers — A type of spyware that changes the settings on a computer without the user's knowledge or permission.

dialer — A type of spyware that changes the settings of a computer that uses a telephone line to connect to the Internet.

Fair and Accurate Credit Transactions Act (FACTA) Disposal Rule of 2005 — A ruling that dictates how personal data should be destroyed.

Fair and Accurate Credit Transactions Act (FACTA) of 2003 — A federal law that grants consumers the right to request credit reports.

Google phishing — An attack in which phishers set up their own search engines to direct traffic to illegitimate sites.

identity theft — A malicious theft that occurs when an individual uses the personal information of someone else to impersonate that individual with the intent to commit fraud or other crimes.

keylogger (or **keystroke logger)** — A hardware device or a small program that records each keystroke a user types.

Payment Card Industry Data Security Standard (PCI-DSS) — A standard for the payment card industry designed to safeguard cardholder data and prevent identity theft based on stolen credit card information.

pharming — An attack that automatically redirects the user to a fake Web site.

phishing — Sending an e-mail or displaying a Web announcement that falsely claims to be from a legitimate enterprise in an attempt to trick the user into surrendering private information.

spear phishing — A phishing attack that targets specific users.

spyware — A general term used for describing software that violates a user's personal security.

Windows Task Manager — A program that allows a user to observe the programs that are currently running.

REVIEW QUESTIONS

1. _____ is a general term used for describing software that violates a user's personal security.

    a. Intrusionware

    b. Netware

    c. Adware

    d. Spyware

2. Each of the following is a function of spyware except _____ .

    a. advertising

    b. collecting personal information

    c. erasing hard drive data

    d. changing computer configurations

3. _____ occurs when an individual uses the personal information of someone else, such as a Social Security number, credit card number, or other identifying information, to impersonate that individual with the intent to commit fraud or other crimes.

    a. Identity theft

    b. Adware

    c. Web theft (WT)

    d. Social fraud

4. Each of the following characteristics indicate that a computer might be infected with spyware except _____ .

    a. appearance of pop-up advertisements

    b. a new Web toolbar unexpectedly appears and cannot be removed

    c. more e-mail is received in the Inbox

    d. the computer takes longer to complete common tasks

5. Each of the following is a spyware software attack tool except

    _____ .

    a. keyloggers

    b. dialers

    c. dumpster diving

    d. backdoors

6. Frontdoors can be a security risk because they perform a tracking function which monitors a user's activities and then sends a log of the activities to third parties without the user's authorization or knowledge. True or False?

7. Phishing involves sending a specific e-mail to a single user that falsely claims to be from a legitimate enterprise in an attempt to trick the user into surrendering private information. True or False?

8. Google phishing involves phishers setting up their own search engines to direct traffic to illegitimate sites. True or False?

9. A backdoor is either a hardware device or a small program that monitors each keystroke a user types. True or False?

10. Configuration changers are a type of spyware that change the settings on a computer without the user's knowledge or permission. True or False?

11. A(n) _____ is a program that makes changes to the settings of a computer that uses a dial-up telephone line to make a connection to the Internet.

12. A(n) _____ provides an unauthorized way of gaining access to a program or to an entire computer system.

13. _____ helps prevent computers from becoming infected by different types of spyware.

14. A(n) _____ symbol in the sender's address is a technique used to hide the real address.

15. The _____'_____ grants consumers the right to request one free credit report from each of the three national credit-reporting firms every twelve months.

16. Explain why harmful spyware is not always easy to distinguish from legitimate programs that use spyware technology.

17. What is the Payment Card Industry Data Security Standard (PCI-DSS)?

18. How can adware be a security risk?

19. What is phishing?

20. What is the difference between phishing and spear phishing?

HANDS-ON PROJECTS

HANDS-ON PROJECTS

Project 4-1: Using a Keylogger

A keylogger program captures everything that a user enters on a computer keyboard. The program runs invisibly in the background and cannot be detected even from the Windows Task Manager. In this project, you download and use a keyboard logger.

1. Use a Web browser to go to the following Web site:

   www.softdd.com/keystrokerecorder/index.html

2. Click **Download and Run – Primary Download Site**.

3. Save the file to the desired location.

4. After the file has been downloaded, click **Open Folder** in Microsoft Windows XP or navigate to the folder where you stored the file and double-click the filename. If you receive a security warning, click **Run** to continue.

5. When asked if you want to install the Keyboard Collector trial version, click **Yes**.

6. Accept the default values of the installation wizard.

7. The readme.txt file automatically opens when the installation is complete. Read through this file and then close it. Click **Finish** to exit the wizard.

Now that you have downloaded and installed Keyboard Collector Trial, you are ready to set options and log your computer activity.

1. Double-click the **Keyboard Collector Trial** icon on the desktop.

2. Click **Run Keyboard Collector**, and then click **OK**. The keyboard collector options are shown in Figure 4-16.

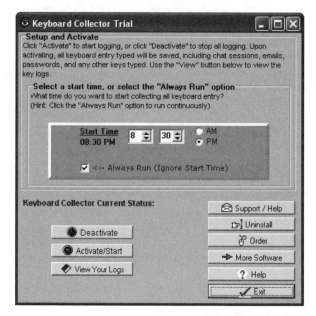

Figure 4-16   Keyboard Collector Trial options

3. Select the **Always Run (Ignore Start Time)** check box, if necessary.

4. Click **Activate/Start**, and then click **Yes** to confirm.

5. Spend several minutes performing normal activity, such as creating a document or sending an e-mail message.

6. Double-click the **Keyboard Collector Trial** icon on the desktop.

7. Click **Run Keyboard Collector**, and then click **OK**.

8. Click **View Your Logs**, and then click **OK**.

9. Scan the log file. Does it contain information that could be used for gathering personal information?

10. Click **Return**, and then click **Exit** to close the Keyboard Collector window.

11. Try to determine if Keyboard Collector Trial is running. Press the Ctrl+Alt+Delete keys simultaneously to open the Windows Task Manager.

12. Click the **Applications** tab to see all of the programs that are currently running. Does Keyboard Collector trial appear in this list? Why not?

13. Close the Windows Task Manager.

Now you can use Keyboard Collector Trial to try to capture a password.

1. Log on to a site that requires you to enter a username and password.

2. Examine the log file of Keyboard Collector. Did it capture your password?

3. Double-click the **Keyboard Collector Trial** icon on the desktop.

4. Click **Run Keyboard Collector**, and then click **OK**.

5. Click **View Your Logs**, and then click **OK**.

6. Click **Delete Key Logs** to remove your log files.

7. Click **Yes**.

8. Click **Return**.

9. Click **Deactivate**, and then click **OK**.

10. Close all open windows.

Project 4-2: Installing Antispyware Software

Antispyware software is an important tool for keeping a computer clean from spyware. In this project, you will download and use Microsoft Antispyware.

1. Use your Web browser to go to the following Web page:

   www.microsoft.com/athome/security/spyware/software/default.mspx.

2. Click **Try it now**.

3. The Validation Required window appears and checks to be sure you are running a genuine copy of Microsoft Windows. Click **Continue**.

4. If you are asked if you want to install the Windows Genuine Advantage Validation Tool, click **Install**. If you are not asked to install the validation tool, click **Continue**.

5. After your copy of Windows has been validated, click **Download**.

6. Click **Run** to begin the download and then install the software onto your computer. Follow the default settings for the installation.

7. Start the Microsoft Antispyware program.

8. Click **File** on the menu bar, and then click **Check for updates**. The program will update the latest spyware definition files.

9. Click **Run Quick Scan Now** to scan the computer for any spyware. If it finds any, the spyware will be listed along with any recommendations regarding what to do. Close the Scan Results window and then click **Continue** to follow the recommended actions.

10. Configure Microsoft Antispyware for automatically downloading updates. Click **Options** on the menu bar, and then click **Settings** to display the Settings window, shown in Figure 4-17. Click the **AutoUpdater** icon in the left pane. Make sure that all three boxes are checked. Under **Check for updates** select a time each day or select **System start up**. Click **Save** and then click **OK**.

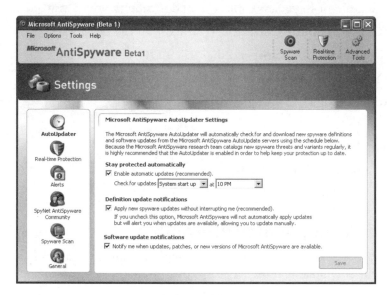

Figure 4-17   Antispyware Settings window

11. Click the **Advanced Tools** icon to display the Advanced Tools window.

12. Click **Browser restore**. The Browser Restore tool allows you to restore specific Web browser settings. If spyware infects the Web browser, it can be reset to these user-defined settings instead of the browser's default settings. Click **Back to Advanced Tools**.

13. The Tracks Eraser will remove information that the system has saved regarding your most recent actions on the computer. Click the Windows **Start** button, and then view the left pane of the Start menu to see all of the programs that you have recently

started. Start your Web browser and click the list arrow in the Address bar to see the Web sites you have recently visited. Close the Web browser.

14. Return to Microsoft Antispyware and click **Tracks Eraser**. Click **Check all** to erase all the tracks. Click **Erase tracks** and then click **Yes**.

15. Now click the Windows **Start** button. Is the list of recently opened files empty? Start your Web browser and check again to see the Web sites you recently visited. What happened?

16. Close the Microsoft Antispyware windows (the program will keep running in the background).

HANDS-ON PROJECTS

Project 4-3: Installing, Using, and Managing a Web Site Detector

Phishers create fake Web sites to look like well-known branded sites such as ebay.com or citibank.com with a slightly different or confusing URL. Software is available that helps to detect these fake Web sites. The software SpoofStick makes it easier to spot a fake site by prominently displaying the relevant information regarding the site to which the browser is pointing. In this project, you will download and install SpoofStick.

1. Use your Web browser to go to the SpoofStick site at the following address:

   www.corestreet.com/spoofstick

2. Click **SpoofStick for Internet Explorer**. Scroll down and click the **Download Now** button.

3. Click **Run** to install the software. Accept all of the default settings.

NOTE

Antispyware software may provide warning messages that SpoofStick is running. If that occurs, click the appropriate button in the warning message to allow SpoofStick to continue.

4. Close your Web browser and then reopen it. Use your Web browser to go to **www-ebay.com**. Notice that below the Address bar, SpoofStick prominently displays the actual Web address the browser is accessing.

5. SpoofStick is a browser add-on that provides additional functionality to a Web browser. On occasion, spyware installs a browser add-on that you want to remove. To manage SpoofStick and other browser add-ons, click **Tools** on the Internet Explorer menu bar, and then click **Manage Add-ons** to display the Manage Add-ons window, shown in Figure 4-18.

6. Scroll down and click **SpoofStick**. Notice that you have the option of disabling the add-on.

7. Close your Web browser.

4

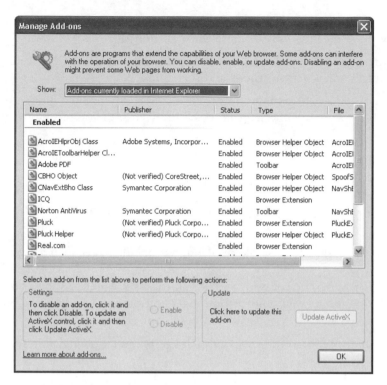

Figure 4-18   Manage Add-ons window

Project 4-4: Blocking Messenger Service

Many pop-up advertisements use a Windows function known as the Messenger Service to display their advertisements. In this project, you will disable that service. Note that if you are using a computer in a networked lab environment, it may not be desireable to block this service. Check with your instructor or support staff to make sure you can perform this project in a lab.

1. Click **Start** and then click **Control Panel**.

2. If Control Panel opens in Category view, click **Performance and Maintenance**, and then click **Administrative Tools**. If Control Panel opens in Classic view, double-click **Administrative Tools**. The Administrative Tools window opens.

3. Double-click **Services**.

4. Double-click **Messenger**.

5. Change the Startup type to **Disabled**. Click **OK**.

6. Close all windows.

Project 4-5: Viewing Credit History Reports

Security experts recommend that consumers receive a copy of their credit report at least once per year and check its accuracy. In this project, you order a free credit report online.

1. Use your Web browser to go to *www.annualcreditreport.com*. Although you could send a request individually to one of the three credit agencies, this Web site acts as a central source for ordering free credit reports. Figure 4-19 shows the Web site.

Figure 4-19   AnnualCreditReport.Com Web site

2. In the Start Here section, select the state in which you live, and then click **Go**.

3. Enter the requested information and click **Next**.

4. Select one of the credit agencies from which to receive your credit report and click **Next**.

5. Click **Next** to be transferred to that credit agency's Web site.

6. Enter the requested information for that site. You may then be asked personal information about your transaction history in order to verify your identity. Answer the requested questions.

7. Follow the instructions to print your report. Review it carefully, particularly the sections "Potentially negative items" and "Requests for your credit history." If you see anything that might be incorrect, follow the instructions on that Web site to enter a dispute.

8. Follow the instructions to exit from the Web sites.

Case Projects

Case Project 4-1: Spyware Quiz

Use your Web browser to go to the following Web site:

www.microsoft.com/athome/security/quiz/spywarebasics1.mspx

Take the Quiz Spyware Basics 1. Now write your own 10-question quiz regarding spyware and what you think users should know about it. Exchange quizzes with other students and see who can earn the highest score.

Case Project 4-2: Phishing Test I

Use your Web browser to go to the following Web site:

http://survey.mailfrontier.com/survey/quiztest.cgi

Click "The MailFrontier Phishing IQ Test" to see ten Web sites or e-mail messages that may or may not be phishing. Identify whether they are "Legitimate" or "Fraud." If you think a Web site or e-mail message is a fraud, write down your reasons why. Now review your score. Did you score as highly as you expected? What were the reasons that you may have missed some of the phishing sites? How could this help people be more selective regarding e-mail messages that they receive?

Case Project 4-3: Phishing Test II

Use your Web browser to go to the following Web site:

www.antiphishing.org/phishing_archive.html

View an archive of actual phishing e-mail messages. Click at random five messages. Although each message contains information about why it is fraudulent, see if you can identify several indications before reading the explanation. If you were to give yourself a score regarding your ability to tell why an e-mail message is a fake, what score would you receive? Why?

Case Project 4-4: Locating Spyware Help Sites

The Internet contains several spyware help sites that provide useful information regarding spyware and recent attacks. Use a search engine to locate the top five spyware sites. Choose one site, record the Web address, and write a one- or two-sentence description of this site and why it is in your list of top five. Share your list with other students. You may want to compile a master list for the class as a resource.

4

Case Project 4-5: Baypoint Computer Consulting

As a community service, Baypoint Computer Consulting (BCC) has decided to design a flyer regarding the risks of spyware and how to prevent it. This flyer will be distributed free of charge at a local festival later in the month. BCC has hired you to assist them with this project.

Create a flyer using Microsoft Word, Publisher, or a similar program. In the flyer, define spyware, explain why it is dangerous, and describe how people can defend against it. Because you are creating the flyer for a general audience, your flyer should not contain a large amount of technical terms and concepts.

As a follow-up, the president has asked you to prepare a presentation that includes some of the information from your flyer. Create a PowerPoint presentation with 6-9 slides that would be appropriate for users of different technology backgrounds.

5
NETWORK SECURITY

After completing this chapter you should be able to do the following:

➤ Explain how a network functions

➤ Discuss how to defend against network attacks

➤ Describe the types of attacks that are launched against networks and network computers

Security in Your World

Greg set his backpack on the empty shelf. He had just started working as a Computer Information Systems (CIS) intern at Walker Enterprises. He chose Walker because he had heard good things about their IT department. Greg was excited to be working with Brian, the security administrator at Walker Enterprises. Brian's job required him to have technical knowledge and supervisory skills because he managed the daily operations of Walker's security technology.

"Hi, Greg," said Brian. "How were your classes this morning?" "Good," said Greg. "Should I finish that documentation I started yesterday?" Brian moved his chair away from the monitor. "Come look at this first. I've been monitoring our new intrusion detection system and we've been getting a lot of bites on our network." Greg sat down next to Brian. "What do you mean by 'bites'?"

"Bites are what we call attacks on our system from hackers," said Brian. "We log both bites and scans, which are probes hackers send out to see if they can find a way in." "How many bites do you have?" asked Greg. Brian glanced at the computer screen. "By the end of the day, we'll have over 500 scans and about that many bites."

"What?" said Greg. "We've had that many attacks on our network in just one day? What should we do?" Brian shook his head. "Well, so far none of the attacks has penetrated our network security. I just read an article yesterday about a college in Israel that received about 100,000 scans and 80,000 bites in a two-week period." "That's incredible," said Greg. "Where's it all coming from?" "If I remember correctly," said Brian, "they traced the attackers to 99 different countries."

"I had no idea there were that many attacks," said Greg. Brian walked over to his desk. "Yes, and we're seeing it growing all the time. They're not just after businesses anymore, but people with computers and networks at home are really getting hit hard, too," he said. "And most home users don't know what to do to keep their networks safe." Greg thought, "I'd better double-check my network security when I get back to my apartment tonight."

Computer networks, once used only in businesses, are now a standard commodity in homes, apartments, and dorm rooms. As users install computers in home offices, bedrooms, kitchens, and children's rooms, a network is essential to tie all of the devices together so that they can share a single Internet connection, a laser printer, and software. Because operating systems such as Microsoft Windows come with networking capabilities, creating a home or small office network is as easy as turning on a wireless access point or plugging in a network cable.

However, some security experts fear that home networking has become *too* simple. Because setting up a home network requires no knowledge of networking standards or techniques, many users are unaware of how to make their networks secure. Computer networks are one of the prime targets of attackers, because once the network is breached, every device on the network might be vulnerable. Networks, no matter how large or small, can and should be defended against all types of attackers.

This chapter examines network attacks and security. It starts by defining a computer network and explaining how it functions. It continues by exploring some types of attacks launched against computer networks. Finally, it discusses how to defend networks and their computers.

How Networks Work

A personal computer can be used to perform a broad range of tasks, such as create a document, calculate a complex formula, or draw an image. Because these computers are *personal*, they are also *isolated* from other computers. The functionality of one personal computer is limited to the software installed on that computer and the hardware directly connected to it. Figure 5-1 shows that a personal computer has its own programs (such as a payroll program), data (such as the employee names and telephone numbers), and devices (such as a printer). This configuration results in higher costs (a copy of the payroll program and a printer must be purchased for each user), and it increases the risk of errors (for example, a change to an employee's telephone number on one comptuer may not be changed on all other computers).

The productivity of someone using a personal computer is greatly improved if the user can access the software and hardware on other computers. This enhanced access can be accomplished by connecting computers and devices to form a **computer network**. The purpose of a computer network can be summarized in a single word: *share*. As shown in Figure 5-2, instead of installing a copy of the employee data program on each employee's computer, a single copy is stored on one central computer (known as the **server**), which all employees can access from their computers (assuming they have the proper authorization). Likewise, because the data is centralized in one place, there is only one copy of it, so errors are less likely. In addition, devices such as printers can also be shared across the network.

Types of Networks

Computer networks are assigned to different classifications. One way in which they are classified is by how close the computers are to one another. A computer network that has all of the computers located relatively close to each other is called a **local area network (LAN)**. The proximity of computers in a LAN is generally limited to the buildings and land that is owned by the organization. For example, networked computers that are located on one floor of an office building or in a classroom of a college is considered a LAN.

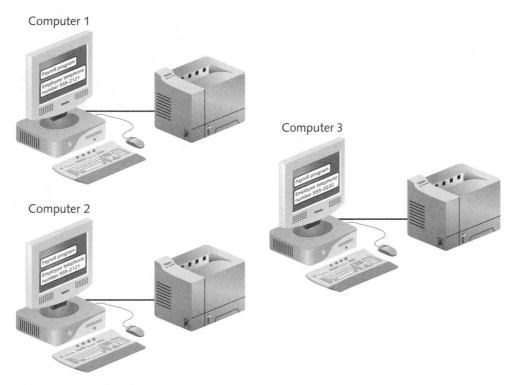

Figure 5-1   Isolated computers

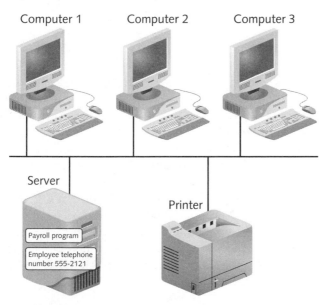

Figure 5-2   Computer network

NOTE

The number of computers in a LAN can range from two to several hundred.

In contrast to a LAN, a **wide area network (WAN)** connects computers over a larger geographical area than a LAN. The technical definition of a WAN is a network that connects computers and LANs that must cross over a public thoroughfare, such as a road, highway, or railroad. LANs and WANs are illustrated in Figure 5-3.

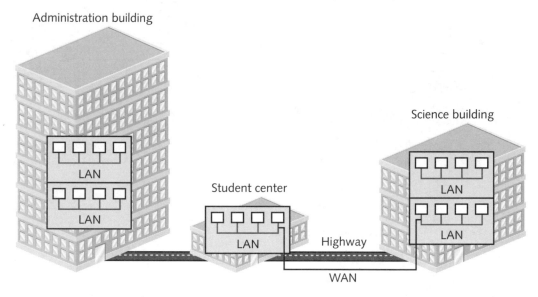

Figure 5-3 LANs and WANs

One special type of LAN that has experienced phenomenal growth in recent years is a **wireless local area network (WLAN)**, also known as **Wi-Fi (Wireless Fidelity)**. WLANs are based on a standard that transmits data at fast speeds over a distance of up to 115 meters (375 feet). A home WLAN can connect a laptop computer, desktop computer, and laser printer into a computer network without running cables between the devices. A WLAN can also connect the devices to the Internet, so users can check e-mail and surf the Web from any room in the house, without a cable connection. A home WLAN is illustrated in Figure 5-4. WLANs can also wirelessly connect televisions and stereo systems to the computer network. This allows people to use their televisions and stereos to access pictures, MP3 songs, and movies that are stored on their computers. They therefore get the benefit of a TV screen that is larger than most computer monitors and a stereo system that offers higher-quality sound than most computer speakers.

5

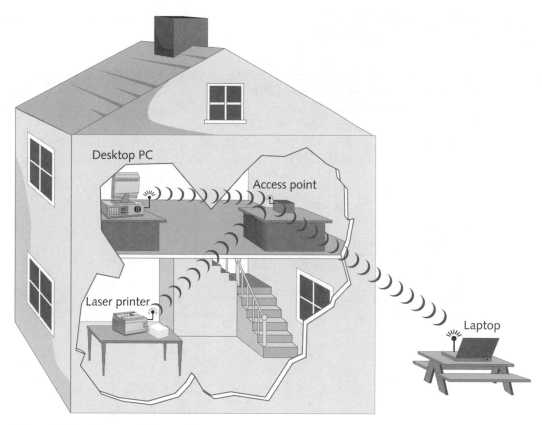

Figure 5-4   Home wireless LAN

Although WANs can also operate in a mode that does not connect the wireless local area network to the Internet and other networks, this is rare.

NOTE

Transmitting Network Data

For data to be transmitted through a network, both the sending and receiving devices must follow the same set of rules. These rules are known as **protocols**. The most common set of protocols used on networks is called the **Transmission Control Protocol/Internet Protocol (TCP/IP)**.

A key to TCP/IP computer networks is that each computer or device on the network must be assigned a unique number. This number, called the **IP address**, uniquely identifies this computer from all other computers on the network (just as a street address uniquely identifies a house from all other houses in the neighborhood). When data is transmitted from one computer to another, the unique IP address of the sending and receiving computer is attached to the data (just as an envelope has the unique street address of the sender and receiver). An IP number is four sets of digits, with the sets separated by periods, such as 198.146.118.20.

The transmission of data through a computer network is accomplished by dividing the data to be sent into smaller units called **packets**. As shown in Figure 5-5, the sending computer divides the data into individual packets, and it labels each packet with information such as the number of the packet, the sender's IP address, and the IP address of the destination computer. These packets are then individually sent through the network. When the receiving computer gets the packets, it reassembles them in the correct sequence.

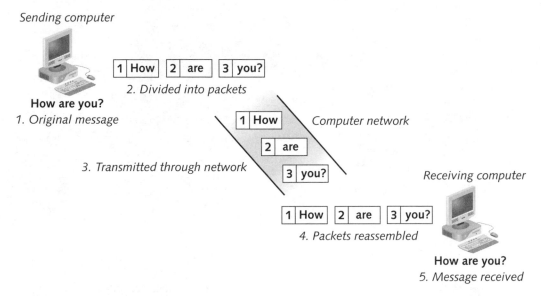

Figure 5-5   Sending data by packets

Network Devices

There are different types of computer hardware devices on a network that perform various functions. The hardware that connects a computer to a wired network is called a **network interface card (NIC)**, sometimes called a **client network adapter**. A NIC connects the computer to the network so that it can send and receive data. For desktop computers connecting to a wired network, an internal NIC is used. One end of the NIC is connected inside the computer, while the other end has an external jack for a cable connection, as shown in Figure 5-6. The cable connects the NIC to the network, thus establishing the link between the computer and the network. Laptop computers may use either an internal NIC or an external NIC, which plugs into the laptop.

Figure 5-6   Internal network interface card

A network interface card for a wireless network performs the same functions as a NIC for a wired network with one major exception: it does not use a jack for a wired connection to the network. In its place is an antenna that sends and receives signals. Figure 5-7 illustrates different types of external wireless NICs.

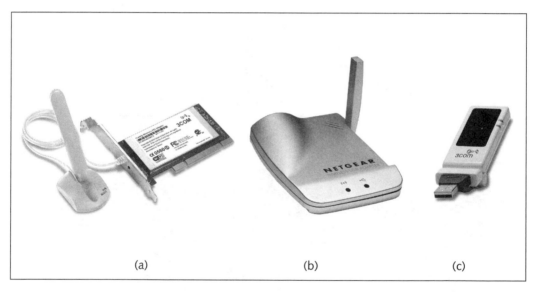

(a)   (b)   (c)

Figure 5-7   External wireless NICs

Wireless networks also require an **access point (AP)**, shown in Figure 5-8. An AP consists of two major components. First, it contains an antenna and a radio transmitter/receiver to send and receive signals. Second, it has a jack that allows it to connect by cable to a standard wired network. An AP acts as the base station for the wireless network. All of the devices that have a wireless NIC can transmit to the AP, which in turn redirects the signal to the other wireless devices. The second function of an AP is to act as a bridge between wireless and wired networks. Because the AP can use a cable to connect to other networks and the Internet, all of the wireless devices can in turn access these networks through the AP, as shown in Figure 5-9.

Figure 5-8   Access point

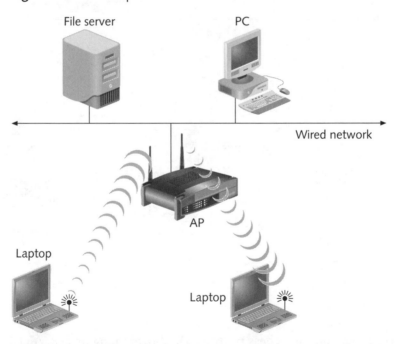

Figure 5-9   Access point as a bridge

Other network devices are responsible for sending packets through the network. One of the network devices that help move packets is a **router**. A router directs packets towards their destination. Because of the number of computers on a network and how the network is configured, a router may not necessarily send the packet directly to the receiving computer.

It may instead send the packet to another router or device that is connected to the destination computer.

Figure 5-10 illustrates a very basic computer network. In order to keep the network and computers connected to it secure, a defensive perimeter is established around the network. This perimeter consists of products (network hardware devices and software), procedures (plans and policies), and people (individuals who follow the procedures and use the products) that form a secure line of defense against attackers.

5

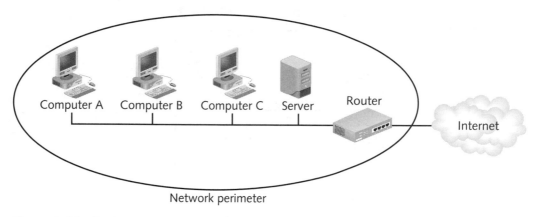

Figure 5-10   Basic computer network

ATTACKS ON NETWORKS

Several types of attacks are directed towards networks and the computers that are attached to them. These include denial of service, zombies and botnets, man-in-the-middle attacks, spoofing, and sniffing.

Denial of Service (DoS) Attacks

Under normal network conditions, a computer contacts a network server with a request, such as to display a Web page or open a file. The server responds to the computer with an acknowledgement that it received the initial request and then waits for a reply. To allow for a slow connection, the server might wait several minutes for the reply. Once the computer replies, the data transfer can begin.

In contrast to a normal network situation, a **denial of service (DoS)** attack attempts to make a server or other network device unavailable by flooding it with requests. In a DoS attack, several computers make requests to the server; the server responds with appropriate acknowledgements, and then waits for a reply. However, the computers that launched the attack do not reply to the server's response. The server continues to hold the line open and waits for responses (which are not coming), while receiving more false requests and keeping more lines open for responses. After a short period, the server runs out of resources and can no longer function. Figure 5-11 shows a server waiting for a response during a DoS attack.

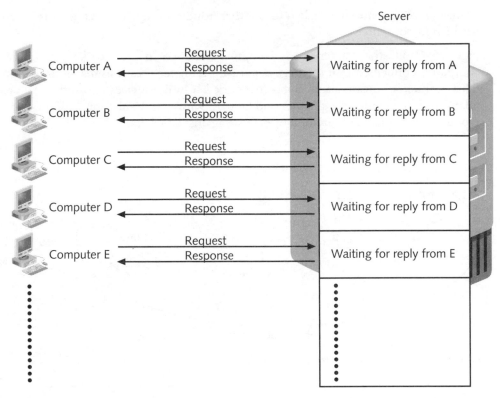

Figure 5-11   Server waiting for response

A variant of the DoS attack tricks computers into responding to a false request. On a computer network, a user might want to know if another computer is turned on and functioning properly. The user can send an "Are you there?" message (called a **ping**), to which the receiving computer immediately replies if possible. An attacker can send a request to all computers on the network that makes it appear that the server is asking for a response. Each of the computers then responds to the server, overwhelming it and causing the server to crash or be unavailable to legitimate users. This is called a **smurf** attack.

Another variant of the DoS is the **distributed denial of service (DDoS)** attack. Instead of using one computer, a DDoS may use hundreds or thousands of computers to flood a server with requests. This makes it impossible to identify and block the single source of the attack. Figure 5–12 illustrates a DDoS attack.

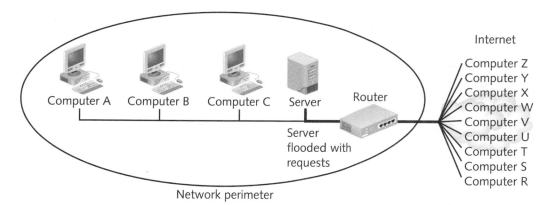

Figure 5-12   DDoS attack

Zombie and Botnets

The computers that perform a DDoS and other network attacks are often normal computers that have been hijacked by attackers to carry out malicious network attacks. A typical
DDoS works in the following stages:

1. An attacker breaks into a large computer with plenty of disk space and a fast
   Internet connection. This computer is called the **handler**.

2. Special software is loaded onto the handler computer to scan thousands of
   computers, looking for those that have a software vulnerability in the operating
   system.

3. Once a vulnerable computer is located, the handler installs software on this
   computer, turning it into a **zombie**, and then the handler looks for another
   computer to infect. The user of the zombie has no indication that his or her
   computer has malicious software installed.

4. At some point, the handler links all of the zombie computers together to form a
   botnet and instructs it to flood a specific server with requests. A botnet can
   consist of up to 50,000 computers under single control.

NOTE

According to the security organization Ciphertrust, 143,074 computers were
turned into zombies each day during a two-month period in early 2005, adding
to the total of one million Internet zombies.

In addition to using zombies for DDoS attacks, zombies can also be put to work to send
spam and messages used in phishing scams, as well as act as hosts for fake Web sites. Users
who have their computers performing as zombies are unaware that they are acting in a
malicious manner.

Zombies and botnets have become such a serious problem that the Federal Trade Commission (FTC) has intervened. Beginning in late 2005, Internet service providers (ISPs), such as AOL, Comcast, and BellSouth, will begin receiving reports on the zombies that lurk on their customer networks. Several ISPs have also taken measures to prevent zombies connected to their network from sending spam. One technique allows an ISP to make sure that members' computers only send e-mail that originates from its server and not from a spammer's server. In addition, most ISPs use techniques such as rate limiting, which control the number of e-mail messages that a member can send.

One prominent ISP has almost 12 percent of its customer's computers acting as zombies.

NOTE

However, some security experts say that these measures are not enough, claiming that service providers should improve customer education and also force users to scan their computer for known vulnerabilities before going online. Some experts even recommend that ISPs should monitor their networks closer for traffic generated by zombies and cut off Internet connections for customers who don't carry out preventive measures.

Man-in-the-Middle Attacks

Suppose that Alice, a high school student, is in danger of receiving a poor grade in math. Her teacher mails a letter to Alice's parents requesting a conference. However, Alice waits for the mail, takes the original letter from the mailbox, and replaces it with a counterfeit letter that praises her for her math work. She also forges her parents' signature on the original letter to decline a conference, and mails it back to the teacher. The parents read the fake letter and compliment Alice on her hard work, while Alice's teacher wonders why Alice's parents do not want a conference. Alice has conducted a **man-in-the-middle** attack by intercepting communication from her teacher to her parents and forging a response to the teacher.

Man-in-the-middle attacks on computer information are common network attacker tools. This type of attack makes it seem that two computers are communicating with each other, when actually they are sending and receiving data with a computer between them, or with the "man in the middle." In Figure 5-13, Computer A and Computer B are communicating without recognizing that an attacker, "a man in the middle," is intercepting their transmissions.

Hijacking and Spoofing

With a man-in-the-middle attack, the attacker intercepts messages that are intended for a valid device. What if the attacker sets up a fake device and tricks other users into sending their messages to it? That is essentially what **hijacking** involves.

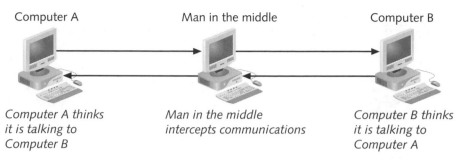

Figure 5-13   Man-in-the-middle attack

With wired networks, hijacking uses a technique known as **spoofing**, which is the act of pretending to be the legitimate owner when in reality you are not. One particular type of spoofing tricks the computer into sending information to the wrong address. Remember that each computer using TCP/IP must have a unique IP address. In addition, certain types of LANs must also have another address, called the **media access control (MAC)** address, to move information around the network. The MAC address is permanently recorded on the network interface card when it is manufactured. Computers on a network keep a table that links an IP address with the corresponding MAC address, as shown in Figure 5-14.

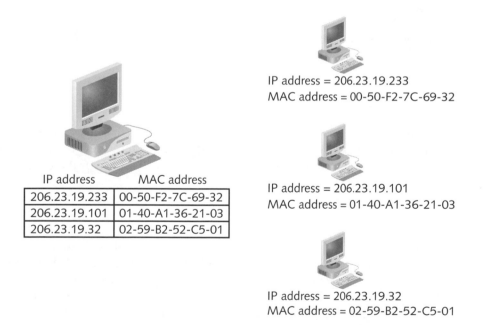

Figure 5-14   Address table

In a spoofing attack, an attacker changes the table so that packets are redirected to his or her computer, as shown in Figure 5-15. The result is that the computer now sends information from the user's computer to the attacker's computer instead of to a valid computer.

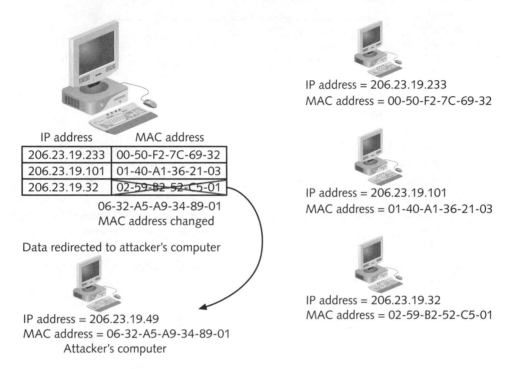

IP address	MAC address
206.23.19.233	00-50-F2-7C-69-32
206.23.19.101	01-40-A1-36-21-03
206.23.19.32	02-59-B2-52-C5-01

06-32-A5-A9-34-89-01
MAC address changed

Data redirected to attacker's computer

IP address = 206.23.19.49
MAC address = 06-32-A5-A9-34-89-01
Attacker's computer

IP address = 206.23.19.233
MAC address = 00-50-F2-7C-69-32

IP address = 206.23.19.101
MAC address = 01-40-A1-36-21-03

IP address = 206.23.19.32
MAC address = 02-59-B2-52-C5-01

Figure 5-15 Spoofing

On wireless networks, hijacking can add a new twist. Because all wireless devices communicate with an access point, an attacker can set up an imposter access point and trick all wireless devices to communicate with that access point instead of with the legitimate one. Figure 5-16 shows hijacking on a wireless network.

Sniffing

Because network traffic is divided into smaller segments called packets, an attacker can capture packets as they travel through the network using a technique called **sniffing**. The hardware or software that performs such functions is called a **sniffer**. Figure 5-17 shows the output from a sniffer. The Source column displays the sender of the packet, while the Destination column shows the receiver. The Info column and data in the bottom pane display the contents of the packet. Attackers with sniffers can capture usernames, passwords, and other secure information without being detected.

Attackers typically position sniffers near targets that contain the most sensitive information, such as a server that provides financial data to a bank.

NOTE

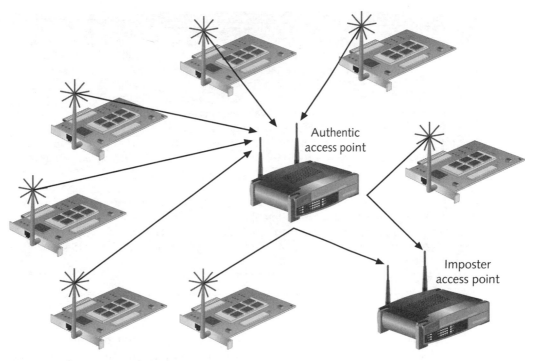

Figure 5-16   Wireless network hijacking

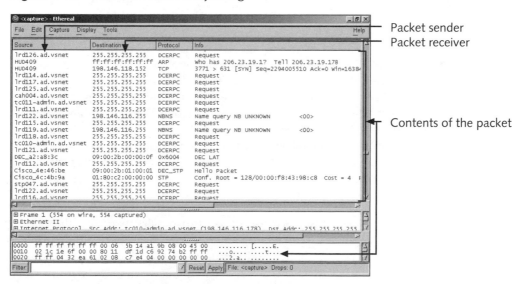

Figure 5-17   Packet sniffer output

SECURITY IN YOUR WORLD

"Is that the firewall?" asked Greg, pointing to a device in the rack. "Yes, it is," said Brian. "I've been thinking about what you said earlier today about the attacks on our network," said Greg. "Don't we have firewalls that stop attacks?"

Brian pushed away from his desk. "Well, yes and no," he said. "Yes, we are using some of the best firewalls available to protect our network. But no, a firewall does not stop every attack. They are not intended to do so. Take viruses, for example. A firewall won't stop a virus. I try to tell our users that it's like getting a flu shot. That shot may stop some strains of the flu, but not all of them."

"Then what do we do for protection?" asked Greg. "There are several things," said Brian. "You may have to install different security devices to stop different classes of attacks. And you've got to keep on top of things. Security is something where you can never really say, 'We're all done.' You're always checking, testing, and keeping alert to the latest attacks."

NETWORK DEFENSES

The importance of protecting a network and its data cannot be underestimated. Attacks directed at networks and computers can destroy a business. It is estimated that an average of $78,000 per hour is lost when a large computer network is not functioning, and 93 percent of organizations that experienced a significant data loss are out of business within five years, according to the Gartner Group.

NOTE

Organizations that cannot tolerate any company network downtime, such as an airline reservation system, often state the need for network availability by the "nines," or the percent of time that the network must be running. A network that must be available "four nines" or 99.99 percent of the time means that the network could not be down for more than 52 minutes each year (based on a year containing 31.5 million seconds). A network that must be available "five nines" or 99.999 percent of the time means that it could be down a maximum of 315 seconds annually. "Six nines" (99.9999 percent) translates to only 32 seconds of annual downtime.

The primary defenses against network attacks can be classified into three groups. These include devices that can thwart attackers, designing the layout or configuration of a network that will reduce the risk of attacks, and testing the network security. Because it is fundamentally different from a wired network, defending a wireless LAN from attacks requires additional steps for protection. First, we will examine the three defenses for wired networks.

Network Devices

Several network devices can be used to thwart attackers. These include firewalls, network address translation (NAT) systems, intrustion detection systems (IDS), and proxy servers.

Firewalls

A firewall, sometimes called a **packet filter**, is designed to prevent malicious packets from entering the network or computers. A firewall can be software-based or hardware-based. A software firewall runs as a program on a local computer (called a **personal firewall**) to protect it against attacks, while hardware firewalls are separate devices that typically protect an entire network. Hardware firewalls usually are located outside the network security perimeter as the first line of defense, as shown in Figure 5-18.

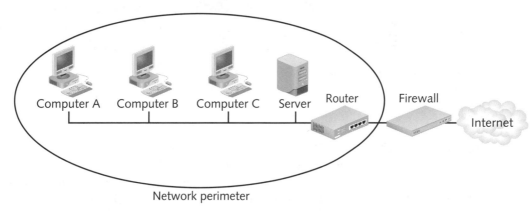

Figure 5-18 Hardware firewall position in network

Security experts recommend that home users should have both a hardware firewall for the entire network as well as a personal firewall running on each computer. This "double layer" of protection helps prevent different types of attacks from breaking through.

The foundation of a firewall is a **rule base**. The rule base establishes what action the firewall should take when it receives a packet. The three typical options are:

- *Allow*—Let the packet pass through and continue on its journey
- *Block*—Prevent the packet from passing to the network and instead destroy it
- *Prompt*—Ask the user what action to take

Packets can be filtered by a firewall in one of two ways. **Stateless packet filtering** looks at each incoming packet and permits or denies it based strictly on the rule base. For example, a user from inside the protected network may send a request to a Web server located on the Internet for a Web page. A rule in the firewall similar to those in Table 5-1 would allow the Web page to be transmitted back to the requesting computer.

Table 5-1 Stateless packet filtering rule

Rule or State Description	Explanation	Filtering
Source address = any	The source IP address is that of the Web server on the Internet.	Because you cannot know in advance what the IP address of a Web server is, this rule allows a packet coming from anywhere to enter the network.
Destination address = internal IP address	The destination address is the IP address of the computer on the internal network where the packet is being sent.	This rule allows packets directed to this internal computer to pass through, but it blocks packets that do not have the correct destination address.
Port = 80	The port indicates what this packet contains, namely an HTML document.	No other types of content besides HTML documents are allowed.

Ports and HTML are covered in Chapter 3.

Although a stateless packet filter does provide some degree of protection, attackers can easily bypass the protection. In the previous example, attackers only have to discover a valid internal IP address of the computer network. Then they can send an attack using that IP address and falsely change the packet to indicate it is an HTML document (port 80).

Firewalls can filter outgoing traffic as well. For example, an organization can use a firewall to prevent users from viewing an offensive Web page or downloading software.

The second type of firewall provides a greater degree of protection. **Stateful packet filtering** keeps a record of the state of a connection between an internal computer and an external server and then makes decisions based on the connection as well as the rule base. For example, a stateless packet filter firewall might allow a packet to pass through because it is intended for a specific computer on the network. However, a stateful packet filter would not let the packet pass if that internal network computer did not first request the information from the external server. Table 5-2 illustrates stateful packet filtering rules.

Table 5-2   Stateful packet filtering rule

Rule or State Description	Explanation	Filtering
Source address = any	The source IP address is that of the Web server on the Internet.	Because you cannot know in advance what the IP address of a Web server is, this rule allows a packet coming from anywhere to enter the network.
Destination address = internal IP address	The destination address is the IP address of the computer on the internal network where the packet is being sent.	This rule allows packets directed to this internal computer to pass through, but it blocks packets that do not have the correct destination address.
Destination address = internal IP address	Did this computer on the internal network request this information from the Web server?	This observation of the "state" of the computer prevents packets from entering that were not first requested by an internal computer.
Port = 80	The port indicates what this packet contains, namely an HTML document.	No other types of content besides HTML documents are allowed.

Firewalls are a critical tool for protecting a network and computer from attacks. However, firewalls are not the final answer in network defense. First, they do not stop all types of attacks such as viruses and Trojan horses. Also, a firewall is only as strong as its rule base. A firewall must be properly configured with the correct rules to be an effective deterrent to attacks.

According to Microsoft, 67 percent of the home computers in the U.S. do not use a firewall.

NOTE

Network Address Translation (NAT)

BLOCK ATTACKS

Another means of preventing attackers from sending malicious packets into a network is to disguise the IP addresses of the computers on the internal network. If the attacker does not know the IP address, then it is more difficult to send a packet past the firewall. Devices that perform this hiding function are known as **network address translation (NAT)** devices. A NAT hides the IP addresses of network devices from attackers. The location of NAT devices in a network is shown in Figure 5-19.

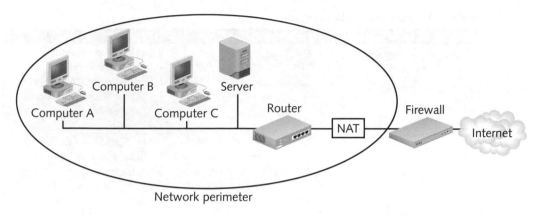

Figure 5-19   Network address translation (NAT) position

As a packet leaves the network, NAT removes the original IP address from the sender's packet and replaces it with an alias IP address, as shown in Figure 5-20. The NAT software maintains a table of the original address and the corresponding alias address. When a packet is returned to the NAT, the process is reversed. An attacker who captures the packet on the Internet cannot determine the actual IP address of the sender. Without that address, it is more difficult to identify and attack a computer.

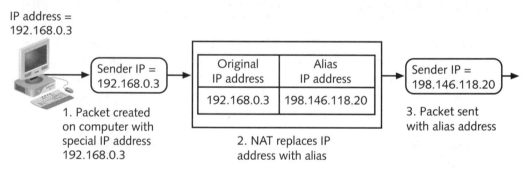

Figure 5-20   Network address translation (NAT)

A variation of NAT is **port address translation (PAT)**. Instead of giving each outgoing packet a different IP address, each packet is given the same IP address but a different port number. This allows a single IP address to be shared by several users. PAT is typically used on home networks that allow multiple users to share one IP address received from an ISP.

Intrusion Detection Systems

Although not found on home or small business computer networks, a device that establishes and maintains network security for large organizations is an **intrusion detection system (IDS)**. An IDS monitors the activity on the network and what the packets are doing (instead of just filtering packets based on where they come from, like a firewall does). An IDS performs a specific function when it senses an attack, such as dropping packets or tracing the source of an attack.

Network-based IDS systems monitor all network traffic and are located just behind the firewall, as shown in Figure 5-21. This system examines the type of data being transmitted and analyzes activity on the network to determine if an attack is occurring. Some IDS systems look for attacks based on a database of attack signatures, similar to how antivirus software detects a virus. If an attack signature is not in the database, however, the system generally does not know about it. Other IDS systems are based on behavior, which means the IDS watches network activity and reports abnormal behavior.

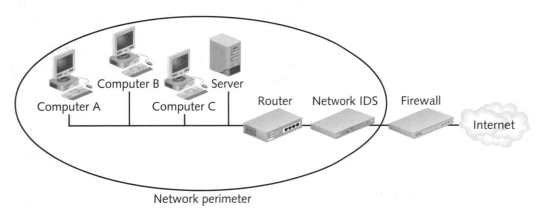

Figure 5-21   IDS system

Network-based IDS systems can also work with other network security devices. For example, if an attack is identified, the network-based IDS can send an instruction to the firewall to block all packets from this source so they cannot enter the network.

When an IDS system identifies an attack, it can send an alert message to an administrator through an e-mail, a pager, or a cell phone.

Proxy Server

 The primary goal of a **proxy server** is to conceal the identity of the computers within a protected network. Although proxy servers function in a manner similar to a NAT system, they can also inspect the packets of data for viruses and other malicious content.

BLOCK ATTACKS

A proxy server intercepts requests sent to a server and replaces the original IP address with its own address, thus preventing a direct connection to the server. The packet is then sent to the server. When the server replies, the packet is sent to the proxy server, which reinserts the original IP address before sending the packet. The location of a proxy server in a network is shown in Figure 5-22.

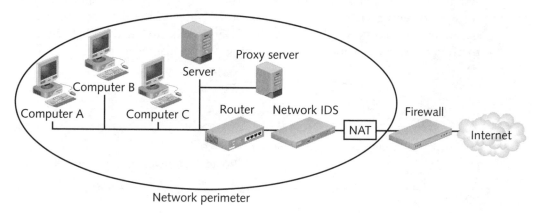

Figure 5-22   Proxy server location

Network Design

Network security devices cannot provide the protection needed to ward off attackers if the network is not properly designed. One key to designing effective network security is to create a single point of entry into the network. Much like a drawbridge on a castle, if the enemy has only one way to enter, it is easier to set the defenses. However, it is difficult to maintain a single point of entry in a network. Employees may install their own unauthorized equipment and thus poke holes in the security perimeter. As an example of multiple network entry points, Figure 5-23 shows that the user of Computer C has installed a modem in his office to dial into a fantasy football server. This user has inadvertantly opened another entry point into the network, completely bypassing the firewall and other devices. An attacker can take advantage of this hole in the security perimeter and gain access to the network. User installation of unauthorized equipment that compromises a network security perimeter is a constant threat to an organization.

In addition to restricting the number of points of entry, the security of a network can be enhanced by properly configuring the overall design of the network. Two technologies that are frequently used are demilitarized zones and virtual private networks.

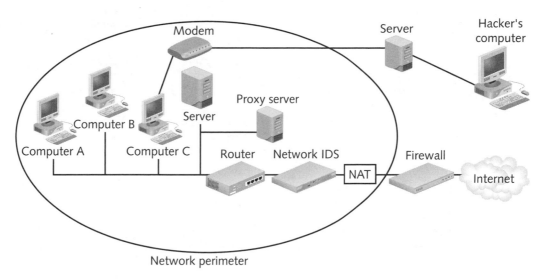

Figure 5-23 Multiple network entry points

Demilitarized Zones

**BLOCK
ATTACKS**

A **demilitarized zone (DMZ)** is another network that sits outside the secure network perimeter. Outside users can access the DMZ, but cannot enter the secure network. In Figure 5-24, a DMZ has been set up outside of the secure network perimeter. The DMZ contains a Web server and an e-mail server, two servers that are continuously accessed by outside users. However, outside users never enter the secure network—only the DMZ. Placing these servers in a DMZ restricts the access of outside users to the secure network.

NOTE

For an extra level of security, some networks use a DMZ with two firewalls.

Many home networks allow users to set up DMZs, as shown in Figure 5-25. The DMZ feature allows one local computer to be exposed to the Internet to use a special-purpose service such as Internet gaming or videoconferencing. DMZ hosting opens all the ports of one computer, exposing the entire computer so all users on the Internet can see it.

NOTE

Because of the high security risk, setting up a DMZ is not recommended unless it is absolutely necessary.

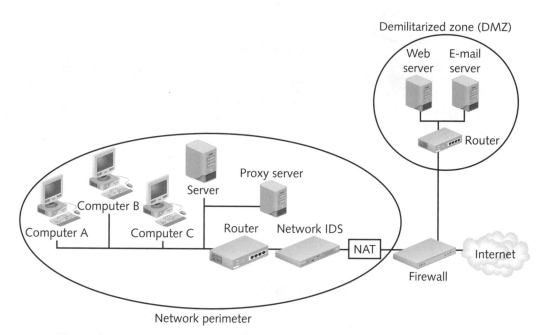

Figure 5-24   Demilitarized zone (DMZ)

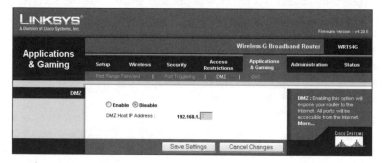

Figure 5-25   Home DMZ

Virtual Private Networks (VPN)

One of the great strengths of the Internet is that it can be accessed from almost anywhere. This makes it especially attractive for traveling business users who can access their company's e-mail and corporate data over the Internet. However, because the Internet is a public network that anyone can access, it should never be used to transmit unprotected, sensitive, or private data. The risk is simply too great for someone to intercept the packets and see the information.

One way to securely transmit data through a public network is using a **virtual private network (VPN)**. A VPN creates a secure network connection over a public network. VPNs are used extensively because they allow employees to access private data from almost anywhere an Internet connection can be located. A VPN is illustrated in Figure 5-26.

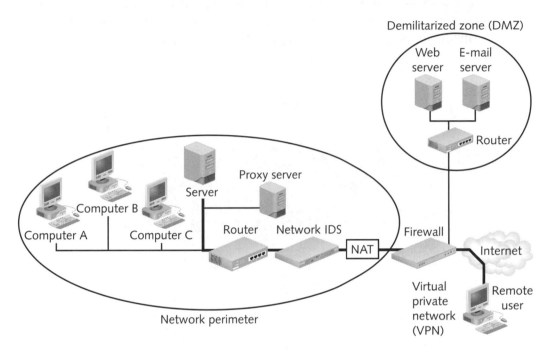

Figure 5-26   Virtual private network (VPN)

When using a VPN, a unique connection known as a **tunnel** is first set up between the sender and receiver. Only those computers or servers that are designated as belonging to the tunnel can participate in the transmission. The packets that are to be transmitted are enclosed within another packet. This helps protect the integrity of the data as it is being transmitted and hides information such as the IP addresses. Then, as an added degree of security, the packets are encrypted using digital certificates. Finally, the recipient must be authenticated as an authorized user to receive the packets.

A VPN can be set up using software that runs on both computers, or a separate hardware device, or a combination of the two.

NOTE

Testing Network Security

A key to establishing a good network security defense is to periodically test the defenses to ensure their strength. Several kinds of programs can probe a network to determine if any vulnerabilities exist. Figure 5-27 shows the results of a port scan, in which the major ports of a computer are tested from the outside to see if a port is open. An open port can be exploited by an attacker as an open hole into the network.

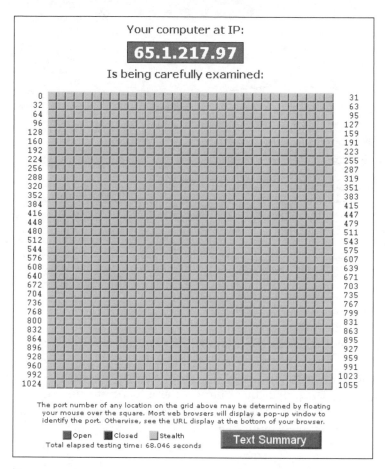

Figure 5-27   Port scan

It is recommended that network security be tested at least once a month for a home network or more frequently if it appears that the network may be a target of attacks. In addition, the network security should be checked when the network configuration or the security settings change.

SECURITY IN YOUR WORLD

Greg clicked OK to open a window showing his network connections. He had just spent the last few minutes reading the online manual about his wireless network after he had checked his firewall and antivirus software. "As long as I'm looking at this stuff, I may as well poke around some of these other settings," he thought to himself.

The window on his computer screen showed two computers on his network—his laptop computer and another computer named "Furgie." I wonder what's going on here, Greg thought to himself. He knew that his computer was the only one on his network. Thinking that perhaps he was picking up a signal from another wireless network nearby, Greg looked at his wireless settings. He realized that although he was not picking up another signal, someone else was picking up *his* wireless signal.

"Who is this?" Greg said aloud. He decided to click the Furgie computer icon. He could see the contents of that computer's hard drive. Greg opened a folder named "My Pictures" and clicked the first file. It was a photo of Mike, a student who lived in the apartment above Greg's.

"I can't believe it!" Greg said. Some of his friends bragged that they drove around town picking up wireless signals and using the connection for free Internet access, but he was shocked to realize he was now the victim. "I ought to march right up there and tell him to get off my connection," Greg thought. "I know that he's surfing the Internet for free on my connection while I'm struggling to pay for it each month." Greg put down his notebook computer and started to put on his shoes.

He suddenly stopped. "If I can see stuff on Mike's computer," he thought, "can he see what's on mine?" Greg turned off his computer and walked over to his bookcase to pull a book off the shelf. "I've got some more security work to do," he said to himself.

WIRELESS LAN SECURITY

Wireless data networks are springing up everywhere. Travelers can wirelessly access their e-mail during flights on airplanes or on trains, while waiting in airports, and in their hotel rooms. Businesses have found that employees who have wireless access to data during meetings and in conference rooms can increase productivity up to two hours each day. Free wireless Internet connections are available in restaurants across the country, and in select football and baseball stadiums fans can order concessions wirelessly and have them delivered to their seats. There is hardly a sector of the economy that has not been dramatically affected by wireless data technology.

Studies bear this out. The number of public **hotspots**, or locations where wireless data services are available, increases at a rate worldwide of almost 350 percent per year. CMP Media estimates that by 2007 more than 155 million wireless data devices will be sold (up from 22 million in 2003), that 98 percent of all laptop computers will be wireless, that more than 25,000 hotels in the United States will provide wireless data access to their customers, and that revenue from hotspots will exceed $9 billion. It is truly becoming a wireless world.

When hurricane Katrina struck New Orleans and Mississippi in 2005, it wiped out cell phone communications. However, wireless hotspots were quickly set up that allowed users to make Internet-based phone calls.

The list of advantages for implementing a wireless LAN is impressive. WLANs provide true mobility for users and do not restrict them to their desks to access network resources. This greater flexibility can result in substantial productivity increases by employees. Another advantage of wireless technology is the relative ease of installation. No longer are wired cable connections required for each computer on the network; instead, a single wired connection to an access point is all that is needed. This both decreases installation costs and allows for wireless networks to be installed in locations where previously it would have been difficult or impossible to install wiring, such as in older buildings or large warehouses.

Despite the advantages of wireless networking, security is a concern. When compared to wired networks, wireless LANs have several features that make them more vulnerable to attacks. These include:

- *Access to the wireless network*—With a wired network, an attacker must have physical access to the network to attempt to gain entry. Access to a wired network can be restricted by locked doors that keep intruders away from the network. However, the signals from a wireless network may reach outside the walls of a building. An attacker sitting in a parked car nearby can pick up the signal and break into the network.

- *View wireless transmissions*—Because the wireless data transmissions are not restricted to a cable, attackers can intercept those transmissions and view passwords, credit card numbers, and other information that is being transmitted.

- *Weaknesses in wireless security standards*—The original wireless security standards were not properly implemented and could be circumvented by attackers. Users who used these security technologies were left unprotected and exposed to attacks.

Security has been the Achilles heel of wireless networking for many years. However, much of that is changing. According to many experts, by implementing new wireless security technologies, WLANs can be made as secure as their wired counterparts. This requires the user to implement the proper steps to make the WLAN more secure.

First, it is important to *turn off broadcast information*. Every wireless network has a unique network name known as the **Service Set Identifier (SSID)**, which by default is broadcast from the access point to everyone. This may allow anyone who comes into its signal area to connect to the network. This feature should be turned off, as shown in Figure 5-28. Although advanced attackers can still use other tools to discover the SSID, turning it off prevents casual users from accessing the network.

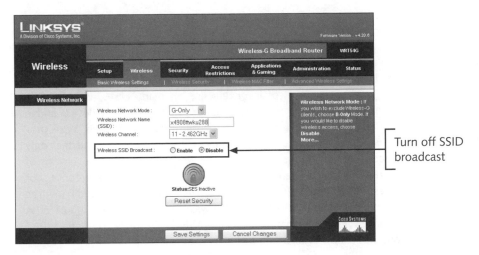

Turn off SSID broadcast

Figure 5-28   Disable SSID broadcast

NOTE

It is also recommended that the SSID of the wireless network not be a name that can easily identify the location of the access point. An SSID such as "Smith-Family" can easily reveal the source of the wireless signal. As shown in Figure 5-28, make the SSID cryptic.

BLOCK ATTACKS

Second, because each network device has a unique MAC address, the access point can be programmed to permit only specific devices into the network, based on their MAC address, or to deny access to specific devices. This is known as **MAC address filtering** and is illustrated in Figure 5-29. Much like turning off the broadcast information, advanced attackers can still use other tools to discover the MAC address. However, turning it off prevents casual users from accessing the network.

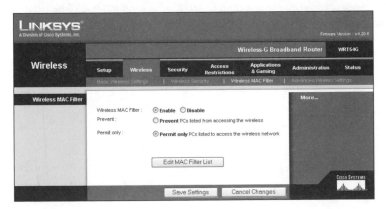

Figure 5-29   MAC address filtering

BLOCK ATTACKS

A final step is to use the advanced security techniques that have recently been developed. In October 2003, a new security implementation for WLANs was introduced, and is known as **Wi-Fi Protected Access (WPA)**. WPA replaces the original WLAN security method called **Wired Equivalent Privacy (WEP)**, which contained security weaknesses. WPA was designed to address WEP vulnerabilities with a minimum level of inconvenience. In many cases, WPA can be implemented with only a software upgrade on the wireless device and a firmware update on older access points. When properly installed, WPA provides a high level of assurance that data will remain protected and that only authorized users can access the wireless network. There are two versions of WPA: WPA Personal (intended for home users) and WPA Enterprise (for businesses). In September 2004, an advanced version was introduced known as **Wi-Fi Protected Access 2 (WPA2)**, which was the second generation of WPA security. Like WPA, there are two versions of WPA2: WPA2 Personal and WPA2 Enterprise, as shown in Figure 5-30.

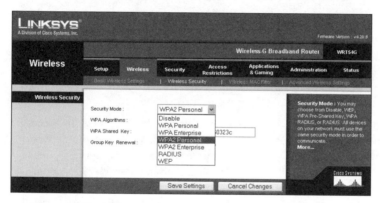

Figure 5-30   Advanced wireless security settings

NOTE

If an older wireless network cannot support WPA or WPA2, WEP may be used as a temporary alternative. However, because of its weaknesses, it should only be considered a transitional phase until a migration to stronger wireless security is possible.

CHAPTER SUMMARY

5

- The purpose of a computer network is to allow computers and devices to share data, programs, and hardware. One type of computer network is known as a local area network (LAN), in which the computers are located relatively close to one another. A wide area network (WAN) connects computers over a larger geographical area. A special type of local area network is a wireless local area network (WLAN) that connects computers without the use of cables. The most common set of protocols used today on networks is called the Transmission Control Protocol/Internet Protocol (TCP/IP), which requires each computer to have a unique IP address. The transmission of data through a computer network is accomplished by dividing the data into smaller units called packets. Network interface cards connect computers to the network; access points connect wireless devices to the wired network; and routers send packets through the network.

- A denial of service attack attempts to make a server unavailable by flooding it with requests. A variation of this attack tricks computers into responding to a false request from the server. This is known as a smurf attack. A distributed denial of service attack uses hundreds or thousands of computers to flood a server with requests. Attackers infect unprotected computers and use them to attack other computers. A network of these infected computers, called zombies, is known as a botnet.

- A man-in-the-middle attack intercepts communication between two computers. Hijacking involves setting up a fake device and tricking other users into sending their messages to it. Hijacking uses a technique known as spoofing, which is the act of pretending to be the legitimate owner when in reality you are not. A packet sniffer is hardware or software that can capture and view packets as they travel through the network.

- Several network devices can be used to thwart attackers. The most commonly used device is a firewall, sometimes called a packet filter. It is designed to prevent malicious packets from entering the network. Network address translation devices hide the IP address of network devices from attackers. Intrusion detection systems monitor the activity on the network and what the packets are doing. A proxy server is designed to conceal the identity of the computers within a protected network.

- In addition to using network devices to ward off attacks, properly designing the network is also important. A demilitarized zone is another network that sits outside the secure network perimeter. A virtual private network creates a secure network connection over a public network.

- Security for wireless LANs remains a primary concern for wireless users. Several techniques should be followed in order to secure a wireless LAN, including allowing only specific devices on the network and implementing the latest version of WPA, which is a standard for improved wireless security.

Key Terms

access point (AP) – A base station that connects wireless devices to a wired network.

botnet – A network of zombie computers.

client network adapter – A hardware device that connects a computer to a wired network.

computer network – A collection of interconnected computers and devices.

demilitarized zone (DMZ) – A part of a network that sits outside the secure network perimeter.

denial of service (DoS) – An attack that attempts to make a server or other network device unavailable by flooding it with requests.

distributed denial of service (DDoS) – An attack that uses hundreds or thousands of computers to flood a server with requests.

firewall – A device designed to prevent malicious packets from entering the network or computers.

handler – A large computer from which an attacker launches attacks to enlist zombies.

hijacking – Setting up a fake device and tricking other users to send their messages to it.

hotspots – Locations where wireless data services are available.

intrusion detection system (IDS) – A device that monitors the activity on the network and what the packets are doing.

IP address – A number that uniquely identifies one computer from all other computers on a network.

local area network (LAN) – A computer network in which all of the computers are located relatively close to each other.

MAC address filtering – The process of permitting or denying specific devices into the network based on their MAC address.

man in the middle – An attack that intercepts communication and then forges a response to the sender.

media access control (MAC) address – A computer address required by certain types of LANs.

network address translation (NAT) – A process of hiding the IP addresses of network devices from attackers by substituting fake IP addresses.

network interface card (NIC) – A hardware device that connects a computer to a wired network.

packet filter – A device designed to prevent malicious packets from entering the network or computers.

packets – Small pieces of data that are transmitted through a computer network.

personal firewall – A software-based firewall that runs on a personal computer.

ping – An "Are you there?" message sent by one computer to determine if another computer is functioning.

port address translation (PAT) – A process of hiding the IP addresses of network devices from attackers by substituting port addresses.

protocols – Rules for how data is to be transmitted through a network.

proxy server – A device that conceals the identity of the computers within a protected network.

router – A network device that moves packets.

rule base – A set of rules that establishes what action a firewall should take when it receives a packet.

server – A central computer that provides services to a network.

Service Set Identifier (SSID) – A unique wireless network name.

smurf – An attack that tricks computers to respond to a server with "I am here" messages.

sniffer – A hardware device or piece of software that performs sniffing.

sniffing – The process of capturing packets as they travel through the network.

spoofing – Pretending to be the legitimate recipient of a computer message.

stateful packet filtering – A type of firewall that keeps a record of the state of a connection and makes decisions based on the connection as well as the rule base.

stateless packet filtering – A type of firewall that looks at an incoming packet and permits or denies it based strictly on the rule base.

Transmission Control Protocol/Internet Protocol (TCP/IP) – The most common set of protocols used on networks.

tunnel – A VPN connection between the sender and receiver.

virtual private network (VPN) – A technique for creating a secure network connection over a public network.

wide area network (WAN) – A computer network in which the computers are distributed over a large geographical area.

Wi-Fi (Wireless Fidelity) – A local area network that does not use wires to connect computers together.

Wi-Fi Protected Access (WPA) – A standard for wireless security.

Wi-Fi Protected Access 2 (WPA2) – The enhanced wireless security standard.

Wired Equivalent Privacy (WEP) – The original standard for wireless security that contained security weaknesses.

wireless local area network (WLAN) – A local area network that does not use wires to connect computers together.

zombie – A vulnerable computer that follows the commands of an attacker.

REVIEW QUESTIONS

1. The central computer on a computer network is known as the _____ .

   a. workstation
   b. TelnedND
   c. server
   d. Network Interface Device (NID)

2. Another name for a wireless local area network is _____ .

   a. Wi-Fi

   b. Wireless communication system

   c. Radio frequency identification resource

   d. Wireless network adapter system

3. The most common set of protocols used on networks is _____ .

   a. Transmission Control Protocol/Internet Protocol (TCP/IP)

   b. Wireless IP Configuration (WIPC)

   c. NetDOS

   d. Network Internetwork Procedure

4. Wireless networks require a(n) _____ , which has a jack that allows it to connect by cable to a standard wired network.

   a. access point (AP)

   b. wireless network interface card

   c. wired NIC adapter

   d. routing IDS

5. A _____ attack attempts to make a server or other network device unavailable by flooding it with requests.

   a. key logger

   b. ping-pong

   c. denial of service (DoS)

   d. distributed ping-pong (DPP)

6. A distributed denial of service (DDoS) attack uses only one computer, but it is located more than 500 miles away. True or False?

7. A zombie contains several botnets. True or False?

8. Man-in–the-middle attacks make it seem that two computers are communicating with each other, when actually they are sending and receiving data with a computer between them. True or False?

9. With wired networks, hijacking uses a technique known as spoofing, which is the act of pretending to be the legitimate owner when in reality you are not. True or False?

10. Because network traffic is divided into smaller segments called packets, an attacker can capture packets as they travel through the network using a technique called sniffing. True or False?

11. The most widely used network device to guard against attacks is a(n) _____ .

12. As a packet leaves the network, the _____ removes the original IP address from the sender's packet and replaces it with an alias IP address.

13. A(n) _____ monitors the activity on the network and what the packets are doing (instead of only filtering packets based on where they come from, like a firewall does).

14. A(n) _____ is another network that sits outside the secure network perimeter.

15. A(n) _____ creates a secure network connection over a public network.

16. Explain the difference between stateful packet firewalls and stateless packet firewalls.

17. Explain how a virtual private network works.

18. How does turning off broadcast information protect a wireless LAN?

19. What is MAC address filtering?

20. Why are wireless LANs more vulnerable to attacks than wired LANs?

HANDS-ON PROJECTS

**HANDS-ON
PROJECTS**

Project 5-1: Performing a Network Security Scan

It is important to test network security on a regular basis. In this project, you perform a scan using an Internet-based scanner and you download and use a local scanner.

1. Use your Web browser to go to the Steve Gibson Research Web site at **www.grc.com**.

2. Click **ShieldsUp!!**.

NOTE

Content on this Web site periodically changes. You might need to search the site for a link to the ShieldsUp!! page.

3. Scroll down and click **ShieldsUp!!**. If you receive a security alert that you are now viewing a secure page, click **OK**.

4. Click the **Proceed** button. If you receive a security alert that you are now leaving a secure page, click **Yes**.

5. On the ShieldsUp!! page, click the **File Sharing** button. Shields Up!! probes your computer to identify basic security vulnerabilities. Print this page when finished.

6. Scroll down to the ShieldsUp!! Services menu.

7. Click the **All Service Ports** button to scan open ports on your computer. A grid is displayed indicating which ports are open (red), closed (blue), or hidden (green), also called "stealth." When the scan completes, scroll through the report to view the results. Print the report.

8. Use your Web browser to go to the Tenable Network Security Web site at the following address:

   www.tenablesecurity.com/newt.html.

9. Click the **download request form** link.

10. Fill out the requested information, and then click the **Submit** button.

11. Go to your e-mail account. Retrieve the e-mail from Tenable and click the embedded link.

12. Click **I accept the terms of this license**.

13. Follow instructions to download, save, and install Tenable NeWT.

14. When prompted, enter the product key code found in the e-mail message. Then update the plug-ins from the Internet.

15. To determine the IP address of your computer, click **Start** on the Windows taskbar, and then click **Run**.

16. Type **cmd** and then press **Enter**.

17. Type **ipconfig/all** and then press **Enter**. Record the IP address displayed next to Default gateway.

18. Type **exit** and then press **Enter**.

Now you are ready to use the NeWT Security Scanner to scan your system for vulnerabilities.

1. Start NeWT Security Scanner.

2. Click **New Scan Task**.

3. Enter the IP address you recorded in Step 18 above (such as 192.168.2.1). Click **Next**.

4. Click **Enable all but dangerous plugins (Recommended)**.

5. Click **Scan now**.

6. Depending on the configuration of the network and computers, the scan may take some time. You can let the scan run for several minutes and then stop it. A report is generated regarding what ports are open and vulnerabilities discovered.

7. Which product (Shields Up!! Or NeWT Security Scanner) provides information that is more helpful?

8. Close all windows.

Project 5-2: Configuring Microsoft Windows Firewall

The Microsoft Windows Firewall included in Windows XP Service Pack 2 is a stateful packet filter firewall. Although it is not as full-featured as other personal firewalls, it does provide basic protection. In this project, you turn on and configure the firewall.

If you are using a computer in a school's computer lab or a computer at work, talk to your network administrator before performing this project. You may need special permissions set before you can change these configuration settings.

5

1. Click **Start**, click **Control Panel**, and then click **Security Center** if the Control Panel opens in Category view. If the Control Panel opens in Classic view, double-click **Security Center**.

2. In the Manage security settings for section, click **Windows Firewall**.

3. Click the **Advanced** tab to display the advanced settings. You use the Advanced Settings dialog box to configure the rule base for the firewall. These settings are all for filtering *inbound* traffic; other than checking the source IP address, Windows Firewall does not inspect any outbound packets.

4. Click the **Exceptions** tab and then the **Add Port** button. This allows you to open a port on your computer so that packets can enter. Click **Cancel** and then click the **Advanced** tab.

NOTE

A personal firewall allows you to open a specific port for a program, or you can just specify the program and the firewall will determine the port and open it for you.

5. In the Security Logging section, click **Settings**. You use this dialog box to select the firewall activities you want to log.

6. Check the **Log dropped packets** and **Log successful connections** boxes. Click **OK**.

7. In the ICMP section, click **Settings**. Click **Allow incoming echo request**. Click **OK** to close the dialog box, and then click **OK** to close the Log Settings dialog box.

8. Close all open windows.

Now you can test the firewall connections, which may be difficult because an enterprise firewall should already be protecting the network, and suspicious packets would not reach the local Windows Firewall. Before performing the following steps, record the IP address of your computer and then go to another computer that is connected to the Internet.

1. Click **Start** and then click **Run**. The Run dialog box opens.

2. Type **cmd** and then press **Enter**. The Command Prompt window opens.

3. At the command prompt, type **ping** ip-address where *ip-address* is the IP address of the system for which you want to test the ICF connection (for example, ping 192. 168.2.1). Then press **Enter**.

4. Type **exit** and then press **Enter** to close the Command Prompt window.

5. Open and view the ICF log file (the default location is C:\WINDOWS\pfirewall.log) of the first computer to see if a ping was received and dropped.

6. Close all windows.

Project 5-3: Stopping Zombies

A zombie is a computer that has been manipulated by a handler to launch attacks. In this project, you download software that would instruct zombies to stop attacking during a DDoS attack.

1. Use your Web browser to go to the following Web page:

   **www.bindview.com/Services/RAZOR/Utilities/Windows/
   ZombieZapper_form.cfm**

2. Scroll down and click **Zombie Zapper**.

3. Read through the license agreement and click **Zombie Zapper[tm] Windows NT Executable v1.2** to download the ZZ.exe file. (This version works with Windows NT, Windows 2000, and Windows XP.) If necessary, navigate to a folder that you use for downloads, and then save the file.

4. Close your Web browser, and then start Zombie Zapper by double-clicking the **ZZ.exe** file to display the Zombie Zapper dialog box, shown in Figure 5-31.

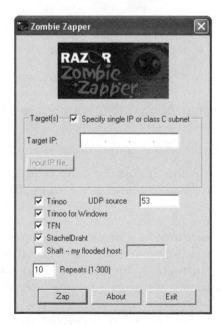

Figure 5-31   Zombie Zapper dialog box

5. The Target IP text box is the address of the system which is attacking you. For this activity, in the Target IP text box, type the address of another system on your network with which you are familiar. If you are unsure of the IP address of a system, ask

your system administrator. *Do not* enter the IP address of an unknown system outside of your network.

6. Accept the default settings and click **Zap** to begin. During a DDoS attack, Zombie Zapper sends ten "kill packets" to that zombie to stop the flood of packets. If you receive a message regarding a domain administrator, ask your system administrator for more information.

7. Close all windows when you are finished.

Project 5-4: Identifying Shared Network Files

Files and directories can be shared across a computer network, allowing other users to access these files. A frequently overlooked security vulnerability is to have sharing enabled on sensitive computer files. In this project, you download and use a program to identify shared files.

1. Use your Web browser to go to the following Web page:

   www.sysinternals.com/Utilities/ShareEnum.html

2. Click **Download ShareEnum**.

3. Click **Save**.

4. When the download is finished, click **Open**.

5. Click **Extract all files**. Follow the steps in the wizard to unzip the files.

6. Double-click **ShareEnum.exe**. In the list box, select each of the domains listed, one at a time clicking the **Refresh** button after each selection. A report similar to the one shown in Figure 5-32 appears.

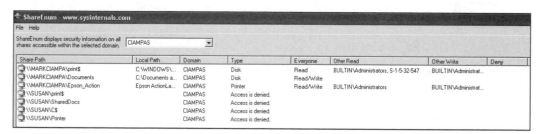

Figure 5-32 Shared folders

7. Each of these shared folders could be accessible to attackers. To close a shared folder so it is no longer accessible, click **Start** and then click **My Computer**.

8. If a folder is being shared, locate that folder. Right-click the shared folder, and then click **Sharing and Security** on the shortcut menu. The Sharing and Security dialog box opens. Select the **Do not share this folder** option button. What happens if your turn off file sharing? Right-click that folder again, click **Sharing and Security** on the shortcut menu, and then turn sharing on by clicking **Share this folder**.

9. Close all windows.

Project 5-5: Setting WLAN Security

You must set the proper security on a wireless network to defend against attackers. In this project, you set the security on a Linksys WRT54G wireless device.

1. Using your Web browser, access the Linksys wireless device by entering its IP address. The default IP address is 192.168.1.1.

2. Enter the username and password. The Linksys Setup dialog box opens.

3. Click the **Wireless** tab.

4. In the Wireless SSID Broadcast section, click **Disable**.

5. Click the **Wireless MAC Filter** tab.

6. In the Wireless MAC Filter section, click **Enable**.

7. Click **Permit only** PCs listed to access the wireless network.

8. Click **Edit MAC Filter List**.

9. If the computers that are to be permitted to access the wireless network are already connected to the network, click **Wireless Client MAC List** and a list of the computers appears under the Active PC heading. To add that computer to the list, check **Enable MAC Filter**. Click **Update Filter list**.

10. For any other computers that are to be permitted but are not already connected, enter their MAC address (use no punctuation).

NOTE

To determine a computer's MAC address, click Start, click Run and then enter CMD. Enter ipconfig/all and record the "Physical Address."

11. Click **Save Settings** and close the window.

12. Click the **Wireless Security** tab.

13. Enter the following:

    Security Mode: Select **WPA2 Personal**

    WPA Algorithms: Select **TKIP+AES**

    WPA Shared Key: Enter **abcd594445219762283412c**

    Group Key Renewal: Enter **3600**

14. Click **Save Settings**.

15. Close the browser.

Now you are ready to set the necessary wireless network properties.

1. On the computer that is to be part of the wireless network, click **Start**, point to **Connect To**, and then click **Show all connections**.

2. Double-click the wireless network connection.

3. Click **View Wireless Networks**.

4. Click **Properties**.

5. Click the **Wireless Networks** tab.

6. In the Preferred networks section, click **Add**.

7. In the Network name (SSID) section, enter the SSID for this network.

8. In the Network Authentication section, select **WPA-PSK**.

9. In the Data encryption section, select **TKIP**.

10. In the Network key section, enter the WPA shared key **abcd594445219762283412c** and re-verify in the Confirm network key section.

11. Click **OK** and close all windows.

CASE PROJECTS

Case Project 5-1: Network Map

Draw a map of the computer network at your home or computer lab. Label each network device that you can. Then try to identify the number of entry points into the network. Would you say this network is secure? Why or why not?

Case Project 5-2: Who Is Responsible for Zombies?

Should users be held responsible if their computers are turned into zombies? Should the users of computers that are attacked be able to demand compensation from zombie owners? Should Internet service providers automatically deny users whose computers are zombies? Write a paragraph regarding the ethical implications of zombie computers and who should be held responsible for the damage caused by zombie computers.

Case Project 5-3: Packet Sniffing

What would you do if you discovered a neighbor using your wireless signal without your permission? Using the Internet, try to find what Internet service providers say regarding the unauthorized use of a wireless signal. Should it be illegal to use a network without the owner's permission? Write a one-paragraph summary on what you find about ISPs and another paragraph on your opinion of what the law should allow or not allow.

Case Project 5-4: Sniffing

Until recently, sniffers cost many thousands of dollars and were only used by network professionals. However, now sniffers are freely available and are one of the primary tools used by attackers. Is this a good thing? Should sniffers be regulated and licensed? Should they be controlled, and if so, how? Write a one-page paper on your findings.

Case Project 5-5: Baypoint Computer Consulting

A local florist, Village Flowers and Gifts, wants to set up a wireless hotspot for its customers to use when they come into the store. However, they are concerned about security. Baypoint Computer Consulting (BCC) has asked you to help.

Create a PowerPoint presentation that lists the vulnerabilities of wireless networks. Use the Internet to identify types of wireless attacks that have been launched and describe their consequences. Include your opinion regarding whether Village Flowers and Gifts should do this. Your presentation should be 6-8 slides in length.

You have now been asked to create another presentation regarding ways in which WLANs can be protected and safeguarded. Create a 5-8 slide presentation that would be appropriate for users of different technology backgrounds.

ENTERPRISE SECURITY

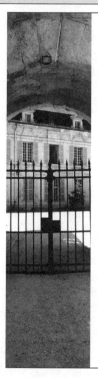

Security in Your World

Hunter looked up as the door to the room opened and Caitlin entered. This was Hunter's first day on the job working for a large company after graduating from college last month. He had just finished his orientation with the human resources assistant director and now was waiting to meet the IT associate director.

"Hi, Hunter. I'm Caitlin, and I'll be handling the next part of your orientation," she said. "It's nice to meet you," said Hunter. "Are you with the IT department?" "Yes," said Caitlin, "I'm the associate director of IT on this campus." "Great," said Hunter. "I guess you're the one who gives me my computer password." Caitlin smiled. "Yes, I'll be giving you your password. But that will come towards the end of this session. First, there are several other things we have to cover."

Hunter looked surprised. Caitlin smiled and said, "I know you thought this would be quick and easy. Most of our new employees do. But this orientation session on IT is one of the most involved sessions you'll have. Because computers and networks play such a critical role in our company, we take it very seriously. We feel it's essential that our employees have a good understanding of our IT policies and procedures."

Caitlin continued, "Let's go ahead and get started. I promised your supervisor that I would be finished with you in four hours." "Four hours!" Hunter exclaimed. "There really must be a lot to cover!" "See? I told you we were serious about it," Caitlin said. "First, we need to pick up your key card so you can get into the building and your cubicle. Come on, we'll walk down to pick it up. I can start our orientation on the way there."

Computer security for a large business, often called **enterprise security**, involves many of the same security tasks that would be performed by a home or small business computer user. These tasks include installing firewalls, antivirus software, antispyware, and other security protections.

Other aspects of enterprise security differ significantly from home security. Besides the obvious difference of needing to secure hundreds of computers and a wide variety of computer networks, enterprise security follows more formal policies and procedures. Whereas users might make a mental note to back up their hard drive every Friday afternoon, in a large organization this procedure would be clearly outlined as a policy that describes steps that must be performed, identifies who should perform the steps, explains what to do in the event of a problem, and tells how to document that the backup was performed. One reason for this more formal approach is to ensure that all the necessary activities are performed and documented.

In this chapter, we will examine enterprise security for an organization. We will start by identifying the tools used to physically protect computers and networks. Next, we will explore the policies and plans that an enterprise uses to establish and maintain computer security. Then, we will discuss how security training can take place at the enterprise level. Finally, we will conclude by looking at ethics and the role it plays in applying practical security in your world.

PHYSICAL SECURITY

One of the first lines of defense against attacks is adequate physical security. **Physical security** protects the equipment itself and has one primary goal: to prevent unauthorized users from reaching the equipment to use, steal, or vandalize it. Although physical security seems obvious, in practice it is frequently overlooked because so much attention is focused on preventing attackers from reaching a computer electronically. However, ensuring that devices or the data on those devices cannot be reached physically by attackers is equally important.

The first step is to secure the device itself. For user computers, many organizations remove or disable hardware that can provide access to a computer, such as floppy disk drives, USB ports, and CD-ROM or DVD drives. This prevents an attacker who reaches the computer from installing her own programs to provide access through a backdoor.

Disabling hardware has another benefit for an organization. It prevents sensitive data from being stolen by being copied onto a CD, USB flash drive, or other removable media.

Securing network servers in an organization is equally important. Most servers are **rack-mounted servers** such as the one shown in Figure 6-1. A typical rack-mounted server is 1.75 inches (4.45 centimeters) tall and can be stacked with up to 50 other servers in a closely confined area. These units can be locked to the rack to prevent theft. Instead of having a separate monitor, mouse, and keyboard, rack-mounted units are typically connected to a single **KVM (keyboard, video, mouse) switch**, which in turn is connected to a single monitor, mouse, and keyboard. KVM switches are shown in Figure 6-2. Connection ports on KVM switches allow analog or digital connections from rack-mounted servers or connections over network cables. For security purposes, some KVM switches have a lock that restricts access. Even an attacker who gets into the server closet can't access the server with a locked KVM switch. For additional security, some organizations use KVM switches that require the user to enter a username and password in order to access the KVM switch.

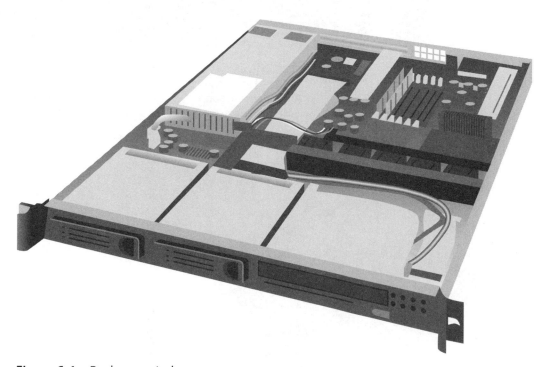

Figure 6-1   Rack-mounted server

   Some KVM switches can accommodate up to eight users and 128 rack-mounted servers.

NOTE

In addition to securing the device itself, it is also important to secure the room containing the device. Two basic types of door locks require a key. A **preset lock**, also known as the **key-in-knob lock**, shown in Figure 6-3, is the easiest to use because it requires only a key for unlocking the door from the outside. When the door is closed, it automatically locks behind the person, unless it has been set to remain unlocked. The security provided by a preset lock is minimal. An attacker can wedge a thin piece of plastic (such as a credit card) between the lock and the door face to open it, or if that fails, the attacker can break off the knob or handle with a sharp blow by a hammer.

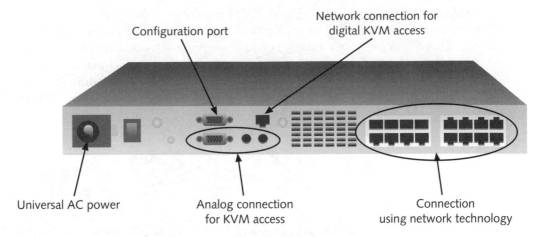

Configuration port

Network connection for
digital KVM access

Universal AC power

Analog connection
for KVM access

Connection
using network technology

Figure 6-2   KVM (keyboard, video, mouse) switch

Figure 6-3   Preset lock

Although preset locks afford the least protection for physical security, they are
the ones used most often because they are the least expensive.

NOTE

The second type of door lock also requires a key, but is more secure. Known as a **deadbolt
lock**, this lock extends a solid metal bar into the door frame, as shown in Figure 6-4.
Deadbolt locks are much more difficult to defeat than preset locks. The lock cannot be
broken from the outside like a preset lock, and the extension of the bar prevents a credit card
from being inserted to "jimmy" it open. Deadbolt locks also require that the key be used to
both open and lock the door.

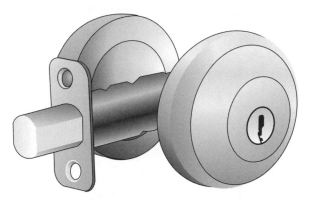

Figure 6-4 Deadbolt lock

Door locks that require a key to open them are the most common defense against an attacker, but unfortunately, they offer the least degree of security in protecting equipment. This is because keys can be lost, stolen, or duplicated. To achieve the most security when using keyed door locks, most enterprises observe the following practices:

- Change locks immediately upon loss or theft of keys.
- Inspect all locks on a regular basis.
- Issue keys only to authorized persons.
- Keep records of who uses and turns in keys.
- Keep track of keys issued, with their number and identification, for both master keys and duplicate keys.
- Do not mark master keys in any way that identifies them as masters.
- Secure unused keys in a locked safe.
- Set up a procedure to monitor the use of all locks and keys, and update the procedure as necessary.
- Mark duplicates of master keys with "Do Not Duplicate," and wipe out the manufacturer's serial numbers to keep duplicates from being ordered.

An alternative to a key lock is a cipher lock, shown in Figure 6-5. **Cipher locks** are combination locks with buttons that a user must push in the proper sequence to open the door. Although cipher locks may seem to be similar to a combination padlock, they have more "intelligence." You can program a cipher lock to allow only the codes of certain individuals to be valid on specific dates and times. For example, an employee's code may be valid to access the computer room only from 8:00 AM to 5:00 PM Monday through Friday. This prevents the employee from entering the room late at night when most other employees are gone. Cipher locks also keep a record of when the door was opened and by which code. Because cipher locks are typically connected to a networked computer system, they can be controlled from one central location.

Figure 6-5   Cipher lock

Cipher locks do have disadvantages. Basic models can cost several hundred dollars each, while advanced models can be even more expensive. In addition, users must be careful to conceal which buttons they push to keep someone from seeing the combination, a technique known as **shoulder surfing**.

In addition to locking doors, other physical vulnerabilities in an office should also be addressed. These vulnerabilities include:

- *Suspended ceilings*—A **suspended ceiling** is composed of a metal grid that supports lightweight ceiling tiles. Suspended ceilings can hide pipes, ducts, and cables from view as well as serve as a sound barrier. However, attackers can easily enter a locked room by passing through the suspended ceiling. Equipment that must be secured should never be placed in a room with a suspended ceiling that permits access from adjoining rooms.

- *HVAC ducts*—Attackers can attempt to crawl through the ductwork that supports heating, ventilation, and air conditioning (HVAC) to enter a building and move around unnoticed. HVAC grates should be secured in place so that they cannot be easily removed.

- *Exposed door hinges*—A door that opens "out" always exposes its hinges and pins. An attacker can remove the hinge pins in seconds to access a locked room. Hinges should always be installed on the inside of the locked door.

- *Insufficient lighting*—An attacker's best friend is a dark place. The inside as well as outside perimeter of a network should be well lit, with the lights left on from dusk to dawn. Because it is easy to defeat motion detector lights, they should not be used.

- *Dead-end corridors*—A hallway that provides only one exit may be an ideal location for an attacker because there is no risk of encountering someone who happens to pass by. Dead-end corridors that may provide opportunities for attackers should be monitored with cameras or security guards.

NOTE

In addition to restricting physical access by door locks, other security measures can prevent unauthorized users from entering secure areas. These include minimizing the number of entry points into a building or area, using guards at entrances to check identification, and installing cameras.

SECURITY IN YOUR WORLD

Caitlin pulled out another thick document from her folder and placed it on the desk in front of Hunter. "And this is our acceptable use policy, which outlines what you may and may not do with the computers here. Along with our security and privacy policies that I already gave you, these are probably the three most important documents you'll see today," Caitlin said.

Hunter flipped to the back page, picked up his pen and started to sign his name on the document. "Wait a minute, Hunter. We haven't even gone over them yet." "Well, I know about policies," Hunter said. "At my college, we had to verify online that we had read all of the policies and would abide by them. But nobody ever did that. I know that these policies are just formalities you have to go through so that you can get your computer account." Caitlin leaned forward. "It may have been that way at your college, but I can assure you it's not that way here. All employees are expected to read and understand the policies and then abide by them on a daily basis. I will tell you that we have terminated three employees already this year exclusively because they violated the company's policies."

Hunter set down his pen. "I'm sorry. It looks like you are really serious about this." Caitlin leaned back in her chair. "Yes, we're very serious. Do you want to sign that policy that says you have read, understood, and will abide by it, or should we first go through them together?" Hunter turned back to the beginning of the policy. "Is page one a good place to start?" he asked.

ENTERPRISE POLICIES

BLOCK ATTACKS

A **policy** is a document that outlines specific requirements or rules that must be met. A policy has these characteristics:

- Policies communicate a consensus of judgment.
- Policies define appropriate behavior for users.
- Policies identify what tools and procedures are needed.
- Policies provide a foundation for human resource action in response to inappropriate behavior.
- Policies make the process of prosecuting violators clearer and more fair than prosecution without policies.

A policy is the correct vehicle for an organization to use when it is establishing information security. A **standard** is a collection of requirements specific to the system or procedure that must be met by everyone. For example, a standard may describe how to protect a computer at home that remotely connects to the organization's network. Users must follow this standard exactly if they want to be able to connect. A **guideline** is a collection of suggestions that should be implemented. These are not requirements to be met but are strongly recommended.

Almost all enterprises design and follow three policies. These include a security policy, an acceptable use policy, and a privacy policy.

Security Policy

A **security policy** is a document that outlines the protections that should be enacted to ensure that the organization's assets face minimal risks. Many organizations require employees to read the security policy and sign a document indicating they understand the policy and will abide by it. An information security policy is usually not a single large document, but a series of specific security documents that address a single asset or procedure, such as a password management policy or a firewall security policy.

To create an effective security policy, an enterprise must carefully balance two elements: trust and control. There are three models of trust:

- *Trust everyone all of the time*—This is the easiest model to enforce because there are no restrictions. However, it is impractical because it leaves the computers and network vulnerable to attacks.
- *Trust no one at any time*—This model is the most restrictive and therefore the most secure, but is also impractical. Most people would not work for an organization that did not trust its employees.
- *Trust some people some of the time*—This approach exercises caution in the amount of trust given. Access is provided as needed with technical controls to ensure the trust is not violated.

NOTE The model of trusting no one at any time is found mostly in high-security government organizations.

A security policy attempts to provide the right amount of trust by balancing no trust and too much trust. It does this by trusting some of the people some of the time and by building trust over time. Deciding on the level of trust may be delicate: too much trust may lead to eventual security problems, while too little trust may make it difficult to find and keep good employees.

The second balancing act deals with control. One of the major goals of a security policy is to implement control. Deciding on the level of control for a specific policy is not always clear. The security needs and the culture of the organization play a major role when deciding what level of control is appropriate. If policies are too restrictive or are too hard to implement and comply with, employees will either ignore them or find a way to circumvent them. Management must commit to the proper level of control that a security policy should address.

Not all users have positive attitudes about security policies. Users sometimes view security policies as barriers to productivity and as a way to control behavior. Others assume the requirements will be difficult to understand and implement. This negative outlook is particularly common in organizations where, in the past, policies did not exist or were loosely enforced. Table 6-1 summarizes how different groups may react to security in an organization.

Table 6-1   Attitudes towards security

User Group	Attitude toward Security
Users	Want to be able to get their work done without restrictive security controls
System support personnel	Concerned about the ease of managing systems under tight security controls
Management	Concerned about the cost of security protection for attacks that may not materialize

Overcoming pessimistic attitudes about a security policy is sometimes the greatest challenge of implementing a policy. Getting all sides to agree about all parts of a policy may not be practical. Instead, reaching a reasonable consensus is often the best approach.

Acceptable Use Policy (AUP)

An **acceptable use policy (AUP)** defines what actions the users of a system may perform while using the computing and networking equipment. The users may be employees, vendors, contractors, or visitors, with different standards for each group. AUPs typically cover all computer use, including Internet, e-mail, Web, and password security.

An AUP should have an overview regarding what is covered by this policy, as in the following sample:

> Internet-related systems, including but not limited to computer equipment, software, operating systems, storage media, network accounts providing electronic mail, and Web browsers, are the property of Organization A. These systems are to be used for business purposes in serving the interests of the company, our clients, and our customers in the course of normal operations.

The AUP should also provide explicit prohibitions regarding security and proprietary information:

> Keep passwords secure and do not share accounts. Authorized users are responsible for the security of their passwords and accounts. System-level passwords should be changed every 30 days; user-level passwords should be changed every 45 days.
>
> All PCs, laptops, and workstations should be secured with a password-protected screensaver with the automatic activation feature set at 10 minutes or less, or the computer user should log off when the host is unattended for 10 minutes.
>
> Postings by employees from an Organization A e-mail address to newsgroups should contain a disclaimer stating that the opinions expressed are strictly their own and not necessarily those of Organization A, unless posting is part of the employee's business duties.

Unacceptable use should also be outlined by the AUP, as in the following sample:

> The following actions are not acceptable ways to use the system:
>
> - Introducing malicious programs into the network or server.
>
> - Revealing your account password to others or allowing use of your account by others; this includes family and other household members when work is being done at home.
>
> - Using an Organization A computing asset to actively engage in procuring or transmitting material that is in violation of sexual harassment or hostile workplace laws in the user's local jurisdiction.
>
> - Any form of harassment via e-mail, telephone, or pager, whether through language, frequency, or size of messages.
>
> - Unauthorized use, or forging, of e-mail header information.

Acceptable use policies are often considered to be the most important information security policies that should be implemented. All organizations, particularly educational institutions and government agencies, should have an AUP in place.

Privacy Policy

Because privacy is of growing concern today, most enterprises have a privacy policy. A **privacy policy** outlines how the organization uses information it collects. A typical policy to consumers may state:

> In general, you can visit us on the Internet without telling us who you are and without giving any personal information about yourself. There are times, however, when we or our partners may need information from you. You may choose to give us personal information in a variety of situations. For example, you may want to give us information, such as your name and address or e-mail, to correspond with you, to process an order, or to provide you with a subscription. You may give us your credit card details to buy something from us, or a description of your education and work experience in connection with a job opening for which you wish to be considered. We intend to let you know how we will use such information before we collect it from you. You may tell us that you do not want us to use this information to make further contact with you beyond fulfilling your request. If you give us personal information about somebody else, such as a spouse or work colleague, we will assume that you have permission to do so.

SECURITY IN YOUR WORLD

"I'm a little confused about the difference between these policies we talked about earlier and these plans," Hunter said to Caitlin. He was looking at another stack of documents that Caitlin had given to him. Caitlin smiled and said, "I think some of our employees who have worked here a long time also get confused. Think of it this way: our policies say what we will do, while a plan outlines exactly how we will do it."

"So a policy is putting the theory into practice?" asked Hunter. "Well, it's something like that," said Caitlin. "Let's go through the first one and I think it will make more sense."

ENTERPRISE PLANS

A policy is a document that outlines specific requirements that must be met; that is, it sets guidelines that define an organization's approach to security, acceptable use, and privacy. A **plan** is a "call to action" outlining specifically what must be done. In other words, a policy defines the goals that are then specified in the plan.

Organizations typically have plans that outline what action to take when a security attack or similar incident means the business cannot perform its normal operations. The two types of plans that are often used are a business continuity plan and a disaster recovery plan.

Business Continuity Plan

Security attacks on a business do not always come electronically through a connection to the Internet. Instead, they may also be acts of vandalism, fire, or disruption of utilities intended to destroy or make data unavailable. Other acts that can destroy data are not man-made. Hurricanes, floods, tornados, and other natural disasters also pose a serious risk to computers and their data. For this reason, it is important for organizations to have plans to protect data against cyberattacks as well as natural disasters.

Business continuity is the process of assessing risks and developing a management strategy to ensure that the business can continue if the worst possible risks materialize. These risks could be external, such as a successful security attack or a power failure, or they could come from within the organization, such as a disgruntled employee's sabotage of a computer system. Business continuity is concerned not only with recovering after a disaster; it also addresses anything that could affect the continuity of service over the long term, such as the shortages of staffing in specialized areas.

Business continuity management is concerned with developing a **business continuity plan (BCP)** that addresses how the organization can continue in the event that risks materialize. The basic steps in creating a BCP are:

- *Understand the business*—The goals of the organization, its mission-critical process, and external influences must be clearly identified.

- *Formulate continuity strategies*—These strategies may vary depending on the event. The strategies could be to do nothing, change or end the process, or adjust the business itself to minimize the impact.

- *Develop a response*—A response addresses what should be done if the risk materializes. For example, should a new initiative be placed on hold if key workers leave the company?

- *Test the plan*—A realistic test of the components of a BCP should be conducted and analyzed so that modifications can be made as necessary.

Although business continuity should cover a broad range of risks, some common factors are usually addressed. These include how to maintain utilities and creating and maintaining enterprise backups.

Maintaining Utilities

The disruption of utilities, such as the loss of electricity, water, sewage disposal, or natural gas, can quickly force an organization's building to be abandoned. However, it is not practical to mitigate all of these utility disruptions, such as holding in reserve thousands of gallons of water or maintaining dual sewage disposal systems. Fortunately, these types of utilities on average are not as volatile as other utilities.

Some utility problems such as disruption to a telephone service may be temporarily dealt with by employees using their cellular telephones.

NOTE

The primary utility that a BCP should address is electrical service. Whereas some organizations could cope for a short period with no water, a disruption in electrical power would immediately cause the organization to cease operations. There are contingency options for a lack of electrical power. An **uninterruptible power supply (UPS)** is an external device located between the outlet for electrical power and a computer device. The primary purpose of a UPS is to continue to supply power in the event that the electrical power fails. The UPS is much more than a large battery. UPS systems, for example, can communicate with the software on the network server to ensure that an orderly shutdown occurs. Specifically, if the power fails, a UPS can complete the following tasks:

- Send a message to the network administrator's computer, or page or telephone the network manager to indicate that the power has failed

- Notify all users that they must finish their work immediately and log off

- Prevent any new users from logging on
- Disconnect users and shut down the server

In addition to providing power, a UPS can also "clean" the electrical power before it reaches the server to ensure that the correct and constant level of power is delivered to the server. The UPS can also serve as a surge protector, which keeps intense spikes of electrical current, common during thunderstorms, from reaching the server.

NOTE   A UPS can provide temporary power only. For long periods without electrical power, an external generator may be required. Using diesel fuel as its power source, a generator can supply electrical power for hours or even days to an entire building. However, building generators are expensive, must be properly maintained, and should be regularly tested to ensure that they can handle the demand for electrical power by the organization.

Creating and Maintaining Backups

Just as performing regular backups is essential for a user's individual computer, backups are critical for an enterprise. Any organization that loses its customer records, employee databases, and inventory files without a means to immediately replace that information will cease to function. Because of the importance of backups, most organizations create a series of backups.

NOTE   Enterprise backups are usually performed "transparently" or without the users knowing that the backup took place.

There are four basic types of enterprise backups: full backup, differential backup, incremental backup, and copy backup. These are summarized in Table 6-2.

Table 6-2   Types of enterprise backups

Type of Backup	Description	How Used
Full backup	Copies all files	Part of regular backup schedule
Differential backup	Copies all files that have changed since the last full backup	Part of regular backup schedule
Incremental backup	Copies all files that have changed since the last full or incremental backup	Part of regular backup schedule
Copy backup	Copies selected files	Copies files to a new location

Developing a strategy for performing backups is important. One of the most widely used schemes is called a **grandfather-father-son backup system**. This system divides backups into three sets: a daily backup (son), a weekly backup (father), and a monthly backup (grandfather). During a typical month, a daily (son) backup is performed each Monday through Thursday. Every Friday, a weekly (father) backup is done instead of the daily backup. On the last day of the month, a monthly (grandfather) backup is performed. Grandfather-father-son backups are illustrated in Figure 6-6.

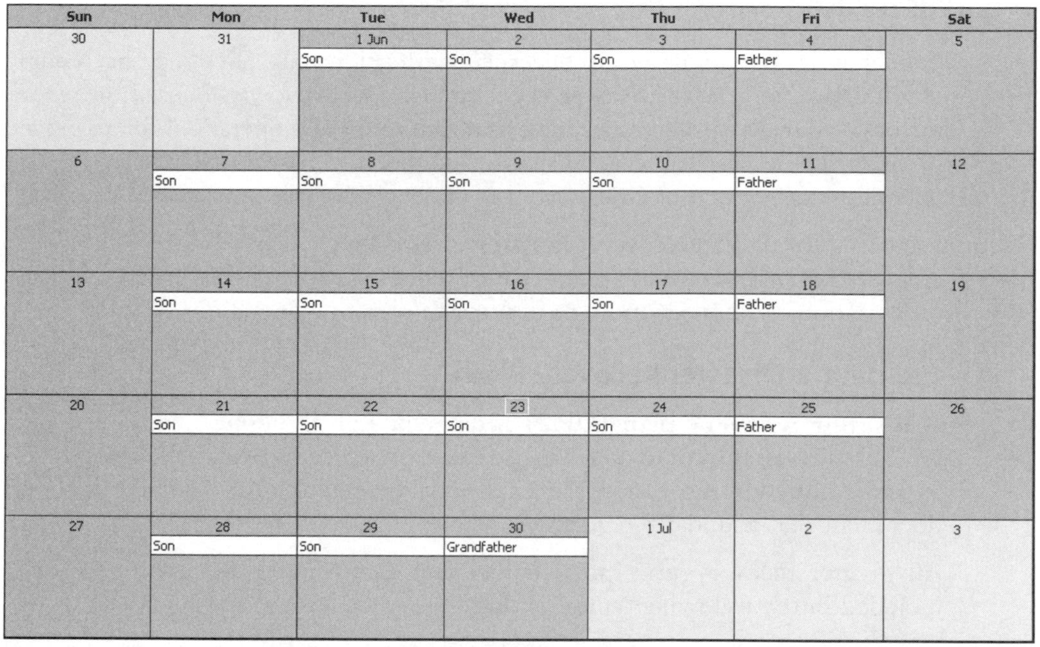

Sun	Mon	Tue	Wed	Thu	Fri	Sat
30	31	1 Jun Son	2 Son	3 Son	4 Father	5
6	7 Son	8 Son	9 Son	10 Son	11 Father	12
13	14 Son	15 Son	16 Son	17 Son	18 Father	19
20	21 Son	22 Son	23 Son	24 Son	25 Father	26
27	28 Son	29 Son	30 Grandfather	1 Jul	2	3

Figure 6-6 Grandfather-father-son backup system

The grandfather-father-son backup system reuses backup tapes on a regular basis. For example, referring back to Figure 6-6, the tape for Tuesday the 1st is stored until the following Tuesday the 8th, when it is used again. This tape is reused on each Tuesday (the 15th, 22nd, and 29th). The tapes for Monday, Wednesday, and Thursday are likewise reused each week. On the first Friday of the month (the 4th), the weekly (father) tape is used and stored away until the first Friday of the next month. Likewise, the monthly (grandfather) tape on the last day of the month (the 30th) is used again, but generally not on the last day of the next month. Instead, it is reused every three months (January, April, July, and October) so that there are three monthly (grandfather) tapes. This system provides the most comprehensive coverage and the best use of tapes.

NOTE
A critical part of backups is to test the reliability of the tapes. Many network managers thought they were performing good backups, but when they tried to restore the data after a disaster, they discovered that the tapes were blank. To test the reliability, a backup should be performed and then all of the data should be restored from the tape onto another server, and finally the restored data should be tested. Although this can be a timely and costly process, it is critical to know that the backups are sound.

Disaster Recovery Plan

While business continuity is concerned with addressing anything that could affect the continuation of service, **disaster recovery** is more narrowly focused on recovering from major disasters that could cause the organization to cease operations for an extended period of time. These disasters can be man-made (such as a security attack, war, terrorism, or chemical spill) or acts of God (such as a flood, earthquake, tornado, or hurricane).

Preparing for disaster recovery always involves having a plan in place. Because most disaster recovery typically deals with catastrophic events, many companies have a remote site that the organization can quickly move to in order to continue operations, albeit at a reduced level.

Creating a Disaster Recovery Plan

A **disaster recovery plan (DRP)** is different from a business continuity plan. A DRP typically addresses what to do if a major catastrophe occurs that could cause the organization to cease functioning. Comprehensive in its scope, a DRP should be a very detailed document that is updated regularly.

All disaster recovery plans are different, but they should address the common features included in the following typical outline:

- *Unit 1: Purpose and Scope*—The reason for the plan and what it encompasses should be clearly outlined. Those incidences that require the plan to be enacted should also be listed. The following topics are usually listed as part of Unit 1:
  - Introduction
  - Objectives and constraints
  - Assumptions
  - Incidents requiring action
  - Contingencies
  - Physical safeguards
  - Types of computer service disruptions
  - Insurance considerations

- *Unit 2: Recovery Team*—The team that is responsible for directing the disaster recovery plan should be clearly defined. Each member must know his or her role in the plan and should be adequately trained. This part of the plan must be continually reviewed as employees leave the organization, home telephone or cell phone numbers change, or new members are added to the team. The Unit 2 DRP should address the following:
  - Organization of the disaster/recovery team
  - Disaster/recovery team headquarters
  - Disaster/recovery coordinator
  - Recovery team leaders and their responsibilities

- *Unit 3: Preparing for a Disaster*—A good DRP should not only list the steps to follow when a disaster occurs, but also the procedures and safeguards that should constantly be in force to reduce the risk of the disaster. Topics for Unit 3 include:
  - General procedures
  - Software safeguards

- *Unit 4: Emergency Procedures*—What should happen when a disaster occurs? Unit 4 outlines the step-by-step procedures that should occur, including the following:
  - Disaster recovery team mobilization
  - Vendor contact list
  - Use of alternate sites
  - Off-site storage

- *Unit 5: Recovery Procedures*—Now that the initial response has put in place the procedures that allow the organization to continue functioning, how to fully recover from the disaster and return to normal business operation should be addressed. This unit should cover:
  - Central facilities recovery plan
  - Systems and operations
  - Scope of limited operations at central site
  - Network communications
  - Microcomputer recovery plan

Identifying Secure Recovery

Major disasters may require that the organization temporarily move to another location. This is particularly true for businesses where any downtime is unacceptable. Three basic types of alternate sites are used during or directly after a disaster.

NOTE

One type of operation that cannot afford any downtime is a reservation system. The airline reservation system for American Airlines and Travelocity.com, known as Sabre, handles 35 percent of all worldwide travel reservations and processes 15,000 transactions per second. It has gone down only once since 1957: in 1989, a bug in disk drive software caused the system to be unavailable for 12 hours.

A **hot site** is a building run by a commercial disaster recovery service that a business can use in the event of a disaster to continue computer and network operations. A hot site has all the equipment needed for an organization to continue running, including office space and furniture, telephone jacks, computer equipment, and a live telecommunications link. If the organization's data processing center becomes inoperable, it can move all data processing operations to a hot site, typically within an hour. A **cold site** provides office space, but the customer must provide and install all the equipment needed to continue operations. A cold site is less expensive, but it takes longer to get an enterprise in full operation after the disaster. A **warm site** has all of the equipment installed, but does not have active Internet or telecommunications facilities. This is much less expensive than constantly maintaining those connections as with a hot site; however, the amount of time needed to turn on the connections and install the backups can be as much as half a day or more.

NOTE

Typically, a business pays a monthly service charge as part of an annual contract with a company that offers hot and cold site services. Some services also offer data backup services so that all company data is available regardless of whether a hot site or cold site is used.

SECURITY IN YOUR WORLD

"I've got a question for you," said Hunter. He and Caitlin had spent almost two hours on his orientation session and were taking a short break. "I know that all new employees go through these orientation sessions with you, and you said that everyone must take a refresher course each quarter. Do you conduct the refresher courses the same way as this one?" Caitlin set down her cup on the table. "Basically, yes. I lecture to groups of about 30 employees at a time for an hour in our training center. Why do you ask?"

Hunter sat down in the chair and said, "I'm certainly no expert on this, but there sure is a lot of material to go over in these sessions, even if it's just a refresher session. Maybe you could create some PowerPoint presentations or videos and put them on the internal Web site for everyone to view before they take a refresher course. That might get everyone prepared for the sessions and leave more time for questions. As a teaching assistant at college, I had to do some training, and when I offered online presentations beforehand, it always seemed to help. I know that everybody learns differently, so the more ways you give the material the better."

Caitlin smiled. "That's a great idea. Tell me some other ideas you have about making this better."

EDUCATION AND TRAINING

A common misperception regarding security in an organization is that keeping computers and networks secure is the exclusive role of the technology staff, and that users do not have to do anything regarding security. Nothing could be further from the truth. All computer users share a responsibility in protecting the assets of an organization. Users need to receive training regarding the importance of securing information, the roles that they play in security, and the necessary steps they need to take to ward off attacks. Because new attacks appear regularly and new security vulnerabilities are continuously being exposed, this training must be ongoing. User awareness is an essential element of security, and as such, all users need constant training in the new security defenses and must be reminded of company security policies and procedures.

 Education in an enterprise is not limited to the average employee. Human resource personnel also need to keep abreast of security issues because in many organizations it is their role to train new employees on all aspects of the organization, including security. People in upper management need to be aware of the security attacks that the organization faces, if only to acknowledge the necessity of security in planning, staffing, and budgeting.

Organizations should provide education and training at set times and on an ad hoc basis. Opportunities for security education and training can be any of the following:

- A new employee is hired.
- A computer attack has occurred.
- An employee is promoted or given new responsibilities.
- A department is conducting an annual retreat.
- New user software is installed.
- User hardware is upgraded.

One of the challenges of security education and training is first to understand how individuals learn. People learn in different ways: for example, some individuals are visual learners, while others are auditory learners. An enterprise should tailor training to meet those differences.

How Learners Learn

Learning involves communication: information developed by a person is communicated to a another person. However, learning is much more than filling a head with knowledge. Many influences affect how individuals learn, such as the cultural setting in which a person was raised. Generational traits also influence how people learn. Table 6-3 lists the generations of individuals born in the U.S. since 1946, along with traits that are common to those individuals, according to BridgeWorks LLC.

Table 6-3   Generational traits

Generation	Year Born	Traits	Number in U.S. Population
Traditionalists	Prior to 1946	Patriotic, loyal, faith in institutions	75 million
Baby boomers	1946-1964	Idealistic, competitive, question authority	80 million
Generation X	1965-1981	Self-reliant, distrustful of institutions, adaptive to technology	46 million
Millennials	1982-2000	Pragmatic, globally concerned, computer literate, media savvy	76 million

In addition to generational traits of learners, training style also affects how people learn. The way that one person was taught may not be the best way to teach all others. Most people are taught using a **pedagogical** approach, which comes from a Greek word meaning *to lead a child*. However, for adult learners, an **andragogical** approach (the art of helping an adult learn) is more appropriate. Some of the differences between pedagogical and andragogical are summarized in Table 6-4.

Table 6-4   Pedagogical and andragogical traits

Subject	Pedagogical Approach	Andragogical Approach
Desire	Motivated by external pressures to get good grades or pass on to next grade	Motivated by higher self-esteem, more recognition, desire for better quality of life
Student	Dependent upon teacher for all learning	Self-directed and responsible for own learning
Subject matter	Defined by what the teacher wants to give	Organized around situations in life or at work
Willingness to learn	Students informed about what they must learn	Change triggers a readiness to learn or students perceive a gap between where they are and where they want to be

People typically learn in three ways: visually, auditorily, and kinesthetically. While most people use a combination of the styles, they usually have one that is dominant. Visual learners learn through taking notes, being at the front of the class, and watching presentations. Auditory learners tend to sit in the middle of the class and learn best through lectures and discussions. In the third style, kinesthetic, students learn through a lab environment or other hands-on approaches. Many information technology professionals are kinesthetic learners.

NOTE To truly aid in knowledge retention, trainers should incorporate all three learning styles into a course and present the same information using different techniques. For example, a course could include a lecture (for auditory learners), PowerPoint slides (for visual learners), and an opportunity to work directly with software and replicate what is being taught (for kinesthetic learners).

Learning Resources

An organization can provide educational content in several ways. The first is through seminars and workshops. These training sessions may be conducted by a variety of sources, such as a workshop offered by the organization itself on company security policies and practices. Most organizations have mandatory workshops for new employees and refresher sessions every three to six months. Other venues for workshops include those conducted by security vendors, trade shows, and local or regional user groups. Seminars and workshops are a good means of learning some of the latest technologies and networking with other security professionals in the area.

NOTE Although most seminars or workshops conducted by training vendors contain valuable information, remember that the vendor may present material from a perspective other than that of your organization. It is always good to compare information obtained from one vendor to that of other vendors as a counterbalance.

Another resource for learning content is print media. Reputable publishers produce factual and unbiased material that contains solid information on security and defenses. Magazines and journals are also good sources for the most recent material.

The Internet contains a wealth of information that can be used on a daily basis to keep informed about new attacks and trends. Web sites can be classified as those maintained by vendors, by trade associations, by vendor-neutral organizations, and as those that offer software tools. What may be more important than identifying a specific site is to become fluent with the use of search engines. Web sites come and go everyday, and their addresses change frequently. Users who can use search engines to regularly locate solid sources of information can keep well informed of security procedures.

SECURITY IN YOUR WORLD

"Our last document for today is our company's code of conduct," Caitlin said as she pulled a set of papers out of her folder. "Code of conduct?" asked Hunter. "What's that?" "I think that it's one of the most important documents that we have developed in the last two years. It's very useful in helping you with everyday decisions and to ensure that those decisions coincide with the company's mission," said Caitlin. "Why don't you just have a list of everything you can do?" Hunter asked.

Caitlin set down her cup. "That would certainly make it much easier, but I'm afraid that's not practical. There are so many things that come up that require judgment decisions, we couldn't possibly list all of them." "Caitlin," said Hunter. "This sounds like the code of conduct gets into ethics." "Yes, it does," said Caitlin. "We are very concerned about our ethical behavior as an organization, just as most companies are today. And that applies to everyone, starting with our president." "If it's important to him," said Hunter, "then it's important to me. Where do we start?"

ETHICS

The corporate world has been rocked by a series of high-profile scandals in recent years. Once-powerful organizations have declared bankrupcy as they recover from losses involving "insider trading" and creating "sham corporations." In many instances, the knowledge and approval of such actions came from the top of the organization. The result was billions of dollars lost by investors and shareholders and thousands of employees suddenly unemployed and without promised pension benefits. These scandals have resulted in new federal legislation that require organizations to act in a responsible manner.

Many people think that the only way to reduce the number and magnitude of such scandals is to refocus attention on ethics in the enterprise. Although defining ethics can be difficult, one approach is to compare ethics with values and morals:

- *Values*—**Values** are a person's fundamental beliefs and are the principles used to define what is good, right, and just. Values provide guidance in determining the right action to take. Values can be classified as moral values (fairness, truth, justice, and love), pragmatic values (efficiency, thrift, health, and patience), and aesthetic values (attractive, soft, and cold).

- *Morals*—**Morals** are values that are attributed to a system of beliefs that helps the individual define right from wrong. These values typically derive their authority from something outside the individual, such as a higher spiritual being or an external authority (such as the government or society). Moral concepts that are based on an external authority may vary from one society to another and can change over time as the society changes.

- *Ethics*—**Ethics** may be defined as the set of principles and behaviors that people understand and agree to be good and right. When people act in ways consistent with their moral values, they are said to be acting ethically. Ethics are behaviors and instruct people how to act in ways that meet the standard they set for themselves according to their values.

Defining what is ethical is not left up to the individual. If it was correct, then it could be argued that what Adolph Hitler did was ethical because his actions conformed to his personal definition of right, fair, and good. Ethics are defined by a group, not individually.

It is not the role of the organization to tell employees what their values should be, because these come with people when they enter the workplace. However, it *is* the company's responsibility to set ethical behavioral standards and to train employees so they understand those standards.

Many enterprises have a written **code of conduct** intended to be a central guide and reference for employees in support of day-to-day decision making. This code is intended to clarify an organization's mission, values, and principles, and then link them with standards of professional conduct. A code should be an open disclosure of the way an organization operates, and it should provide visible guidelines for behavior. The code of conduct also serves as a communication tool that reflects the agreement that an organization has made to uphold its most important values, dealing with such matters as its commitment to employees, its standards for doing business, and its relationship with the community.

NOTE A code is also a tool to encourage discussions of ethics and to improve how employees or members deal with the ethical dilemmas, prejudices, and gray areas that are encountered in everyday work. A code is meant to complement relevant standards, policies, and rules, not to substitute for them.

Computer security is closely tied to the subject of ethics. In fact, we need computer security because attackers conduct themselves in an unethical fashion. Although some attackers like to portray themselves as "white hat" attackers who perform a valuable function by exposing security vulnerabilities, not all agree with this self-portrait. According to many security experts, anyone who attacks a computer or network—no matter what the motive—is violating ethical standards.

However, unethical behavior is not limited to attackers. An employee who borrows a list of customers from his employer and then starts a competing company by contacting and attempting to recruit those customers acts unethically. Similarly, if an organization's code of conduct prohibits employees from using company equipment for personal use, an employee who uses company computers and Internet access to download songs or movies exhibits unacceptable behavior. All employees should be aware of their organization's code of conduct and should follow high ethical standards.

NOTE When an ethical decision is required, one of the best approaches is to ask how you would like to be treated if you were in that same situation, or "Do unto others as you would have them do unto you."

CHAPTER SUMMARY

▫ One of the first lines of defense against attacks is adequate physical security. Physical security protects the equipment itself. Computers can be protected by removing or disabling hardware that provides access to the computer. Network servers can be protected by using KVM (keyboard, video, mouse) switches. Door locks are likewise necessary tools to provide physical security. Door locks can be preset locks, deadbolt locks, or cipher locks.

▫ A policy is a document that outlines specific requirements or rules that must be met. A security policy is a document that outlines the protections that should be enacted to ensure that the organization's assets face minimal risks. An acceptable use policy (AUP) defines what actions the users of a system may perform while using an organization's computing and networking equipment. A privacy policy outlines how the organization uses information it collects.

▫ A plan outlines specifically what must be done. Business continuity is the process of assessing risks and developing a management strategy to ensure that the business can continue if the risks materialize. Business continuity management is concerned with developing a business continuity plan (BCP) that addresses how the organization can continue in the event that risks materialize. BCPs typically address electrical service outages and backup procedures. While business continuity is concerned with addressing anything that could affect the continuation of service, disaster recovery is more narrowly focused on recovering from major disasters that could cause an organization to cease operations for an extended period of time. Disaster recovery may outline a temporary move to another location if the primary location is no longer accessible.

▫ Users need to receive training regarding the importance of securing information, the roles that they play in security, and the necessary steps they need to take to ward off attacks. Organizations should provide education and training at set times and on an ad hoc basis. Because people learn in a variety of ways, different techniques should be used in order to reach all users.

▫ Ethics may be defined as the study of what people understand to be good and right behavior and how people make those judgments. When a person acts in ways that are consistent with their moral values they are said to be acting ethically. It is the company's responsibility to set ethical behavioral standards and train employees so that they understand those standards.

KEY TERMS

acceptable use policy (AUP) – A document that defines what actions the users of a system may perform while using an organization's computing and networking equipment.

andragogical – An instructional approach for teaching adults.

business continuity – The process of assessing risks and developing a management strategy to ensure that the business can continue if the risks materialize.

business continuity plan (BCP) – A plan that addresses how the organization can continue if risks materialize.

cipher lock – A combination lock with buttons that a user must push in the proper sequence to open the door.

code of conduct – A written document intended to be a central guide and reference for employees in support of day-to-day decision making.

cold site – A location that provides office space, but the tenant must provide and install all the equipment needed to continue operations.

copy backup – A backup that copies only selected files.

deadbolt lock – A lock that extends a solid metal bar into the door frame for extra security.

differential backup – A backup that copies all files that have changed since the last full backup was performed.

disaster recovery – A narrowly focused document outlining how to recover from major disasters.

disaster recovery plan (DRP) – A document that addresses what to do if a major catastrophe occurs that could cause the organization to cease functioning.

ethics – A set of principles and behaviors that people understand and agree to be good and right.

full backup – A backup that copies all files onto a secondary storage device.

grandfather-father-son backup system – A backup system that divides backups into three sets: a daily backup (son), a weekly backup (father), and a monthly backup (grandfather).

guideline – A collection of suggestions that should be implemented.

hot site – A location generally run by a commercial disaster recovery service that a business can use in the event of a disaster to continue computer and network operations to maintain business continuity.

incremental backup – A backup that copies all files that have changed since the last full or incremental backup.

key-in-knob lock – A lock that requires only a key for unlocking the door from the outside.

KVM (keyboard, video, mouse) switch – A device that provides a single monitor, mouse, and keyboard access to multiple computers.

morals – Values that are attributed to a system of beliefs that help the individual define right from wrong.

pedagogical – An instructional approach for teaching children and adults.

physical security – Security that protects computer and networking equipment.

plan – A document that outlines specifically what action must be done.

policy – A document that outlines specific requirements or rules that must be met.

preset lock – A lock that requires only a key for unlocking the door from the outside.

privacy policy – A policy that outlines how an organization uses the information it collects.

rack-mounted server – A networked server that can be stacked with other servers in a closely confined area.

security policy – A document that outlines the protections that should be enacted to ensure that an organization's assets face minimal risks.

shoulder surfing – Watching over a person's shoulder as he or she enters a code.

standard – A collection of requirements specific to the system or procedure that must be met by everyone.

suspended ceiling – A metal grid that supports lightweight ceiling tiles.

uninterruptible power supply (UPS) – An external device located between an outlet for electrical power and a computer device.

values – A person's fundamental beliefs and the principles used to define what is good, right, and just.

warm site – A location that provides network equipment an organization needs, but does not have active Internet or telecommunications facilities.

REVIEW QUESTIONS

1. _____ security protects the equipment itself and has the primary goal of preventing unauthorized users from reaching the equipment to use, steal, or vandalize.
   a. Physical
   b. Network
   c. Server
   d. Actual

2. Many organizations routinely remove a computer's _____ to prevent an attacker from installing any programs onto the system.
   a. hard drive
   b. floppy disk drive
   c. radio frequency identification resource
   d. mouse

3. _____ can be stacked together with up to 50 other similar devices in a closely confined area.
   a. Rack-mounted servers
   b. Wireless access points (WAPs)
   c. Keyboard, video, mouse switches
   d. Network Interface Cards

4. A _____ is the easiest to use because it requires only a key for unlocking the door from the outside.
   a. preset lock
   b. cyberlock

c. deadman's cylinder

d. USB lock

5. Although _____ ceilings can hide pipes, ducts, and cables from view as well as serve as a sound barrier, they can also allow an attacker to easily enter a locked room.

a. drag

b. suspended

c. covered

d. metal

6. A policy is a document that outlines specific requirements or rules that must be met. True or False?

7. An acceptable use policy (AUP) defines what actions the users of a system may perform while using the computing and networking equipment. True or False?

8. Business continuity is the process of assessing risks and developing a management strategy to ensure that the business can continue if the risks materialize. True or False?

9. An uninterruptible power supply (UPS) is a device located inside a computer that provides continuous electrical current. True or False?

10. Once a backup is made, it is not necessary to test the backup for reliability. True or False?

11. A(n) _____ is a document that outlines the protections that should be enacted to ensure that an organization's assets face minimal risks.

12. A(n) _____ backup copies all files that have changed since the last full or incremental backup.

13. A(n) _____ system divides backups into three sets: a daily backup, a weekly backup, and a monthly backup.

14. While business continuity is concerned with addressing anything that could affect the continuation of service, _____ is more narrowly focused on recovering from major disasters that could cause an organization to cease operations for an extended period of time.

15. Adult learners prefer a(n) _____ approach to learning.

16. What are ethics?

17. What is the purpose of a code of conduct in an enterprise?

18. What is the difference between a hot site, a cold site, and a warm site?

19. Explain how a grandfather-father-son backup system functions.

20. What is the difference between a policy, a standard, and a guideline?

HANDS-ON PROJECTS

Project 6-1: Performing a Total Security Audit

Now that you have learned about applying practical security in your world, it is time to test your computer to see how secure it is. In this project, you perform an audit using the Microsoft Baseline Security Analyzer (MBSA).

1. Use your Web browser to visit the following Web page:

   www.microsoft.com/technet/security/tools/mbsahome.mspx

2. Click **MBSA 2.0**.

 Content on the MBSA Web site periodically changes. You might need to search the site for a link to the latest version of the Microsoft Baseline Security Analyzer.

NOTE

3. Scroll down to Download Now, and then click **English**.

4. Click **Continue** in the Validation Required section. If necessary, follow the instructions to install the Genuine Windows Validation Component.

5. Click **MBSASetup-EN**.msi and then click **Save**. Select a location to save the file and then click **Save**.

6. When the file has completed downloading, click **Run**. If you receive a security warning, click **Run** again.

7. Follow the steps to install MBSA.

8. Double-click the **Microsoft Baseline Security Analyzer 2.0** icon on the desktop.

9. Click **Scan a computer**.

10. Accept the default settings for the scan by clicking **Start scan**.

11. When the scan is complete, a report appears similar to the one shown in Figure 6-7.

12. Items with a green mark indicate that the item passed the scan. An item with a yellow or red mark means the scan has located a vulnerability that should be attended to. Scroll down to any item that has a yellow or red check and click **What was scanned**. Close that window when you're done.

13. Next, click **How to correct this**. Follow the instructions to correct any vulnerabilities in this system.

14. Close all windows when completed.

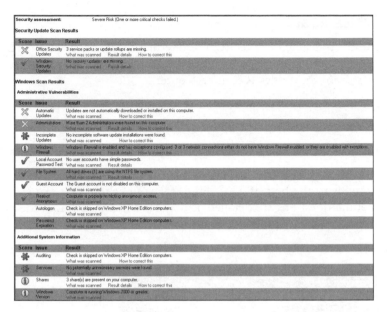

Figure 6-7   MBSA results

Project 6-2: Online Security Policy Generator

A good starting point for creating a security policy is to use one of the security policy generators available online. In this project, you will use the Cisco Security Policy Builder.

1. Use your Web browser to visit the following Web page:

   www.ciscowebtools.com/spb/

NOTE

Content on the Cisco Web site periodically changes. You might need to search the site for a link to the latest version of the Cisco Security Policy Builder.

2. Click **Launch Security Policy Builder**.

3. Click **SECURITY POLICY INTERVIEW**.

4. Answer the questions to the best of your ability for your school or organization.

5. When prompted, enter your e-mail address and check **I accept the disclaimer above**. Click **Send Security Policy**.

6. Retrieve the policy and read it. Does it contain helpful information? Could you use this as a starting point for a security policy?

7. Close all windows when you're finished.

Project 6-3: Ethics Test

Online tools are available to gauge the effectiveness of ethics in an organization. These tools can help raise the level of awareness regarding ethics among employees. In this project, you will use an online test from the Ethics Resource Center.

1. Use your Web browser to visit the following Web page:

   www.ethics.org/quicktest/index.cfm

2. Note the rating scale that is being used, and then click **Continue to online Quick Test**.

3. Answer the questions to the best of your ability for your school or organization. Because many of the questions are detailed, it may be difficult to know the precise response, but use your best judgment.

4. A profile will appear similar to the one shown in Figure 6-8.

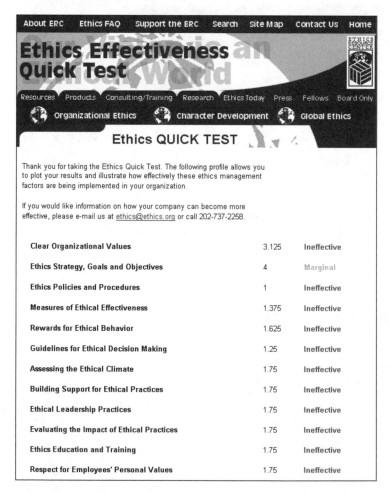

Figure 6-8   Ethics profile

5. Does this profile reflect the ethics at your school or organization? Do you feel that this tool would be helpful for employees and managers to use?

6. Close all windows when you're finished.

CASE PROJECTS

Case Project 6-1: Ethics

Defining ethics and determining the ethical standards in an organization can be a challenging task. Using the Internet, research the definition of ethics and how it is used. Then, find two ethical policies of organizations. What are their good points? What are their bad points? Do they truly address ethics in the proper way? Finally, create your own one-page ethics policy for your school.

Case Project 6-2: Physical Security Audit

Conduct a physical security audit of several computer rooms in your school or organization. What type of locks do they use? Are there suspended ceilings? What about the lighting? Create a one-page document that outlines your observations. Include suggestions regarding how it could be improved.

Case Project 6-3: Security Policy Review

Locate the security policy for your school or organization. Based on what you now know about security, is it sufficient? Does it adequately address security for the organization? Is it up-to-date? What changes would you suggest? Write a one-page paper on your findings.

Case Project 6-4: Acceptable Use Policy

Create your own acceptable use policy for access to the computers and network at your school or organization. Be sure to cover computer use, Internet surfing, e-mail, Web, and password security. Compare your policies with other students in the class. Finally, locate the acceptable use policy for your school or organization. How does it compare with yours? Which policy is more strict? Why? What changes would you recommend? Write a one-page paper on your findings.

Case Project 6-5: Baypoint Computer Consulting

Garrison Towing is a regional automobile towing and wrecker service. Because of several recent incidents, Garrison Towing has decided that they need an acceptable use policy for their employees. Baypoint Computer Consulting (BCC) has asked you to help.

Create a PowerPoint presentation for the board of directors of Garrison Towing that defines an acceptable use policy and outlines what it should contain. Also, provide some brief suggestions regarding what items you feel that Garrison Towing should include. Your presentation should contain eight or more slides.

After your presentation, Garrison Towing started to create their own acceptable use policy. However, they cannot agree on a policy regarding e-mail use. They have asked you to create a one-page document that outlines acceptable and unacceptable use of e-mail facilities.

Index